Colonized Schooling Exposed

This book presents a novel perspective on colonialism, education and other related issues. It unveils the effects of colonialism on the learning and well-being of students and workers, including marginalized groups such as women, Native Americans, Latino/as, Asians, Blacks, and African Americans. It is a collection of essays combined with in-depth interviews and conversations with committed social justice educators and activist-scholars genuinely concerned with educational issues situated in the context of western renewed forms of colonialism and neoliberalism. This book covers many interwoven and pressing issues echoed through authentic voices of progressive educators and scholars. Anyone interested in decolonizing schools and transcending neoliberal and colonial mentality must read this book.

Pierre Wilbert Orelus is assistant professor at New Mexico State University. His recent books include: Whitecentricism and Linguoracism Exposed (2013); The Race Talk (2012); and Radical Voices for Democratic Schooling (with Curry Malott, 2012).

Curry S. Malott is assistant professor in the Department of Professional and Secondary Education, West Chester University of Pennsylvania, US. Some of Dr. Malott's most recent books include *Critical Pedagogy and Cognition: An Introduction to a Post-Formal Educational Psychology* (2011); *Teaching Joe L. Kincheloe* (2011) co-edited with Rochelle Brock and Leila Villaverde; and *Radical Voices for Democratic Schooling* (2012), co-edited with Pierre W. Orelus.

Romina Pacheco is doctoral candidate in the Department of Curriculum and Instruction at New Mexico State University. Her research interests include critical pedagogy, Black and Latina/Chicana Feminist Thought, critical multicultural education, and radical participatory democracy in the classroom.

Routledge Studies in Education and Neoliberalism

SERIES EDITOR DAVE HILL, *University of Northampton, UK*

1 **The Rich World and the Impoverishment of Education**
Diminishing Democracy, Equity and Workers' Rights
Edited by Dave Hill

2 **Contesting Neoliberal Education**
Public Resistance and Collective Advance
Edited by Dave Hill

3 **Global Neoliberalism and Education and its Consequences**
Edited by Dave Hill and Ravi Kumar

4 **The Developing World and State Education**
Neoliberal Depredation and Egalitarian Alternatives
Edited by Dave Hill and Ellen Rosskam

5 **The Gates Foundation and the Future of US "Public" Schools**
Edited by Philip E. Kovacs

6 **Colonized Schooling Exposed**
Progressive Voices for Transformative Educational and Social Change
Edited by Pierre Wilbert Orelus, Curry S. Malott, and Romina Pacheco

Colonized Schooling Exposed

Progressive Voices for Transformative Educational and Social Change

Edited by
Pierre Wilbert Orelus, Curry S. Malott, and Romina Pacheco

Routledge
Taylor & Francis Group
NEW YORK LONDON

First published 2014
by Routledge
711 Third Avenue, New York, NY 10017

and by Routledge
2 Park Square, Milton Park, Abingdon, Oxon OX14 4RN

Routledge is an imprint of the Taylor & Francis Group, an informa business

Library of Congress Cataloging-in-Publication Data

Colonized schooling exposed : progressive voices for transformative educational and social change / edited by Pierre Wilbert Orelus, Curry S. Malott, Romina Pacheco.
pages cm. — (Routledge studies in education and neoliberalism ; 6)
Includes bibliographical references and index.
1. Transformative learning. 2. Critical pedagogy. 3. Neoliberalism—Social aspects. 4. Postcolonialism—Social aspects. 5. Social change.
I. Orelus, Pierre W. II. Malott, Curry, 1972– III. Pacheco, Romina.
LC1100.C65 2013
370.11'5—dc23
2013023749

ISBN13: 978-0-415-84036-1 (hbk)
ISBN13: 978-0-203-76782-5 (ebk)

Typeset in Sabon
by IBT Global.

Contents

Introduction

Pierre Wilbert Orelus, Curry S. Malott, and Romina Pacheco

For many critical educators, colonialism is still at work; its legacy continues to shape the practices of many institutions, such as schools, governments, churches, workplaces, and the mass media. Concealed under the umbrella of Western neoliberalism, colonialism has been implemented through different educational, socioeconomic, and political policies that have had a negative impact on the school system and the economy of many countries, particularly formerly colonized countries as well as those that are currently occupied. The educational, socioeconomic, political, and cultural disaster that colonialism has engendered may not be as obvious as its renewed form, neoliberalism, partly because those in power have used the corporate media to gain the consent of people, including the poor, leading them to believe that they have benefited from global capitalism and the *free market*.

However, those who have presence of mind, and are thus able to critically reflect on their direct experience with neocolonialism and neoliberalism, know this system mostly works for the rich who have created it. Likewise, neoliberalism has not only impacted factory and sweatshop workers, though they are most affected by it; it has also affected many institutions, such as universities and colleges, and people who are the engines of these institutions, like students, professors, and staff. This book aims at shedding light on these issues, which will be analyzed in depth throughout the book. In the section that follows, we provide a brief overview of the impact of neoliberalism and neocolonialism on the well-being of people in general and the learning of students and teachers' teaching practices in particular.

THE CORPORATE MODEL: A CURRENT TREND RUNNING THROUGH UNIVERSITIES AND COLLEGES

Over the last two decades or so, many universities and colleges have been following and implementing an externally imposed corporate and militarist model of education (Aronowitz, 2000; McLaren, 2005; McLaren and Faramandpur, 2001a; Schugurensky, 2007). The corporate takeover of higher education and the intensified focus of using the knowledge factory in the service of military innovations can best be understood as a consequence of competition between capitals. That is, since before Columbus washed up on the shores of Haiti in 1492, European powers used military force to conquer lands and gain access to resources, labor, and potential markets.

Today is no different. Another reason for the militarization of higher education is related to the self-preservation of capitalists themselves. That is, because the competitive drive for profits and access to markets perpetually pushes capitalism toward crisis and because unproductive production, such as "the means of destruction" (Callinicos, 2011, p. 231), offsets this tendency, universities have deepened their investments in this sector of the economy. Explaining what "waste production" is and why it offsets the tendency toward crisis, Callinicos (2011) notes:

> The military struggle between national capitals has . . . been crucial to the comparative stability and great prosperity which the world economy enjoyed in the 1950s and 1960s, for the diversion of resources to the production of destruction paradoxically reduces some of the pressures on the system which force it toward crises. To understand why this is so we have first to recall that Marx identified two main sectors of the economy . . . means of production . . . and goods for consumption. . . . The commodities produced [here are] . . . productively consumed . . . they are used to produce more commodities. The means of production—machinery, infrastructure, and so on—are obviously necessary if more goods are to be made. But consumer goods too are used to keep labor power alive and working efficiently. There is, however, a third sector of the economy . . . whose output is not productively consumed. . . . Arms are . . . not used to make other commodities. . . . Arms production is waste production. . . . The effects of competition is to force capitals to reinvest surplus value in improving their methods of production. So the organic composition of capital—that is, the share of the means of production in total investment—rises, and the rate of profit falls. Waste production, however, offsets this process. (pp. 231–232)

It becomes clear that arms production is therefore needed both to build up the neocolonial militias capital relies on to expand into new markets and to offset the tendency toward overaccumulation and crisis. Despite these efforts, which cannot solve the tendency toward crises, but only postpone or temporarily displace them, the United States entered an economic recession during the 1970s, which, among other factors, was fueled by the corporate competition of Japan, Germany, and other industrialized countries devastated by WWII and the disappearance of cheap oil, which had led to enormous development in related industries. As wages stagnated and the cost of living (i.e., fuel) rose through the 1970s, Reagan took office under promises of economic recovery and a way out of the crisis (Ackerman,

1982). Reagan's solution was a policy of "trickle-down economics," which was based on the assumption that what was prohibiting economic growth was government regulation *getting in the way of the free market.* Consequently, Reagan took drastic steps to deregulate capital, paving the way for the neoliberal era, or the corporate and militarist model of education.

This militarist and corporate atmosphere at many universities and colleges is what many educators, including the authors herein, have witnessed and experienced. Doors of many universities and colleges have been widely opened to corporations, that is, the business world (Aronowitz, 2000). In his breakthrough book *Knowledge Factory,* Aronowitz (2000) eloquently describes the way many universities have followed a corporate model of education aiming to prepare students for the labor force, thus making it much more challenging for progressive educators to do critical work. According to Aronowitz, the content of the curriculum in many schools and the choice students make regarding their majors reflect the logic of the market. Aronowitz argues, "In most cases, their choices of major and minor fields are informed by a rudimentary understanding of the nature of the job market rather than by intellectuals, let alone intellectual passion" (p. 10).

Because higher education began feeling the neoliberal pinch around the mid-1990s, there has been increasing pressure for professors to engage in profitable research. Consequently, professors who bring capital (i.e., grant money) to their institutions are more often the ones who are rewarded and held in high esteem. Those who refuse to sell their souls and minds to corporations but instead decide to question the status quo often do not receive the credit and respect they deserve, even when they are prolific writers, great researchers, and profoundly committed to teaching and helping students to become critical citizens. Worse yet, they are too often the first ones to be denied tenure and promotion.

With regard to the ongoing presence of militarism on college and university campuses, Peter McLaren, a dissident voice in academia, argues

> There is increasing militarism in the universities, much stronger links to military projects and programs, with officers training programs, with the Pentagon providing funds for research; we can all agree that public funding for universities is drying up, that the quality of our universities is suffering in its overall academic programs, especially the liberal arts sector, that, in effect, the universities are abandoning the public sphere and embracing the market-based neoliberal rationality that powers the private sphere. (McLaren, as cited in Orelus, 2011, p. 102)

We concur with McLaren's statement that programs designed to recruit students for the U.S. army have indeed increased nationwide from secondary to higher education. For example, at the community and liberal colleges where the first author, Pierre Orelus, taught, he witnessed and experienced firsthand the aggressive way with which military personnel, established at these institutions (they had their own offices there), tried to recruit students, particularly minority and poor White students. Several military personnel approached him numerous times on campus and tried to convince him to sign up for the army. They told him that his college tuition will be paid for and that he will have great benefits, not clearly explained. When he informed them that he was an instructor, not a student, they responded, saying, "Oh! I am sorry. Do you know any student in your class who might be interested in joining the army? The army offers great benefits."

Furthermore, as Orelus was teaching at a community college in western Massachusetts, his boss invited some people who represented Bank of America to visit the college. Confused, he decided to ask her what those who represented this bank were doing at the college. She informed Orelus that Bank of America had donated money for the computer lab and the tutoring program at the college, so they wanted to see if the donation money was being used properly. She also stated that she had to write a report and submit it to the bank as part of the college's agreement with this bank. This information helped Orelus understand why students that he was teaching and tutoring were strongly advised by their advisors to pursue an associate degree in business. Some of these advisors received grant money from Bank of America. It is safe to argue Orelus's students succumbed to the pressure from their advisors.

While Bank of America was donating money to this community college, Orelus witnessed rampant racial and gender inequalities there. Three single female mothers enrolled in his classes had to miss classes because they did not have transportation to make it to school. In fact, many had to discontinue their schooling because of a lack of support and resources. Specifically, they had to get a second job in the midst of the semester to make ends meet; consequently, they withdrew from their classes. These were committed and serious students of color that Pierre Orelus witnessed dropping out of college because of a lack of support and financial resources.

We ask: Why can't the government allocate resources to create programs at colleges, particularly at community colleges, which most poor working people attend, to support single mothers so they can stay in and finish college? Why does the government spend billions of dollars on wars and yet refuse to allocate adequate resources to educate working-class women? Should we talk about democracy and social justice in a country where certain groups of people have the resources to attend elite colleges and receive high-quality education whereas others do not even have the opportunity to finish an associate degree at a community college?

We share the view of scholars such as Noam Chomsky (1994, 1999, 2004), who argues that democracy was never really intended to exist in the United States because it requires maximal participation; and capitalism, which this country was founded on, requires minimal participation. Similarly, questioning the United States' notion of democracy, Shirley Steinberg asked, "Can democracy be possible?" Steinberg went on to say, "I am not sure. In light of the past forty years, I don't know what democracy is. I see it as a buzzword, which means *we* are right (democracy) and *they* are wrong (everyone else). And no, if democracy can exist, it will not be in a capitalist country. The Darwinian essence of capitalism precludes democracy" (Steinberg, as cited in Orelus and Malott, 2012, p. 30). Chomsky's and Steinberg's statements unveil lies that have been circulated in the media and schools. These lies are intended to make people believe that we are living in a democratic country, and poverty is the consequence of individual deficiencies rather than a structural requirement of capital.

Finally, we have witnessed many business-driven people who have been appointed as provosts and vice-provosts at many universities, including universities we attended and where we have worked. They are mostly powerful heterosexual, Christian, and able-bodied White males. Like many other universities, these White males are the ones who decide whether or not universities should follow a corporate model of education. They are also the ones who decide whether universities and colleges should be under academic censorship and surveillance, or should be a public sphere where academic freedom is valued and embraced. In most cases, we have witnessed they have opted for the former. These are decisions that female faculty, faculty of color, and queer faculty may not be in a position to make.

These decisions have been made on their behalf and often at the expense of their careers and academic freedom. Yet, the empty talk about democracy and freedom continues to be circulated through most schools in the United States. These two notions, embedded in the U.S. pledge of allegiance, have been a daily ritual in schools. Elementary, middle school, and high school students alike are expected to recite this allegiance like a parrot. The empty discourse of democracy, freedom, and social justice has also run through many departments and/or programs at universities that often attempt to silence the voice of dissident and progressive educators.

BOOK ORGANIZATION

Part I

In "Colonialism in the 21st Century: A Critical Analysis," Pierre Orelus unveils the persistent effects of Western colonial legacy on the school, political, and economic systems of countries that were formerly colonized. Orelus unravels the cultural and linguistic impacts of such legacy on the learning and well-being of colonial subjects who have been educated in a colonial-based school system. He concludes this chapter by making concrete proposals to resist the devastating educational, socioeconomic, cultural, and political effects of this legacy maintained through neoliberal policies.

The second chapter, "Violence and the Interstices of Difference: Working With[in] and Around Fanon," works with Fanon's diagnosis of violence to examine the interstices of difference as violence is produced and perpetuated on the racialized colonial encounter of the marginalized and dominant. George J. Sefa Dei and Loren Ola Delaney examine ways the colonized body is conceptualized, produced, and imagined as in included/excluded space and politics of everyday enactment of violence and resistance. In the discussion they narrate a particular incident as a story of how the interstices of difference point to the interlocution of race, gender, class, sexuality, disability, language, and culture in producing a complexity of an event, which defies singular interpretations of the body and the social act. It is pointed out that George J. Sefa Dei and Loren Ola Delaney are multiplicative beings/selves and that they experience events differently and yet in relation to others. Thus, violence perpetuated by the colonized on male and female bodies is different and yet connected [Black] bodies, within a colonial project, where such bodies are feminized to ensure they fit the colonial Manichean divide. In offering a particular critical interpretation of the story, the learning objective is also to show how the colonial interpellation of violence and social difference is about everyday encounters. George J. Sefa Dei and Loren Ola Delaney conclude their chapter by pointing to the pedagogic and instructional need and relevance to understand, respond, and address violence in everyday lived experiences of colonized bodies.

In the third chapter, *Colonialism and Neoliberalism: Twins of Inequities*, Professor Prashad explores the complexities and contradictions of the colonialist relationship between Great Brittan and his native India. This discussion offers another important example of challenging the simplistic dichotomous logic of victims and victimizers, for a more nuanced and complete understanding of two-way colonization and shifts in power rendering the period of British plunder and extreme wealth extraction of the nineteenth century not the only period, but rather just one stage, however much long-term damage it inflicted. Through this discussion, Prashad elaborates on the impact this complex relationship has on his own identity and the status of being a so-called *model minority* in the context of the United States. Prashad's seemingly effortless ability to delve effortlessly into an honest engagement with his own situatedness in the colonialist present offers others, of whatever positionality, an example of fearless self-reflection, necessary for shifting ourselves out of the colonialist/capitalist discursive paradigm that renders us unable to pose real challenges to abstract labor and the global neoliberal capitalist social, political, and economic system it supports and is supported by.

In "Countering the Colonizing Allure of (Pseudo)-Scientific Discourse in Education Research and Policy," Myriam Torres examines and demonstrates the allure of pseudo-scientific discourses in education research and its colonizing effect on the public, including researchers, educators, and parents. Torres describes concrete cases of such pseudoscientific discourses and illustrates how to counter such colonization by using research approaches such as critical discourse analysis (CDA) and participatory action research (PAR) to unveil the intended meaning of those discourses. She calls on concerned educators and other people interested in actions for defending minority languages, public education, and democratic schooling to engage in the battle against dominant discourse aimed at perpetuating various forms of discrimination against marginalized students and groups in schools and society at large.

In the fifth chapter, "Courageous Voices Against Neocolonial Schooling and White Supremacy," Pierre Orelus engages Professor Sandy Grande in a discussion centered on issues concerning primarily indigenous people. Professor Grande starts by talking about how she accidentally got into academia. She then goes on to talk about her experience as the only indigenous female faculty negotiating space with Caucasian colleagues at an institution dominated mostly by White males. Unlike many scholars, Professor Grande unequivocally states that she does not use information that people in her indigenous community share with her and write about it, as she does not know how this information will be consumed by people outside this community. She also refuses to put "the expert on indigenous issues" label on her, even though she writes about issues concerning indigenous communities.

In "Surviving Language as a Refugee," Marisol Ruiz provides a personal account informed by linguistic discrimination practices of her journey from her native land, Chile, to her host land for more than two decades, the United States. In her chapter, Ruiz correctly maintains that language intersects with our identity. She further argues that words are praxis: reflection and action. Ruiz suggests that as critical language pedagogues we must rethink how we use language in the classroom. She also states that we must be aware that words can be evocative of multiple meanings, sensations, emotions, and memories. Many classrooms, insisting on Standard English as the sole vehicle for thought, create word walls that act to exclude students from understanding and belonging. Finally, Ruiz contends that sharing personal experience can help understand how words create consciousness among youth, especially refugee and other children displaced from the narrative forms approved by Standard English.

Similarly, in "Unfair Comparisons: Monolingual Norms and Language Discrimination Against Nonnative English-Speaking Students at U.S. Colleges and Universities," John Katunich examines the ways and the degree to which the predominance of a monolingual English norm within the context of U.S. higher education impacts the academic identities and performance of nonnative speakers of English at U.S. universities. By applying research on stereotype threat that has investigated how negative stereotypes of racial/ethnic minorities and women affect academic identity and performance, his chapter presents the case that a similar phenomenon may explain lived experiences of nonnative speakers of English in U.S. academic contexts. Katunich's chapter further advocates for a reconceptualization of the linguistic environment of U.S. higher education that is not grounded in assumptions of a monolingual, native-speaking English norm.

In "An Arabyyah-Muslimah Queer Feminist Negotiating Gender/Nation/Sexuality/Colonial Discourses," Manal Hamzeh critically examines multiple forms of oppression, including colonial, imperial, racial, gender, and sexual oppression. Professor Hamzeh critically traces back her personal and professional experiences as the first female and lesbian educational audiologist striving to meet the needs of deaf people in her native Jordan. She goes further to talk about the way she has had to negotiate and affirm her multiple identities as a lesbian in a very oppressive and homophobic world and as a transnational female professor of color from a [neo] colonized land living in an imperialist country. Specifically, Professor Hamzeh, who has been inspired by her parents' long history of activism, eloquently explained how she has been profiled and targeted crossing borders in the U.S. imperial land for carrying a Jordanian passport despite her status as a university professor. In addition, Professor Hamzeh illuminates through counternarrative how she has strategically dealt with xenophobic attitudes and behaviors in her own community and the U.S. community as a whole. Finally, while being fully aware of the possible danger she faces as a nonconformist lesbian *Arabyyah-Muslimah*, Professor Hamzeh is determined to continue to use her writing and teaching to challenge students to question the normalization of many forms of oppression/social injustice in society.

In "Fighting Microaggression on University and College Campuses," Marivel Oropeza explores the way that Latina/o students endure different forms of racism on university and college campuses. Specifically, drawing on her personal experience as a Latina and relevant literature, Oropeza illuminates how students of color are confronted with microaggessions on university/college campuses and beyond. She shares three testimonios or testimonies to illustrate the way she has been a victim of microaggressions. In the first testimony, Oropeza recounts an experience of linguicism related to word choice. In the second, she details an incident that transpired under the supervision of a campus administrator, whereas in the third, Oropeza recounts a microaggression of linguicism that she experienced while working with a university professor.

Part II

In *Marxist Scholarship in Neoliberal Times: Social Imagination or Social Revolution?* distinguished professor and dissident scholar Antonia Darder draws on Marxist theoretical framework to unveil the socioeconomic inequities inherent in the capitalist and neoliberal system. Specifically, Darder examines how neoliberalism and neoconservatism have an impact on education, on equality within education, on the standard of public-sector provision, and on the lives of teachers—with increased managerialization and intensification of work. Similarly, in "A Critical Pedagogy of Revolutionary Solidarity Against Neoliberal, White-Supremacist, Petro-Chemical Plunder," Curry Stephenson Malott critically analyzes the harmful effects of corporatization and militarization of schools on student learning and teachers' teaching practices. Malott locates this form of corporatization and militarization in the context of the U.S.-capitalist system. Malott critiques U.S. institutions that have been applying a corporate model of education to fit the logic of the capitalist system. Furthermore, Professor Malott unveils rampant social inequity in the US school system where historically marginalized groups have continued to receive a poor-quality education and have been subjected to regimented, standardized tests, especially with the implementation of the No Child Left Behind Act (NCLB) mandates. Professor Malott provides a sharp critique of NCLB, arguing that it is designed to perpetuate a system of neoliberal educational apartheid. Searching for ever-deeper connections, Malott connects these schooling trends to a sharp critique of the U.S.-capitalist system in general, contending that capitalist schooling has only ever enabled the CEOs of global corporations to maximize their profits at the expense of the poor.

In "Understanding History From the Standpoint of the Oppressed," Pierre Orelus draws on postcolonial theory to examine and challenge the Western version of world history. Through critical analysis of the biased nature of world history, Orelus offers a novel, anticolonial, and an inclusive approach of history, taking into account world historical figures such as Toussaint-Louverture and Simon Bolívar, whose heroic actions and great legacy have been overshadowed. Orelus ends his chapter inviting the reader to deconstruct world history written from a Western perspective.

In "Uncovering the Neoliberal and Neocolonial Western Agenda," Professor Sangeeta Kamat begins by talking about her background growing up in Bombay, India, and her engagement with activist-oriented social work situated in the context of structural adjustment and neoliberal capitalism into an exploration of how that rise in global corporate power has impacted universities in the United States and the historically progressive institution she teaches at, University of Massachusetts, Amherst. Professor Kamat explores how her experience as a woman of color has impacted her work and how she is perceived in that context. Central to this discussion is Kamat's reflection on her ongoing work and life in India and other developing parts of the world, including parts of Africa and Central America. This enlightening interview contributes significantly to our overall understanding of great complexity of the ongoing influence neocolonialism and neoliberalism have on individual lives as well as global patterns of extreme poverty and overwhelming opulence.

Finally, in "Education, Neoliberalism, Neoconservatism, and Class Struggle in Britain and Europe," Dave Hill argues that neoliberalism—marked, inter alia, by the marketization, commodification, degradation, managerialization and privatization/preprivatization of public services—has a twin: neoconservatism. Hill describes and analyzes the neoliberal/neoconservative education revolution in Britain. He isolates, in particular, marketization/competition/choice: "parental choice," league tables and high-stakes testing, and privatization/preprivatization of schooling: the case of (charter school–like) academy schools now more than 50% of high schools in England. And he discusses what he and other critical/Marxist/socialist educators see as a duty to develop critical education. He concludes his chapter by examining effects of neoliberalism and conservatism on teachers in schools: managerialism, surveillance, and control, using a small-scale investigation, located within wider research, into high school (in England, "secondary school") teachers voicing their observations on managerialism, surveillance, and control and the Ofsted inspection regime.

CONCLUDING THOUGHTS

This book, which gathers the courageous voices of many progressive scholars, examines issues such as colonization, corporate model of education, and racism, including the genocide of Native Americans. This book draws on postcolonial, feminist, and Marxist theoretical frameworks and lived and professional experiences of scholars working primarily with marginalized groups to analyze and unmask brutal forms of oppression these groups have experienced in the U.S. school system and elsewhere. It goes on to link these forms of oppression to U.S. racism and White supremacy, colonization, and the larger unequal socioeconomic and political systems. We invite the reader to critically engage the ideas articulated by the authors in this volume. Our hope is that the reader will take the ideas expressed throughout the book and act on them. That is the only way, we believe, real changes will happen.

REFERENCES

Ackerman, F. (1982). *Reaganomics: Rhetoric vs. reality*. Boston: South End Press.
Aronowitz, S. (2001). *The knowledge factory: Dismantling the corporate university and creating true higher learning*. Boston: Beacon Press.
Callinicos, A. (2011). *The revolutionary ideas of Karl Marx*. Chicago: Haymarket.
Chomsky, N. (1994). *Secrets, lies and democracy*. Berkeley, CA: Odonian Press.
Chomsky, N. (1999). *Profit over people: Neoliberalism and global order*. New York: Seven Stories.
Chomsky, N. (2004). *Hegemony or survival: America's quest for global dominance*. New York: Holt Paperbacks.

Schugurensky, D. (2007). Higher education restructuring in the era of globalization: Toward a heteronomous model? In Robert F. Arnove and Carlos Alberto Torres (Eds.), *Comparative education: The dialectic of the global and the local* (pp. 257–276). New York: Rowan & Littlefield.

Steinberg, S. (2012). Democracy and social justice in a capitalist society: Is this possible? A conversation with Shirley Steinberg. In P. W. Orelus & C. S. Malott, (Eds.), *Radical voices for democratic schooling: Exposing neoliberal inequalities* (pp. 222–236). New York: Palgrave Macmillan.

Part I

Unmasking the Wretchedness of Neoliberalism and Neocolonialism

1 Colonialism in the 21st Century
A Critical Analysis

Pierre Wilbert Orelus

> Colonialism denies human rights to human beings whom it has subdued by violence, and keeps them by force in a state of misery and ignorance that Marx would rightly call a subhuman condition.
>
> —Jean P. Sartre, foreword to *The Colonizer and The Colonized* (Memmi, 1965)

Being born and raised in a country with a history of colonialism is one of the greatest challenges that descendants of formerly colonized countries have been facing. The reason is that the shadow of colonialism is deeply imprinted on their psyche and human consciousness and follows them throughout their journey in life. In fact, the legacy of colonialism overshadows the multifaceted aspects of neocolonized subjects' ways of living and being in the world. In this sense, it is reasonable to argue that these subjects are in the best position to know how it is like to be neocolonized and cope with the aftermath and legacy of colonialism, such as continuous colonial domination of the school, political, and economic systems of their native land, and their misrepresentation, including the misrepresentation of their culture and history. This chapter aims at shedding light on these crucial issues. To this end, I begin by reviewing key scholarly work of postcolonial scholars like Albert Memmi and Frantz Fanon. I go on to analyze the ways and the extent to which the legacy of colonialism continues to impact the school system, the economy, and the political apparatus of many formerly colonized countries, such as Haiti and India. I end this chapter making proposals as to what needs to be done to counter the effects of the colonial legacy on people living in countries that were colonized and continue to be victimized by such a legacy.

COLONIALISM STILL AT WORK: A HISTORICAL OVERVIEW

In the *Colonizer and the Colonized*, Albert Memmi (1965) brilliantly dissected the structure of the colonial system. Memmi analyzed how colonialism dehumanized the colonized through brutal exploitation, subjugation, and misery. However, as Memmi made clear, the colonized were not the only ones who suffered from colonialism. The colonizers also suffered from it. They constantly feared that the colonized could violently revolt against the inhumane conditions they were forcibly put in by poisoning or brutally killing their colonizers. Thus, it can be argued that the colonial system rendered both the colonizers and the colonized its slaves. To paraphrase Memmi, the so-called freedom that the colonizers enjoyed could only be maintained by sophisticated weapons, ideological brainwashing, and institutionalized fear. Psychologically, they were not free; to some extent they were just as enslaved as the colonized.

Memmi's economic and political analysis of colonialism is very insightful in that it can help one understand Western neocolonialism. Although Memmi did not explicitly make any claim as to what would happen to formerly colonized countries decades after they were colonized, his ideas, as articulated through his book, were somewhat prophetic. That is, the economic and political situations of colonized countries, as Memmi laid them out in his book, are not so different from the current educational, economic, social, and political situations of countries such as Haiti, Congo, and India. For example, during colonialism the educational, political, and economic system of these countries was dominated and destroyed by European colonial powers' policies. Currently, with the rise of Western neocolonial and neoliberal economic policy, implemented through the World Bank, the International Monetary Fund, and the World Trade Organization, the economic system of Haiti and India, for example, seems to be as bad as it was during colonization. For example, as a result of the implementation of this policy in these countries, many Indian and Haitian farmers have been forced to abandon their farms. This has economically and psychologically affected both the Haitian and Indian farmers and their family. According to Arundhati Roy (2006), sixty wives of Indian farmers committed suicide because they were overwhelmed by the accumulated debt of their husbands who were forced out of work due to Western neoliberal economic policy. Roy put it in those terms while she was commenting on the official visit of former U.S. President George W. Bush in 2006 in India to sign an "economic deal" with the Indian government:

> But I must say that while Bush was in Delhi, at the same time on the streets there were—I mean apart from the protests, there were 60 widows that had come from Kerala, which is the south of India, which is where I come from, and they had come to Delhi because they were 60 out of the tens of thousands of widows of farmers who have committed suicide, because they have been encircled by debt. And this is a fact that is simply not reported, partly because there are no official figures, partly because the Indian government quibbles about what constitutes suicide and what is a farmer. (Roy, interviewed by Democracy Now! host Amy Goodman, May 2006)

Roy's statement illustrates that colonization, through the Western model of globalization, is still happening in formerly colonized countries, albeit manifested in different forms and shapes. It also can be inferred from her statement that Western neoliberal economic policy has mainly served the interest of already existing privileged groups in formerly colonized countries but not that of the poor farmers and factory workers.

Likewise, Memmi's diagnosis of the situation of the colonized and their occupied territories seems relevant today and will most likely remain relevant for decades to come unless neocolonial subjects, including intellectuals, align with the masses to combat Western neoliberal economic policy. Simply put, as long as Western neoliberal policy is still at work, Third World countries will continue to experience educational, economic, and political dominations. With respect to the school system of formerly colonized countries, such system continues to reflect the colonial legacy through its practices, including language policies implemented in these countries.

In the case of former colonized country like Haiti, I argue that any anti-colonial project aimed at rescuing the country from the colonial vestige should first and foremost involve transforming the Haitian school system that is still colonial-based. The earthquake occurring there in 2010 destroyed major historical and school buildings in this country, for example. However, in my view, the colonial mentality that has long inhabited these buildings has not disappeared. In other words, the colonial mentality would persist in many Haitians' minds and souls regardless of the fact these school and historical buildings were collapsed during the earthquake. These minds and souls need to be decolonized (Thiong'o, 1986) if Haiti is to transcend the negative effect of the French colonial legacy in order to become the independent, autonomous, and prosperous Haiti that genuinely concerned and caring Haitians have long wished for. After two hundred years of independence, Haiti unfortunately continues to emulate the French educational system. French, the language of the colonizer, is still valued over the Haitian Creole, the maternal language of all Haitians except those from the upper class who grow up speaking French as their first language.

Haitian students whose minds are still colonized tend to value more the French language than the Haitian Creole. They also tend to show more appreciation for French literature and history than for Haitian literature and history. Until a fundamental change occurs in the Haitian educational system, including a profound transformation of the colonial mentality of many Haitian students, Haiti would continue to be a neocolonized nation. Likewise, until Haitian leaders with human and political dignity join their brilliant minds and souls together to discuss and attempt to solve the pressing educational, socioeconomic, and political problems that Haiti has been facing, it would continue to be a nation that depends on its former colonial and imperial powers, such as France and the United States, respectively, to solve its internal problems. A nation can't shape its destiny and stand on its feet when its people are still trapped in a colonial mentality.

Like Haiti, many formerly colonized countries have been experiencing a new form of colonialism since their "independence." This new form of colonialism, which is analyzed in the book, is perhaps worse than nineteenth-century colonialism because, although subtle at times, it is operational at all levels (e.g., educational, political, social, economic, cultural, and ideological) in non-Western countries particularly. It is worth emphasizing that Memmi's detailed and perspicacious descriptions of the political, economic, and social situations of the colonized to a great extent reflect the political, educational, social, and economic situations of marginalized Haitians, Indians, Somalis, and Sudanese, among others. These neocolonized subjects have been deprived of basic human rights and needs, such as clean and safe water, food, and shelter, while living under the constant threat of imperial and neocolonizing powers such as the United States, Great Britain, and France.

People who have lived under colonialism and/or have to deal with the historical, educational, political, social, cultural, and psychological effects of colonialism do not know what their lives would have been like if their countries were not colonized. But this might not even be relevant or important to them in the final calculation, for after experiencing colonization, what these people do know is the color and taste of exploitation and humiliation resulting from it. Memmi (1965) explains this colonial phenomenon in the following terms:

> We have no idea what the colonized would have been without colonization, but we certainly see what has happened as a result of it. To subdue and exploit, the colonizer pushed the colonized out of the historical and social, cultural and technical current. What is real and verifiable is that the colonized's culture, society and technology are seriously damaged. (p. 114)

Placing Memmi's argument in the context of neocolonialism, I argue that the struggle for political, economic, and cultural autonomies of countries that were formerly colonized must go on even though these countries have been "independent" for decades. The reason is that, despite the fact that White colonial administrators are no longer present in the colony to defend the interest of their superior colonialists in the Western metropolitans, formerly colonized countries are still under the gaze of Western neocolonial powers. Arundhati Roy (2003) eloquently unravels this neocolonial phenomenon in most of her scholarly and activist work. Roy (2003) argues:

> This time around, the colonizer does not need a token white presence in the colonies. The CEOs and their men do not need to go to the trouble of tramping through the tropics, risking malaria, diarrhea, sunstroke, and an early death. They do not have to maintain an army or a police force, or worry about insurrections and mutinies. They can have their

> colonies and an easy conscience. "Creating a good investment climate" is the new euphemism for western repression. Besides, the responsibility for implementation rests with the local administration. (p. 17)

What Roy points out above reflects the sad political and economic realities of most—if not all—formerly colonized countries in Africa, Asia, Latin America, and in the Caribbean. Despite radical nationalist movements that emerged out of mass struggle to resist the hegemonic influence of the West on Third World countries, the former still finds ways to control internal affairs of these countries through complicity of corrupt leaders. These corrupt leaders are often put in power to defend the interests of the West while the majority of people, including journalists, students, and factory workers, are being murdered, exploited, and oppressed. The assassination of the famous Haitian journalist Jean Dominique, in 2000, is a case in point. (See the movie *The Agronomist* for more details.)

Like Memmi, Fanon (1963) addressed issues related to domination and oppression in the colonial context. In *The Wretched of the Earth*, Fanon (1963) clarified the source of the pitfall of national consciousness caused by a national bourgeois class. This bourgeois class uses "the working class of the towns, the masses of unemployed, the small artisans and craftsmen to line up behind its nationalist attitude" (Fanon, 1965, p. 34) for its own political and economic gains. In other words, the bourgeois class uses the masses to take over the colonizer's political and economic positions and to defend its own interests. The current economic and political state of formerly colonized countries, such as Uganda, Haiti, Somalia, Zimbabwe, Congo, and Rwanda, is a prime example of a national bourgeois class whose goal is to have access to and remain in power by using the masses.

After years of independence from the French and British colonial powers, these countries have been destroyed by the greedy elite who, in order to stay in power, have isolated and killed whoever opposed to their hegemonic agenda and violent actions. Moreover, while in power, this elite group usually reproduces the same colonial practices of the colonizer, for its political agenda is to replace the colonizers but not to change the status quo. As Fanon observed,

> The national middle class, which takes over power at the end of the colonial regime, is an underdeveloped middle class. It has practically no economic power, and in any case it is in no way commensurate with the bourgeoisie of the mother country, which it hopes to replace. In its narcissism, the national middle class is easily convinced that it can advantageously replace the middle class of the mother country. (p. 149)

As Fanon noted, being obsessed with power, the emerging middle class from a colonial state has only strived to have access to and remain in power. Given their opportunistic and bourgeois attitude, members of this class throughout history have been known to be reactionary. Like the colonizers, this class, often supported by the West, has proven to be oppressive to the poor masses and its opponents while in power. Some Haitian leaders are good examples of this. As Chomsky (2002) observes, "The United States has been supporting the Haitian military and dictators for two hundred years—it is not a new policy" (p. 35).

Chomsky's statement illustrates a very important point that I wish to make here. It is not merely the French and the British who have been oppressing and exploiting the Haitians, Ugandans, Sudanese, Zimbabweans, Somalis, and the Rwandans; also, the powerful Haitians, Ugandans, Sudanese, Somalis, and Rwandans who, by carrying out the legacy of colonialism and executing the economic order of the West at the expense of the poor, have been torturing and impoverishing their compatriots. The colonizers and occupying empires have "left" the formerly colonized land, but the powerless people living in this land have been experiencing what I would call *intranational colonization* by their own leaders. That is, being supported by and, in some cases, put in power by former Western neocolonial and imperialist powers, such as the United States, Great Britain, and France, these so-called leaders have divided their poor countries into multiple hostile and antagonist groups for their political gains. They have also worked tirelessly to serve and protect both the interests of the Western imperial powers and their own.

Some of these postcolonial leaders have not proven that they are ready to govern and unite their nation and people living within. By making this argument, I do not intend here to justify the distorted view of the colonizers who, in order to maintain the colonial status quo, have repeatedly stated that colonized people are not ready or able to govern and represent themselves and must therefore let the colonial power do it for them. Rather, I am arguing that the real and uncompromising leaders emerging from the mass, or what Gramsci (1971) called organic intellectuals, have not had the chance to lead and govern their countries without being attacked or killed by internal and external opposing forces supported by Western colonial and imperial powers. A good example of this is the Congolese prime minister, Patrice Lumumba, who was assassinated by Western imperial power due to his nationalism and autonomous political and economic decisions to serve his country. (See the movie *Lumumba* for more details about the assassination of Patrice Lumumba by the Belgium and the U.S. governments with the complicity of some national political opponents.)

In *Dying Colonialism,* Fanon (1963) warned us of the danger of having a nationalist bourgeois and elite government take control of the nation after independence. Having assessed the social and political situations of the colonized Algeria, Fanon explained what consequences would result from the deceitful and dishonest political acts of the elite if they ever took over power. Fanon eloquently articulates that the elite have no interest in protecting from the colonizers the inalienable rights of the poor farmers and peasants. On the contrary, like the colonizers, the elite have a lot to gain from torturing the poor in order to have access to power. Said (1993) brilliantly captured Fanon's argument when he argued, "The national bourgeoisies and their specialized elites, of which Fanon speaks so ominously, in effect tended to replace the colonial force with a new class-based and ultimately exploitative one, which replicated the old colonial structures in new terms" (p. 223).

As historically proven, the national elite's "false generosity" (Freire, 1970) would be soon unveiled during national liberation and independence. Once colonized countries gained their independence, the elite of these countries were the first to collaborate with the colonizers in order to have access to power while marginalizing the peasants, farmers, and the rest of the population. The Congolese dictator Mobutu Sese Seko is a case in point. With the help of the former colonial power, Belgium and the United States, he overthrew and participated in the assassination of the populist Congolese prime minister, Patrice Lumumba, whom he succeeded. While in power, he continued to receive support from the Belgian government despite the fact he was murdering civilians who opposed his government, as demonstrated in the movie *Lumumba*. Similarly, in the context of the neocolonial era, the elite of invaded and occupied countries such as Iraq and Afghanistan tend to be the group of people that collaborate with Western imperialist powers like the United States so they can have access to political and economic power. Ruling with a Western mind, this elite class has created space and paved the path for Western empires to continue to invade and Westernize the third world, to whose analysis I turn next.

THE WESTERNIZATION OF THE THIRD WORLD

As amply documented, neocolonizers and occupiers have always tried to subjugate and put formerly colonized and currently occupied countries in a subaltern position. To this end, colonial powers, such as Great Britain, France, and now the United States, have eagerly and tenaciously been trying to control the internal economic and political affairs of formerly colonized countries. What have been the consequences of such imperialist actions? This question can be answered by taking a close look at what the United States and its imperialist ally, Great Britain, have done to Third World countries, such as Haiti, Pakistan, Afghanistan, and East Timor, for decades. They have invaded, brutally exploited, and tried to impose their prefabricated notion of democracy on these countries. In some of these countries, such as Afghanistan and Iraq, they have been somewhat successful by putting in power a puppet government that has been defending their interests. Given such imperialist actions, it is clear that the ideological, political, and economic agenda of these Western imperialist powers has been to Westernize the Third World through their neoliberal policy of ideological, economic, political, and cultural dominations. Westernizing the third world is certainly not a new concept, for it has existed for centuries.

However, its effect nowadays is more obvious than ever before in formerly colonized countries, which dared to fight for and gain their independence from Western countries like Great Britain, France, and Spain. Before going any further to discuss the Westernization of the world, it is worth asking oneself: What is the West and what does it stand for?

The West has been conquering the rest of the world for centuries and has been a champion of the exploitation of the poor. Moreover, the West has monopolized the keys to the most advanced and sophisticated technology so it can control the Third World. The West should be held accountable for the poverty and human misery of Third World countries, yet has gotten away with it without blame; further, the West has been exploiting and trying to politically control the Third World in order to occupy the most powerful position in the world. Finally, the West expects Third World countries to go along with its economic policy of oppression and domination.

Returning to the attempt of the West to Westernize the rest of the world, I argue that such policy aimed at controlling not only the political and economic aspects of Third World countries but also their ideological apparatus. As Said (1993) put it, "Westerners may have physically left their old colonies in Africa and Asia, but they retained them not only as markers but as locales on the ideological map over which they continued to rule morally and intellectually" (p. 25). Said's statement is quite revealing and speaks to imperialist powers' propaganda aimed at ideologically influencing and controlling a great portion of the rest of the world. One of the arguments that the U.S. and British governments have often put forward to justify their invasion and occupation of other countries is that the United States and Great Britain are civilized and democratic nations. Therefore, any country that is not civilized and democratic has to be civilized according to the United States and Great Britain's definition of these concepts.

In other words, in the eyes of these neocolonial and neoliberal powers, the Western definition of democracy, liberty, and freedom is the best one and therefore must be embraced by undemocratic and uncivilized Third World nations. Clearly the message that the West seems to be sending to the rest of the world is that "We westerners we will decide who is a good or bad native, because all natives have sufficient existence by virtue of our cognition. We created them, we taught them to speak and think, and when they rebel they simply confirm our views of them as silly children duped by some of their Western masters" (Said, 1993, xviii).

One would then need to be politically naïve and misinformed to fail to understand that the hidden ideology behind these outright lies of the West is to economically, culturally, and politically dominate the rest of the world. As U.S. imperialism has been trying to politically and economically control a great portion of the world, the West no longer encompasses only the British, French, and Spanish empires, which, for decades, colonized thousands of countries in Africa, the Caribbean, Asia, South and Central America. In other words, as Latouche (1996) brilliantly put it,

> The West no longer means Europe, either geographically or historically; it is no longer even a collection of beliefs shared by a group of people scattered over the earth. I see it as a machine, impersonal, soulless, and nowadays masterless, which impressed mankind into its service. This mad machine has shaken off all human attempts to stop it and now roves the planet, uprooting what and where it will: tearing men from their native ground, even in the furthest reaches of the world, and hurling them into urban deserts without any attempt to adjust them to the limitless industrialization, bureaucracy and technical 'progress' which the machine is pursuing. (pp. 4–5)

The concept machine that Latouche used in defining the West symbolizes, in my view, globalization and its catastrophic socioeconomic and political effects on Third World countries. My argument is that globalization is in itself a machine that corporate Western imperialist countries have been using to widen the gap between the haves and the have-nots, the privileged groups and the underprivileged groups, in Third World countries. Globalization has probably caused more economic harm to countries in the Third World than any operational capitalist machine that Western imperialist countries have historically used for gigantic profits. The supposed initial mission of globalization was to strengthen the economy of countries devastated by the Second World War, to create more jobs, and transport beyond borders goods and medical equipments from which people, especially the poor, could benefit.

However, informed by a Western corporate capitalist agenda, globalization has drastically paralyzed the economy of poorest Third World countries. As the democratically elected president of Bolivia, Evo Morales, eloquently put it, "Globalization creates economic policies where the transnationals lord over us, and the result is misery and unemployment" (Morales, interviewed by *Times* magazine, 2006).

Globalization is not a new economic and political phenomenon, for there has always been trade between countries. However, to paraphrase Kamat (2000) and Robertson (1992), through the Western version of globalization, Third World countries have simply been put under the siege of Western economic expansion and exploitation. In fact, with its ruinous effects, globalization has profoundly impacted the economy of poor countries like Haiti, Bolivia, Guatemala, El Salvador, and India. Roy (2001) describes the impact of globalization on India in the following terms:

> From April 1, 2001, according to the terms of its agreement with the World Trade Organization (WTO), the Indian government will have to

> drop its quantitative import restrictions. The Indian market is already flooded with cheap imports. Though India is technically free to export its agricultural produce, in practice most of it cannot be exported because it does not meet the first world's "environmental standards." (You do not eat bruised mangoes, or bananas with mosquito bites, or rice with a few evils in it . . . In effect, India's rural economy, which supports seven hundred million people, is being garroted. Farmers who produce too much are in distress, farmers who produce too little are in distress, and landless agricultural laborers are out of work as big estates and farms lay off their workers. They are flocking to the cities in search of employment. (pp. 15–16)

As Roy's description of the horrible economic situation of India clearly indicates, globalization is not the solution to the economic and social problems of Third World countries. It has simply been used as part of the neocolonial and neoliberal agenda of the United States, France, and Great Britain to continue exploiting their formerly colonized countries. Like the former White colonial administrators in the French and British colonies, the CEOs of World Trade Organization (WTO), World Bank (WB), and International Monetary Fund (IMF) have local administrators in countries like Jamaica, India, and Haiti to defend the interests of these organizations. As Roy noted earlier, these CEOs do not have to be in these tropical countries and run the risk of getting malaria or other illnesses and deal directly with factory workers there. They can still make millions from these workers' sweat and blood without having to know who they are, let alone interact with them.

As the rhetoric of CEOs of these capitalist corporations seems to suggest, it would be ideal if the objective of IMF, WTO, and WB were to financially help Third World countries to be economically stable. But their corporate agenda is to destabilize to an even greater extent the economy of these countries that rely on the backbone of farmers who are unable to compete with the technological advances and the economic greed-driven attitude of Western countries. Joseph E. Stiglitz (2003) puts it in these terms:

> Forcing a developing country to open itself up to imported products that would compete with those produced by certain of its industries, industries that were dangerously vulnerable to competition from much stronger counterpart industries in other countries, can have disastrous consequences—socially and economically. Jobs have systematically been destroyed—poor farmers in developing countries simply could not compete with the highly subsidized goods from Europe and America—before the countries' industrial and agricultural sectors were able to grow strong and create new jobs. (p. 17)

In addition to Roy's analysis of India's terrible economic situation caused by the Western version of globalization, Stiglitz's critique of this corporate capitalist machine makes clear that Third World countries will get poorer and poorer as long as they continue signing diabolic economic contracts with WB and IMF. Unfortunately, signing this kind of economic contract with these Western organizations is a vicious economic cycle in which many Third World countries have been trapped. This vicious economic cycle has thus far been responsible for the chronic poverty of the poor in the Third World.

I go further to argue that the root of the political, economic, and social problems of these countries seems also to partially lie in the so-called educational, economic, and social programs of the West through non-governmental organizations in Third World countries. Colonialism has unquestionably paralyzed economically, politically, and even culturally Third World countries. However, I assert that neocolonialism appears to be worse than colonialism, because, although subtle, its devastating effects are enormous and unprecedented.

Neocolonialism can be and is indeed implanted in neocolonized lands in an invisible way that might not instantaneously provoke radical mass movements among those who have been marginalized and oppressed. In fact, neocolonialism has been used by Western countries like a slow but an active economic and political poison pill administered by corporate organizations such as IMF, WB, and, to a certain extent, the nongovernmental organizations (NGOs) to which I am now turning my analysis.

ARE NGOS A NEW FORM OF COLONIALISM?

Unlike the policies and regulations of IMF and WB that usually lead to instantaneous reactions from the poor, NGOs have had an easier time being implemented in Third World countries. The reason behind this is that many people in such countries as Haiti and India generally tend to believe that the goal of these organizations is to help the poor without any governmental influence. Consequently, NGOs are perceived to be politically neutral and economically autonomous while carrying out the so-called humanitarian mission. This perception and conception of NGOs has led some activists and intellectuals from the "left" to work with and/or for these organizations.

I am reminded when I was in high school, one of my teachers, who was known to be a leftist, worked for an NGO for over a decade. Through his daily rhetoric he never hesitated to speak in favor of this organization. In fact, he took pride in being one of the representatives of this organization. My teacher's rhetoric about his affiliation with the NGO was so convincing and his influence was so strong that I felt the burning desire to work for this "great organization," as he usually put it. At the time I thought that working with or for this organization would enable me to help the poor without having to deal with the politics of governmental deceit. Thus, my goal after high school was to work for an NGO while pursuing a college degree.

However, what my teacher failed to explain was that, although there might be some NGOs that contribute to some kind of social change, this organization has not yet proven to be capable of helping eradicate chronic social, economic, and political problems that have sabotaged Third World countries. Although, to a certain extent, NGOs might have helped certain social institutions in poor countries remain functional, I argue they simultaneously constitute a barrier to radical social, political, educational, and economic changes in these countries. The reason is that real changes cannot take place without attacking the political apparatus that holds power and privilege and often contributes to the unequal distribution of wealth among citizens.

Yet, as a politically and governmentally "neutral" organization, NGOs do not seem to have any interest in speaking to power. Therefore, it may be argued that these organizations are in direct or indirect complicity with governments that are hostile to radical social and political changes. In fact, the very existence of NGOs in Third World countries works to the advantage of the governments of these countries because these organizations can be used as a façade to mask a country's lamentable educational, economic, and social conditions, and thus the misery of the poor.

I argue that NGOs are part of the Western neocolonialist agenda that operates in a subtle way. By making this argument, I am not suggesting that NGOs should be fought against like neocolonialism should, as some NGOs have somewhat contributed to certain type of social change, such as providing some training to teachers and social services workers, and opening cultural centers for young people. However, my argument is that if NGOs are really serious about effecting social change, they must begin by finding ways in which to influence the political force of the countries where they are operating. One of the ways this can be done is to help the youth be aware of and active in the political affairs of their own countries. Failing to do so, NGOs will simply help maintain the status quo in Third World countries. With that said, I suggest that NGOs should be restructured in order to become part of the organizational machine that runs for social justice and social change in Third World countries.

For example, in Haiti, a country that has been run mostly by NGOs, an important thing that needs to be changed within these organizations is their bureaucratic structure. Among NGO's employees, there are college students, professors, and the so-called leftist intellectuals who only see these organizations as a way to fill up their pockets and embellish their résumés, rather than organizations through which they can work to effect transformative and social change. It goes without saying that corruption from within NGOs is rampant, although it might not be as visible as political corruption that ruins the socioeconomic and political structures of Third World countries. In short, to be effective and truly helpful to Third World countries, NGOs need to be involved in and support the political struggle in which the poor have been engaged. Otherwise, these organizations will merely be a pill that temporarily relieves the pain of educational, social, and economic diseases of Third World countries caused by the West, rather than being a part of the diagnosis and cure of these diseases. Finally, by failing to denounce atrocities of governments that have put Third World countries in a state of political, social, and economic agonies and dependence, NGOs will most likely be accused of perpetuating the legacy of Western colonialism.

WESTERN HEGEMONIC CONTROL OF THE THIRD WORLD

As previously noted, Western neocolonizing countries have no other political and economic agenda for Third World countries but to politically and economically paralyze them. To do so, they have been using all sorts of strategies. The most common strategy has thus far been invasion and occupation of these countries. When Western neocolonizing powers cannot create a climate of terror and fear as an excuse to invade and occupy Third World countries, they try to manipulate puppet political leaders to protect their corporate interests (Chomsky, 2004; Parenti, 1995). In other cases, they train and finance death-squad groups to oust or kill any democratic leader that refuses to obey their political and economic dictates (Chomsky, 2004; Parenti, 1995). Thereafter, they orchestrate a climate of terror aiming to justify their military intervention and invasion in these countries to supposedly help restore peace and order. The climate of economic and political terror ignited by the United States leading to the overthrow of the Haitian president, Jean Bertrand Aristide, is a case in point. Trained and supported by these neocolonizing powers, a group of soldiers politically destabilized Haiti until Aristide was forced to leave the country in 1991 and again 2004.

Immediately after his departure, the United Nations, following the orders of the United States, sent troops to supposedly establish democratic order in the country. I ask: Why did not the UN send the same troop to Haiti to counter the criminal action of these soldiers that helped overthrow President Jean Bertrand Aristide? Alluding to Western neocolonizing countries' rhetoric about promoting and maintaining democracy abroad, I wish to pose another question: How can a country boastfully claim that its goal is to help restore democracy in other countries around the globe while people within its own borders are deprived of their democratic rights? Chomsky (1996) captures this hypocrisy when he argues, "A society that excludes large areas of crucial decision-making from public control, or a system of governance that merely grants the general public the opportunity to ratify decisions taken by the elite groups that dominate the private society and the state, hardly merits the term democracy" (p. 33).

Elaborating on Chomsky's argument, I contend that one cannot talk about a democratic society when the government wants people to be only passive spectators and followers of its political and economic decisions.

Nor can one talk about democracy when it only satisfies and meets the needs of a small elite group. Whereas the West has not proven that it can promote and maintain democracy and freedom in its own land, ironically it has been increasingly determined to export its so-called notion of democracy and freedom abroad. In its own backyard, immigrants and minority groups, such as African Americans, Blacks, Latino/as, Native Americans, and people of Arabic descent, have been unfairly jailed and tortured. Thus, one has to ask if Western neocolonizing empires are not the most hypocritical empires that have ever existed on earth. For example, while unfairly arresting and brutalizing its own citizens who stand for workers', women's, minority's, and prisoners' rights and denying people of color access to decent housing, jobs, health care, and quality education, the West has been trying to sell its "banking concept" (Freire, 1970) of democracy and freedom to Third World countries. I argue that this act in itself is the most convincing evidence that the West is very hypocritical in that it does not practice what it has been preaching to the rest of the world.

Despite the corporate media's attempt to cover up what happened in countries such as Grenada, Panama, Guatemala, Chile, Haiti, Afghanistan, and Iraq, the informed citizens know what the West has done to these countries. They know that in 1982 the U.S. government participated in the assassination of Maurice Bishop because he was defending his country, Granada, from U.S. imperialism. They know that in 1990 the U.S. government invaded Panama to capture its former protégé, Manuel Noriega; that in the Dominican Republic this government supported the bloody dictator Trujillo, who murdered thousands of poor innocent Haitians; that in Guatemala in 1954 the United States participated in the overthrow of the socialist president, Jacob Albenz, who was perceived as a threat to its interests; that in 2003 the United States invaded Iraq for oil purposes but attempted to convince the American people and the world that they did so to overthrow the dictator Saddam Hussein, whom they accused of possessing nuclear weapons; that in Afghanistan in 2002 thousands of innocent children and elderly people lost their lives due to the U.S. invasion motivated by its search of Osama Bin Laden; that in Chile in 1973 the United States plotted the overthrow of a popular socialist president, Salvador Allende; and finally, in Haiti in 1991 and 2004 the U.S. government, with the complicity of corrupt Haitian political leaders and soldiers, twice overthrew the democratically elected president, Jean Bertrand Aristide, who they felt represented a threat to its interests. These actions are undeniable evidence that part of the neocolonizing agenda of Western countries is to have a free zone for big corporate investments in and to gain political and economic control of Third World countries. Said (2003) noted,

> Everything is packaged and up for sale. This is the meaning of the neoliberal market economy, which globalization has foisted on the world, leaving very little room for individual challenge and questioning,

> whereas large organizations, whether governments or corporations, pursue policies that are virtually blind in many instances, causing widespread environmental destruction, widespread genetic destruction, and the possibility for powerful groups to pursue profit without responsibility. (p. 99)

As Said's comment makes clear, what fundamentally matters to Western occupying and neocolonial powers are their corporate interests. The economic greed of Western imperialist countries becomes evident through their participation in the assassination of political activists and the ousting of leaders in Third World countries that they feel represent a threat to their corporate interests. Once their interests are in danger, it does not matter if people are oppressed, starving, or killed. Because of their economic greed, Western empires have been trying to put Third World countries under economic and political siege for decades. Occupying colonial forces were forced by grassroots mass movements to leave formerly colonized and occupied countries, but they left behind Western-trained national armies to protect their own interests. In formerly colonized countries such as Haiti and Congo, among others, most of the presidents have been generals or someone who was affiliated with the army of these countries.

So the colonial power, although not physically there, continues to control the political structure of these countries through the army and the complicity of corrupt leaders and the elite. Presidents who have risen out of a mass popular movement have either been ousted or killed by the Yankee army that has been put in place by Western neocolonizing countries. The short-lived presidencies of Salvador Allende in Chile, Patrice Lumumba in Congo, Thomas Sankara in Burkina Faso, and Maurice Bishop in Grenada are prime examples of this. However, dictators such as the Duvaliers in Haiti, Trujillo in the Dominican Republic, Pinochet in Chile, Mobutu Sese Seko in Congo, Suharto in Indonesia, and Hosni Mubarak in Egypt were protected by Western empires despite all the crimes they committed against their own people and humanity. Chomsky and Herman (1979) cast some light on this historical fact. They state:

> The old colonial world was shattered during World War II, and the resultant nationalist-radical upsurge threatened traditional Western hegemony and the economic interests of Western business. To contain this threat the United States has aligned itself with elite and military elements in the Third World whose function has been to contain the tides of change. This role was played by Diem and Thieu in South Vietnam and is currently served by allies such as Mobutu in Zaire, Pinochet in Chile, and Suharto in Indonesia. (p. 8)

As pointed out above by Chomsky and Herman, it is clear that the agenda of U.S. imperialism is to protect its corporate interest in formerly colonized countries by all means necessary. The complicity of the U.S. government in the assassination of priests and poor farmers in the countries of El Salvador and Nicaragua who stood up against U.S. imperialism in the late 1970s and 1980s are cases in point. For Western imperial powers like the United States, farmers and peasants are not human beings and therefore they can be treated and killed like animals. Ironically, the killing of these farmers has been done in the name of U.S. definition of freedom and democracy. In regard to this hypocrisy, Chomsky (1996) asks: "What kind of freedom is there inside a corporation?" (p. 45).

Chomsky's question is a valid one in that it speaks to the dominance of Third World countries by Western countries. Since their "independence," formerly colonized countries have been used by neocolonizing powers as convenient sites to build factories, where the poor provide cheap labor to make brand-name shoes, shirts, pants, and baseballs to enrich the CEOs of these factories. These products have been made by Haitian, Indian, and Pakistani factory workers for, say, between 25 and 50 cents per hour to be sold for a fortune in countries such as the United States and France. For example, a pair of jeans made by a Haitian factory worker for 30 cents could cost between $25 and $80 in the United States. Chomsky (1994) described such a horrible situation as follows:

> Baseballs are coming along nicely. They're produced in US-owned factories where the women who make them get 10 cents an hour—if they meet their quota. Since meeting the quota is virtually impossible, they actually make something like 5 cents an hour. Softballs from Haiti are advertised in the U.S. as being unusually good because they're hand-dipped into some chemical that makes them hang together properly. The ads don't mention that the chemical the women hand-dip the balls into is toxic and that, as a result, the women don't last long at this work. (p. 78)

As Chomsky points out above, the Western form of globalization has economically paralyzed poor Caribbean farmers and factory workers. Particularly in the case of Haiti, globalization has affected everyone; however, women have been the major victims of it. Haitian women have spent hours laboring for cheap prices in U.S.-owned factories. They barely have time to breast feed their babies. Even when they are sick they still have to go to work in these factories, for there is no law that obliges these foreign factories to provide health insurance and sick-day benefits to Haitian women. However, this horrible working condition to which Third World factory workers have been subjected in U.S. owned factories unfortunately remains unknown to many people in the West because the Western mass corporate media have too often covered it up. I wish to end this chapter making the following points: (1) The so-called version of Western democracy and neoliberal economic policies need to be questioned and fought against because they only serve the interest of Western imperial powers. And (2) given the ruinous economic and political effects of Western colonial and neocolonial policies on the Third World, it is imperative that what happens locally or nationally is linked to what happens internationally. Local, national, and international politics intersect. Therefore, they should not be studied in a disconnected way. Failing to link the national to the global might prevent one from grasping that Western colonial legacy has affected poor people both in the Third World and in the West.

REFERENCES

Chomsky, N. (1994). *Secrets, lies and democracy.* Berkeley, CA: Odonian Press.

Chomsky, N. (1996). *The common good.* Berkeley, CA: Odonian Press.

Chomsky, N. (2002). *Understanding power: The indispensable Chomsky.* New York: The New Press.

Chomsky, N. (2004). *Hegemony or survival: America's quest for global dominance.* New York: Holt Paperbacks.

Chomsky, N., & Herman, E. (1979). *The Washington connection and Third World fascism.* Boston: South End Press.

Fanon, F. (1963). *The wretched of the earth.* New York: Grove Press.

Fanon, F. (1965). *A dying colonialism.* New York: Grove Press.

Fanon, F. (1967). *Black skin white masks.* New York: Grove Press.

Freire, P. (1970). *Pedagogy of the oppressed.* New York: Seabury Press.

Gramsci, A. (1971). *Selections from the prison notebooks.* New York: International Publishers.

Kamat, S. (2000). Globalization/Paradox: Education, culture and the state in India. *Comparative Education Review, 40*(2).

Latouche, S. (1996). *The westernization of the world.* Cambridge, MA: Polity Press.

Morales, E. (2006). Interview. Time Magazine, June 5, 167 (23).

Memmi, A. (1965). *The colonizer and the colonized.* Boston: Beacon Press.

Parenti, M. (1995). *Against empire: A brilliant expose of the brutal realities of U.S. global domination.* San Francisco: City Lights Books.

Robertson, R. (1992). *Globalization: Social theory and global culture.* London: Sage.

Roy, A. (2001). *Power politics.* Cambridge, MA: South End Press.

Roy, A. (2003). *War talk.* Cambridge, MA: South End Press.

Roy, A. (2006, May 24). Interview. *Democracy Now!*

Said, E. (1993). *Culture and imperialism.* New York: Vintage Books.

Said, E. (2003). *Culture and resistance.* Cambridge, MA: South End Press.

Said, E. (1978). *Orientalism.* New York: Vintage Books.

Stiglitz, J. (2003). *Globalization and its discontents.* New York: W.W. Norton & Company.

Sartre, J.-P. Foreword. In A. Memmi (1965), *The colonizer and the colonized.* Boston: Beacon Press.

Thiong'o, N. (1986). *Decolonizing the mind: The politics of language in African literature.* Portsmouth, NH: Heinemann.

2 Violence and the Interstices of Difference

Working With(in) and Around Fanon

George J. Sefa Dei and Loren Ola Delaney

INTRODUCTION

In this chapter we have set out to use Fanon's life and scholarly works, particularly on violence, to interpret and understand a particular actual event as a story that focuses on racial, gender, sexual, and disability violence drawing on the interstices of oppressions. We narrate the story in the first-person pronoun as it speaks to the particularity of the event, as specifically encountered/experienced by one of the authors. But we also want to register how this particularity is a shared common daily experience for certain bodies in our communities. Our learning objective is both to understand Fanon and also to show how the understanding of a Fanonian conception of violence is complicated and defies easy readings. We argue through the story that violence can also be masked in the everyday racist, sexist, ableist, homophobic practices of bodies who wield dominant power. The chapter lends credence to those who argue that Fanon never simply proposed nor valorized violence but instead set out to diagnose the problem of violence (see Austin, 2006; Samuel, 1997). To understand Fanon on violence we must first understand what shaped this man and his ideas. Fanon grew up with violence, which we argue is part of the everyday encounters of racialized, gendered, and sexualized minorities in our dominant culture.

It is actually an understatement to say that the writings and ideas of Frantz Fanon (1921–1961), the psychiatrist, humanist, revolutionary fighter, and a social-political analyst, have significantly influenced anticolonial and antiracist struggles of our times. Those who deny this history have not read Fanon intensely. Although he died at the young age of thirty-six of leukemia, his short life span contrasts sharply with the knowledge that his life work has had significant impact on anti-imperialist, anticolonial, antiracist, civil rights, and Black consciousness scholarship and activism. His intellectual contributions in language studies, cultural studies, postmodernism, anti- and postcolonial theories, political studies, and to some extent sociology are well-known and broadly felt. Born in the French colony of Martinique in 1925, Fanon later went on to study clinical psychiatry in France in the 1950s. He served as a chief medical officer at Blida-Joinville Hospital in Algeria. We learn from those who have studied his life trajectories that Fanon encountered racism on his maiden visit to Algeria that seemed to have somehow eluded him while in Martinique. We are suspicious of this and David Macey (1996) captures Fanon's struggle in Martinique within the politically hostile environment Emmanuel Hansen (1997) describes as an "island [that] [overnight] came to look like 'rape, racism and rioting,'" for which we learn Fanon's "future was by no means certain" (p. 46; 1996, p. 491). To follow, we believe it is precisely for the uncertainty of Fanon's material and immaterial life conditions that he had not yet developed a critical reading and moreover ideological praxis for race and race relations then. In Algeria, Fanon denounced French colonialism and racism and was appalled by the French treatment of the Algerian Front de liberation Nationale (FLN). His work caught the attention of the FLN "Front for National Liberation," a group then engaged with a grueling battle against French colonialism who recruited his services. Later, Fanon was appointed as FLN ambassador to Ghana in the mid 1950s. In Ghana his speeches, which were met with skepticism by some elites, however, became a center of debate among young intellectuals and budding revolutionaries. Through his sojourns, particularly serving as a combat soldier with the Algerian forces in the French army during World War II, Fanon witnessed the horrors of war directly. He was later to berate the French racist separation of their troops from Black West Indians/Caribbean and Africans, who were supposed to be French citizens, as well as the Arabs. He bore witness to German fascism with notions of racial purity and became particularly angered by how the French had hypocritically denounced it. It is without doubt that both World War II and the Algerian liberation struggle influenced Fanon's understanding of violence (Azar, 2000; Cherki, 2006; Geismar, 1971; Hansen, 1974; Wright, 1975; Wyrick, 1997).

We recount this life history in order to understand how Fanon came to conceptualize violence. As noted, there are competing readings of how Fanon spoke of violence. He would argue that the colonial encounter is a violent encounter, and that violence is a perquisite for total liberation from the colonizer/oppressor. Part of such violence is in terms of how the colonizer sets the terms of engagement. But more than that, the violence of the colonized is a response and reaction to the colonizer's violence. It is violence in self-defense, and so is the violent resistance he posits necessary for liberation from the colonial oppression. This is significant. In fact, Fanon writes in his book, *The Wretched of the Earth,* that "the argument the Native chooses has been furnished by the settler." This can be juxtaposed/aligned with Steve Biko, who asks, "Why should we [colonized/Africans] be concerned with a problem we never created?" (see Biko, 1978). Fanon's work was about a practical diagnosis of violence in order to understand and to act to destroy and liberate oneself from violence. Fanon argued that we must see violence as part of the "colonial problem," that is, the violence of the colonial encounter. To respond to that colonial encounter, violence may also be evoked as part of the search for human freedom and liberation. The resister who chooses violence is simply responding to what she or he has been presented with.

In this chapter, we ground some fundamental questions about the Fanonian conception of violence. For example, how does Fanon help us take up the intersections of race, class, gender, sexuality, and disability as sites of oppression and resistance in critical anticolonial work? How does his exposition and diagnoses of violence speak to the issue of our interstices and an understanding of difference through intersectional analysis? The power of the racial/colonial dominant cannot be downplayed. It is to this end that discourses about the intersectionality of social difference (race, class, gender, sexuality, [dis]ability, etc., as linked, intersected, and integrated) must never lose sight of such differences as sites of marginality and resistance. An examination of our multilayered experiences reflecting complexities of identities and their intersections from varied positions of resistance, dissonance, and dislocatedness can only help us understand violence in the Fanonian conception. Fanon clearly sought to understand the genealogy of colonial relations of power and the ways the epidermalization of inferiority is encoded on bodies as raced, classed, gendered, and sexualized Others. In understanding the matrix of domination, he argued that the assumed purity of the White body and of Whiteness rested on a manufactured Blackness as impure and deviant. The colonized body was conceptualized, produced, and imagined as in included/excluded space and politics that gives form to the worldview, underpinning the colonial encounter. Resisting and challenging racist colonial exclusionary and hegemonic practices are key. We must understand ourselves in a holistic prism/paradigm that stresses our mutual interdependencies with everything (e.g., social communities, cultures, and Nature), to recognize our ethics in our anticolonial struggles against violence resides in concrete human practice and not in institutions, nor Nature. Intergroup relations should be about understanding conflict and power relations as manifested in our everyday materiality of existence, human/social interactions, and the institutionalized ways of distributing and allocating the valued social goods and services of societies.

The interstices of difference are also about the interlocution of race, gender, class, sexuality, disability, language, and culture from multiple standpoints to produce a complexity which defies singular interpretations. Understandings derived from multiple interstices of difference, reinforces a sense of holism, and a sense of intricateness, that centers a self and collective intensity of social experience. It speaks to the multidimensionality of self and collective and the fact that we are either implicated or made complicit in events in different and complex ways. For example, violence and violent actions produce a multiplicative effect on bodies and such effects must be read differently and holistically when countered on bodies.

Interstices connect our understandings of identity and subjectivity and a relation between who and what one is. It is about a multiplex self, in which the sense of self, whether determined authentically via the self or experienced as socially constructed, read, and/or imposed upon the body, is nevertheless significant and necessary to the collective experience. With that said, we locate our identities primarily in categories of self, by which we define in the everyday ways of speaking of race, class, gender, [dis]ability, among many notable others, hence, "what I am". In alluding to the positionalities one assumes in one's subjectivity would encompass the lenses through which one sees the world (values, experiences, opinions, morals, desires etc.). It is our orientation to these categories of race, gender, class, sexuality, [dis]ability, and so on, that offers an interpretative relation as to how we choose to live and experience our identities. Thus a gender identity, we assert, cannot be understood without its relations to race, class, sexuality, disability, and so on; and conversely, a gendered subjectivity in its reference to the many positionalities one assumes allows the self and the collective to express the values, experiences, opinions, morals of the community through the subject.

If for nothing at all, the foregoing discussion is to highlight how we are multiplicate beings and also how we experience events differently and yet in relation to others. Thus violence perpetuated by the colonized on male and female bodies is different and yet connected Black bodies, within a colonial project, where bodies are feminized to ensure they fit the colonial Manichean divide. Fanon spoke of this divide as an irrational philosophical dualism which constituted a way of thinking (irrational and oppressive dualisms and binaries as fostered in discourses of anti-difference) that produced colonial rule in the first place. The Manichean divide has been a philosophical recognition of the colonial-binary relationship of Black-White, that is, Black is in relation to White. It is a divide that is intentional and purposive to serve goals of the colonial project and dominant. This divide helps foster a colonial mimicry when Black bodies come to recognize their experiences through Whiteness and believe these said experiences are their own. Fanon speaks of the duality, as dual consciousness that creates two conflicting bodies of knowledge, induced into the psyche of the oppressed.

But it is also not just our bodies that exhibit such dualities. There is the question of difference as multiplicate selves. For example, how is difference (as race/ethnicity, gender, sexuality etc.) relevant and to be situated in the rereading of Fanon (discourse and politics) around struggles for and over liberation from oppressions? The aspects of internal colonialisms which Fanon spoke about in the context of how colonials exploit the nation unequally, creating privileges and hierarchies within that also point to asymmetrical power relations that normalize violence as inevitable social difference. Thus we need a redefinition of the colonial as more than "foreign" and "alien" to anything "imposed" and "dominating." The failure to powerfully note social difference continues to be a legitimate critique of conventional political economic theorizing of political liberation struggles. The context of each body is not separate from its knowledge and knowing and so we must engage social difference. How then do we locate sexuality, gender, disability and other social categories and structures in Fanon's pedagogy of violence?

For colonized bodies violence speaks to us in multiple tongues (e.g., from the sheer physical brutality of colonization, the negation of our historical experiences and collective and cultural memories, a denial of our subjectivities, the (dis)embodiment of our cultural and historical knowledge, the continued struggles against our dehumanization, the Spirit, mental, emotional and psychological pain of engaging in perpetual resistance, to the oftentimes easy and seductive slippage into the form, logic, and implicit assumptions of the very things we are contesting.

We now share an experience narrated as a story by one of the authors to illustrate the complexities of understanding lived experiences and the significance of how difference shapes social action and practice, as well as and how in this case violence is daily enacted on different bodies in multiple spaces. We offer an interpretation of the story to also show how the colonial interpellation of violence and social difference and the pedagogic and instructional need and relevance to understand, respond, and address violence in everyday lived experiences.

> *In the early mornings on the 5th day of October 2012, on route from a birthday celebration in downtown Toronto, I arrived parked in a friend's visitor's parking lot. I stepped out of the car, with my friend still sitting in the passenger seat to keep watch, as I crouched behind another visiting car parked adjacent to my car, to attain what privacy available to me, in order to fix a misaligned area of much sensitivity. Upon my return to the car, I gathered my things to put in my bag. Before getting my purse out of the car, four white male security employees approached us, with flashlights aimed at the car, property within the car, and more importantly our bodies. They introduced themselves abruptly, aggressively, and in a manner alarming enough to announce the violence to transpire.*
>
> *At this moment, we received the impression, all to clearly that we were suspects, cast upon a Black backdrop that offended the Whiteness imbued into the space, indicated through the violence that began to be acted out upon our bodies. At once, I profess I am a daughter, guardian, Black, intelligent, female, androgynous, spiritual, rebel, middle class, bi-sexual, artist, Diasporic and educated. In context, however, we were reduced to simply Black and female, highly suspected to be the perpetrators of an incident that occurred several hours before we were on site. The intersections of our identities, we were reduced to, Blackness and gender, played out unevenly within the context of this encounter, one where our station at a visitor parking lot in one of many socioeconomically disadvantaged communities in Toronto, hailed us into a particular history and location, characterized by the violent ontology of colonization. At approximately 1:30 am, one of the White employees questioned the spatial locality, and what I was doing behind the car. I questioned his inquiry, stating "why"? He became more aggressive and proceeded to try and tell me what I was doing, as I stared at him blankly and disinterested. I told him I*

didn't appreciate the tone of his voice, his accusations and his sense of entitlement that endeared his approach, line of questioning, and flashing lights onto my things and onto my body.

My friend expressed the same sentiments, explaining we were on our way home, and their tone of voice and questioning was highly disrespectful, serving as enough cause for our irritation and civil disobedience. He however, demanded that we confess, and we declined, beginning our walk toward the building. They surrounded us, wailing threats and their allegations, positioning themselves to prevent us from walking away, while growing disturbingly close in spatial proximity to us. We were told we were trespassing and that we must leave. My friend became so angry contesting their demands, questioning under what authority they possessed to require us to leave, and who they thought they were. They threatened to call the police, and with such I told my friend I wanted to go home. I proceeded to walk towards my vehicle, and again I was stopped and told I couldn't leave. It was now 2:30 am, and the situation was unrelenting. Bored, annoyed and tiring, I chimed in on the ongoing verbal battle between my friend and the most vocal of the white employees, saying "what do you want? I want to go home!" He mustered something about trespassing and his co-conspirators looked to grow in amusement by the unfolding situation. I turned to my friend, and turning to look at the most quite of the men, and said "don't you see what's going on, their idiots". I began another attempt to walk to my car, and my friend joined me. As we walked, the white employees followed behind us talking a whole lot of nothing, and my friend would rebut, and then I stopped in my tracks, as I noticed a light cascading my body. I turned around to see the most vocal of the White dominant male body flashing light up and down my body, outlining my physique. I questioned him, "what are you doing!" I wanted to hurt him, and yet still he continued to flash his lights in motion upon my silhouette, not meeting my gaze I kept focused on him with utter disgust. Turning to my friend I belted, "he is getting off on this shit!" She furthered the inquiry into his sexualizing behaviour, questioning his masculinity in relation to the possibility of erection, accusing him of impotence and emasculation. We laughed, so as to harmonize our laughter with the imaginings of the thrall of his penile dysfunction and shrinkage, as she repetitively stated "it must be small", raising and forming her fingers to indicate the inadequacy of size. She asserted that he must be unhappy with his life, with a job that pays 30,000, in which he feels so small to feel the need to provoke us because as she persuasively made the point, "[he is] a . . . toy cop!" And with such, she reverted again to calling into question his penis size, as the cause and consequence for his insignificance, constituting his persistent harassment of our bodies, again, indicating with her fingers the estimated diameter of the inadequacy of the petrified phallus.

He threatened to call the police again, and my friend proceeded to walk over to the crowd of them, huddled now approximately 5 meters from where we had now been standing by the car. She demanded to see their badges, which they followed to obscure with cell phones. The bold move inspired a direct assault toward me from the injured masculinity of the White dominant male body, accused of impotence. He stormed toward me, now leaned on the car, for another attempt at White masculinity, at 3:00 am. He grabbed my arm and told me that I was going to jail, and I stared at him, again, blankly, but yet amused. My friend told him she was calling the cops, while he made small talk about the law, and what jail was like, assuring me I would soon find out. My friend now engaged with a female emergency dispatch officer on the phone, who instructed her to tell me to stop talking, to get in the car, safely securing the locks, while revealing that the security employees were potentially on ambiguous ground, as the incident calling for suspicion occurred hours before our arrival. With that information we hurried into the car, winding the windows up and locking the doors, awaiting the police to arrive.

As we waited, my friend breathed violently, as if to catch her breath, escaping her, in effect due to the wretched demands of the confrontation. Following the police arrival, which happened rather quickly (in 5 to10 minutes maximum), we again were questioned, and I spoke as I was in this moment calm and quite reticent. I informed the police officer that we were scared, and had serious concerns about the White dominant male bodies and their behavior. I told her that we were very confused about what was going on and furthermore at a loss as to how to diffuse or escape the confrontation. The police officer that took our information was a white woman; we immediately noticed the ambivalence written on her body as white, and female in the doubly masculine and White position of an officer. A non-white male officer at this time was engaged with the White dominant male bodies, taking their information and story. The story they construed was of a primitive being urinating behind a car. At once, my Blackness reared its head, and with such located me within a history tainted, fossilized, and made the fact of our Blackness the cause and consequence of a myth of racial degeneracy. The white female officer had left us to join her partner engaged with the White dominant male bodies, to get the details of this narrative, one they discussed for a few minutes, imagining the Other. We viewed them from the car's rear view mirrors, intensely watching the scene unfold.

The white female officer took charge of the situation as the lead officer in charge, soon leaving the men and headed toward the grassy area, behind the car I had been to check for any indication of my racial mark. Speaking directly to the most vocal and now fragile of the White dominant male bodies, an interesting spectacle began. We had predicted that this White dominant male body would come undone, as he appeared to be unraveling since the comment of his penis had been wailed back at him. To satisfy our suspicions, the White dominant's masculine fragility reared its head as he began to speak down to the officer in that aggressive tone he had too long badgered us with. She returned the assault in a 'civil/professional' tone, in which she reframed the exchange to question his volume, and made his point a substantiated reason that we should be intimidated and concerned, which she all too willingly expressed to him. And with such, the officer moved in our direction, and affirmed to us that the white security official was a complete 'asshole', looking for someone to give a hard time. She instructed for me to leave, despite his recantations, emotional instability and confusion, expressing her ambivalence about the safety of my car, as it would be under their authority, stating that 'they did have some authority under property laws and it was better to be safe than sorry'. With that said, I hugged my friend, and asked the officer if she could have them move their car, so I could get out, and requested that she stay to supervise the situation, so as to ensure our safety.

VIOLENCE, INTERSTICES, AND SOCIAL DIFFERENCE: INTERPRETING A STORY

We note of course that this story can be subjected to varied interpretations. Suffice to say we offer an interpretation that allows us to read the intersectionality of social difference and how this plays out when violence is revisited on racialized, gendered, sexualized, and classed bodies. In the foregoing story, it is important to note the direction for which Blackness came to define the frontier as a point in reference, in which the question of who comes to whom, and further who the possession and execution of privilege becomes very reminiscent of the settler experience, warranting careful attention to what Fanon coined the "fact of Blackness." We must question the temporal and geospatial boundaries, in regards to who travels to whom, and why. It is the White privileged dominant who comes to the marginalized/subordinated/colonized, whether in the name of peace, security, aid, and/or surveillance, and at the same time, it is the colonized that cannot access the Whiteness of privilege to settle, to coexist, or leave at their choosing? For this reason, Fanon tells us that the cause always appears as the consequence and the consequence as the cause in the imperialist context of colonialism. Such can explain the discursive rendering of Blackness to become the cause and effect of its own subversion, said to be Blackness concretely and materially, yet through in effectual existence for Whiteness. Fanon captured this dialectic of being of Blackness prophetically, when he writes, "The colonizer created the Negro and the Negro created Negritude," which speaks to the terms of engagement made for Blackness, as one that at once must be contained, and yet resistant to containment through its very multiplicate being in Blackness, to at the same time substantiate and evade Whiteness.

For example, the White dominant male bodies continued movement and unrelenting pursuit of the Blackness marking one's Black skin, one's failed attempts at retreat, and Black conscientiousness that understands there is no retreat, outside of perpetual resistance. This too speaks to Fanon's lessons, as noted, when the colonized take matters into their own hands, which manifest within the violent interstices of their anticolonial and antiracist struggle. We are Black and in the context of White supremacy, there is no space made for such bodies to reclaim our peace, security, in order to renounce the accountability and legitimacy for a history and a consciousness that was not ours to begin with, but theirs independent of our violent resistance. The ideology of choice, in relation to the act of bending, and/or moment of being, can serve only to reify the White dominance moral and value system that substantiates the myth of racial degeneracy, undergirding the Negro as a biological threat. The logic flows to point to the way Blackness is always returned to the ontological dilemma of the Negro, when evaluating whether the Black body can be or not be, whether to resist or not to resist, to escape the totalizing project of colonial sites, targets, and violent occupation. At once the Manichean delirium conduces the being in Blackness to a singularity of racial being, in such a way where the Others' existence is made for others, provided for both the substance and demarcation of Whiteness as dominance. Speaking precisely to Fanon's lessons, which long foretold that the necessity for resistance will be violent, in order for the colonized to counter the violence of the colonizer, and with such reject the colonizer's inhumanity, too often ritualized into a normative co-relational dialectic of humanities.

What are the investments, projections, and desires placed upon Black bodies within the imaginary of Blackness as a biological threat, said to need containment, occupied by the White dominant body, their systems and structures? In the Western gaze, and the authority this gaze afforded these White male dominant bodies, constituted simultaneously, what Fanon tells us is the biological threat the Negro comes to represent in the eyes of the colonizer. A biological threat, one must recognize as sexualized, and so always feminized, made our Black bodies desirable in a fantasy these White dominant bodies possessed in excess. Why? The charge of impotence and a small penis size is telling here by the ways it vivaciously inspires a direct assault onto the body, which is revealing in the way it speaks to what Fanon tells us is at once the product and production of the Manichean delirium. The way one's being in the materiality of Blackness exists at once for silencing and embodiment, outlining the dualism underpinning the Manichean divide, induced through our bodies as Black and for that fact reduced to subhumanity, produced the badge of Whiteness for the establishment of the phallus life and desire in the story. In this way, we must note the praxis of Blackness and how the interstice of the encounter, produces spaces for our resistance that are unavoidably violent, and yet complicit in the sexual colonization of the Black female body. The very attack we ushered onto the White male dominant's impotence in effect disturbed his fragility of White masculinity, returning his interrogation to his phallus, shifting the matter of our Blackness onto the despondent fact of his and others' White masculinity.

In a position, evasive and ambiguously located, we were suspects because we were desirable. "The official questioned my business behind the car, and I questioned his business in my business". The language is telling, again of the distorted what George Dei calls the "co-relational relationship" of the colonizer and colonized, but yet seeks to find legitimacy by way of the demand for dialogue in the form of confession. The confession the White dominant male body in effect desired to satisfy is the desire for Blackness, one in which we were invited to part take in the civilizing project, at once extending our bodies and life force, to constitute and deject ourselves into the inevitable degeneracy made 'rapable' for others. We were not only to be suspects, and biological hazards to the grounds, he was entrusted to guard, but too schematically and corporeally organized as hypersexual-asexual, exacerbating foremost the ambiguity of difference through the forbidden terrain, where gender intersects race. We must note the residency in the building was in that moment erased through a de-racing politic, which immediately was met with anger is precisely how Black bodies become implicated and complict, revealing what Fanon would locate as the colonized proof of his/her humanity and yet too, the psychological scars, from the alienated consciousness conceived in the loss of not belonging to the White space/Whiteness and yet still occupied by and because of it.

As the White dominant male body proceeded with questions, he was in a sense demanding to remove Black bodies, with the intention for them to remove ourselves, a process Fanon terms "lactification" and what he says is the moment of being for others (1967; p. 109). "Dehumanized and sexualized objects, we were called to be, in order to incite the gazing imaginaries of imagined White masculinity". The lactification process explains how colonized bodies come to whiten and de-race themselves in order to survive, to determine a survival self, and to resist. We embodied the de-racing politic Fanon speaks to through "lactification," as we, aware of our 'Otherness' and as such, ways for our resistance can be expounded upon to facilitate what Fanon names colonial mimicry. For at the same time, we were contained by a myth of racial degeneracy, and with such, invited to participate in the legitimation of a historicity of "Blackness."

As we questioned under what authority, and under what suspicion they had to question us, immediately, our agency was received at once as an attack and allure, and with such the urgency of their conquest was given momentum. We question whether the horror was in the fact that we spoke back or that we spoke at al?. Speaking back tells the White dominant body that they too may be others, a haunting dread, sufficed by the Other's ability to speak for oneself, and against their narrative, which at once attempts to return the

White gaze and still flee it. Inevitably our presence remained a constant factor refuted by the White dominant male body, one that insinuates a totalizing rejection of our humanity, in order for the colonialist to garnish a glimpse of his or her own humanity, in the gaze of the Western imaginary.

We must question what the implications and consequence are of an overwhelming police and security presence in this neighborhood, overrepresented with Black bodies, and socioeconomic disadvantage, political oppression (the police presence silencing these voices). Moreover, what are the consequences and demands Blackness places upon the community, diversely made up of Black people? To see one as choosing or having the choice to choose a path of mediation in relation to Blackness too often allows the implicit insertion of a neoliberal narrative of self-determination within the larger metanarrative of the colonial myth and storyline that is antithesis and dependent on such Blackness. Fanon notes the all too wretched reality and near impossibility to "escape the ontology of existing for others" and thus the very arrogance and yet fragility of Whiteness. Fanon teaches us that "the [Negro] has no ontological resistance in the eyes of the [colonizer]" (2008; p. 90). And Nadine Gordimer (2003) articulates these precise sentiments, in her forward of Albert Memmi's deep analysis of the life of the colonized marked by terror and crisis, inflicted by the colonizer through an unrelenting cycle of pathology and myth, underpinned by the colonial encounter in the following:

> "When the colonizer adds . . . that the colonized is wicked, backward person, he thus justifies his police and his legitimate severity . . ." and so "the humanity of thecolonized, rejected by the colonizer becomes opaque . . . [u]seless . . . to try to forecast the colonized actions ('They are unpredictable' 'With them you never know') . . . (Gordimer, 2003, pp. 29).

The discussion speaks precisely to violence that comes to constitute the space as a nonevadable frontier, under constant attack by the White dominant body that penetrates the exterior so that retreat or relief becomes almost impossible for particular bodies. This penetration and surveillance of marginalized bodies takes many forms in different contexts, but the underlining differences that mark both bodies and space hails through the Western imaginary diffused in the despondent construction of Blackness.

GENDER AND VIOLENCE

What other more specific interpretations around gender can be made in this story? In answering such questions, we also know how the police officer, a white woman, took information and noted the racialized nature of a geospatial controversy, and later sensitized our narrative against the White dominant male body. What accounted for this? We must question the roles of particular femininities and masculinities in relation to race, within the production of sexualities and ways femininities operate as a vehicle that establishes and legitimates the White dominant. How do we conceptualize the patriarchal white supremacist, capitalist structures that exist, historicize, and are maintained through an ongoing dehumanizing of the Black body by way of Blackness? We come to see the narrative around femininity, used to resist and injure the colonial masculinity at play, but which had no effect on the racism, as it underpinned the ontology of the violent encounter. The interstices of the white female officer's identity, like ours, we laid bare in our search for hope and gaze to resist the lie that Fanon tells us is the colonial situation (1963; p. 109). The attention we placed onto her Whiteness, as a dominant body both representative of her skin and her badge and thus role of mediator in the situation and neurosis that was not ours, but White, belonging to the legitimacy that placed her in context, on scene, presumably on unsettled land, she was implored to settle. Speaking to the officer again called upon us, as Black bodies, to speak through the silence and yet totality of race. As such we engaged the script through the praxis of gender, in order to counter this vicious racism, naturalized through the inherent race structure as one of too many "normal" procedures, when encountering others.

The arrogance of the colonial situation is lucidly telling, with the encounter playing out predictably, so much so, one can guess with accuracy that injury afflicts those and other White dominant male bodies, engaged in colonial warfare, at multiplicate dimensions, constituting their way for becoming. Dissonance, in any event, is kept in place by White supremacy, unabatedly needing continuous forces to unleash, one with an interlocutrix in Blackness. With that said, returning the Western gaze onto the police officer, a White, but yet female and so feminized, positioned her as what is often termed the "dupe," one placed in the ambiguous middle ground as trying to be one of the "boys," like a Black body trying to be settled in White spaces their very unsettlement constitute, only to come undone in acts of "doing" (race, class, gender, etc.) for White hegemony. Through intersectional analysis, we come to understand the importance of interstices as spaces to resist from a standpoint that locates the self, multiplicate and without currency for colonial White structural domination. For example, the White dominant male body can be understood as a particular subjectivity, one that is fraternized into a community of normalcy hailed through and because of a myth of difference, one heavily invested in Blackness, however, when the space this subjectivity occupies reveals its own ambiguity and de-stabilization, that subjectivity can only find understanding through colonial violence, as the White dominant subject is permitted if not demanded to debase and subordinate bodies marked by any difference, like the female officer in our story for its own containment. This is precisely why the white female officer's corporality as a feminine subject relegated her to the position of Other, or what we have described as the "dupe", which is evident in the paternalistic and aggressive tone that was used to address her, is one that remains to be used to identify, subordinate and remove Others. Thus one can clearly see that the white female officer speaking back and bringing legitimacy to the subjectivity of the Black bodies in our story is in itself a form of resistance, one that is hers, but nevertheless connected to a collective of Others. Though the contradiction remains present that the legitimation of her authority as an officer of the law is upheld, her extrapolation from such authority becomes necessary to the Structure of Whiteness because of her subordinated gender location, in effect is becoming the platform and community ties from which her authority in White supremacy is garnered. In this matter, White dominant bodies are allowed to amply obscure the brunt of their differences, by constituting Whiteness in multiplicated hierarchies of difference and thus on the reduction of one's multiplicated being as indication of Blackness and the perquisite condition that suffices the inherent racist structural divide, undergirding the Manichean delirium and foundation of White domination.

We must always question and speak to the multiple identities multiplicate beings possess, and how they are silenced, reduced, and yet not extinguished by a matter of Blackness. For example, Kobena Mercer tells us that "Fanon knows little about homosexuality, but which then reveals that he knows all too much" (1996; p. 125). Bearing mindfulness to Mercer's insights, we question whether the silencing of our multiple identities within the co-relational relations that mutate can negate us as holistic beings. And if we need to pose this question, why? Mercer draws "our attention to sexual politics as the interior limit of decolonization" in order for us to hold "on to the emancipatory vision which Fanon theorized . . . [for] liberating the subjectivity of coloniser and colonized" (1996; p. 119). We must come to see how Black bodies are at once dislocated from and yet induced into the colonial situation, through the process Fanon tells us is a psychological amputation, in order for the colonized to be caricatured as a subhuman sexualized "thing" and site, and become subordinated to both constitute and resist Blackness through one's very being in the materiality allocated to Blackness, collapsed into a myth of racial degeneracy.

In *Wretched of the Earth*, specifically in the chapter "Colonial War and Mental Disorders," Fanon (1963) describes a series of clinical cases and argues that random violence, random acts of torture, and physical brutality were not normal behavior, although we must be mindful it is this very normalization as a process in itself and its constitution through violence that must be disjointed. The colonizer used violence to achieve his aims and goals of colonization. Thus we come to understand how violence and colonialism go hand in hand. Violence is a vehicle, systematically used to achieve the Other's subjugation. Fanon diagnosed that the mental disorders of many of his patients were directly linked to the colonial condition in what undoubtedly becomes deposed as theirs.

The contemporary lessons of Fanon's location for the justification of violence must be re-visited outside of the framework of its instrumentality, that is, outside of the myth of racial degeneracy, proceeding treatment and inevitable results and consequences. (1988; p. 108). There is also a need for a distinction between the violence exercised by the colonized and that which is exercised by the colonizer, alongside thoughts into why violence becomes an inevitable consequence of colonization and decolonization. Fanon might have rightly diagnosed violence for these reasons, and the complexity he eschews through his readings of the colonial encounter remain reflexive of the dissonance, demoralization and denigration of the colonized life, made as the catalyst for colonial desire, colonial life and the colonizer's trajectory into significance. Yet, we must make mention of Fanon's acute awareness of the transformative potential of his words and, specifically, the revolutionary potential of violence in bringing about social exchange. It could be said, then, that consequently Fanon was informed by the Marxian exhortation our (as educators/academics, etc.) task is not simply to analyze society but to change it. Fanon was aware that violence dehumanizes both the perpetrator and the victim. The violence of Europeans has changed the colonized. Through violence, Europe had destroyed the language, culture, and tradition of the colonized. Yet violence itself can also heal the very wounds that it has inflicted on the colonial subject. Hence, the only violence the colonized subject accesses is "counterviolence," violence in reaction to the settler.

When embarked upon by the colonial subject, such violence is a "cleansing force" (Fanon, 1963; p. 94). It is violence intended to restore the subject's humanity, self-worth, and respect, to deal with his/her inferiority complex and cast away any repressed anger and resentment of the oppressor/settler. Such violence is an expression of the oppressed collective consciousness. It is suppressed fury that must find an outlet. When unleashed, it is the colonized subject re-creating himself/herself. In Fanon's own words, "The rebel's weapon is the proof of her/his humanity" (1963; p. 22).

THE PEDAGOGY OF DISABILITY

In narrating and working with the story we have had to grapple with the question: How do we articulate a Blackness/Black identity and politics which is not read as simply a Black/White duality or a colonial binary? There is always the challenge in bringing a distinctive [Black] voice [our voices] into a form of "leveled coexistence" with other voices (see also Madan, 2012). The concern is not simply with voice location, identifying voice locations, or even understanding the absence of particular voices; but more fundamentally, coming into a consciousness and act on the question of voice dislocation (e.g., where, what, when, and why we come to speak and/or come into voice) (see also bell hooks).

There is a "fallout" from colonial hegemonic structuring of human existence and, in particular, the hierarchical relations or coloniality of power that requires a resistant voice continually pitted against the normality of Whiteness and the colonial dominant. There is a madness about it all which Fanon termed "Manichean delirium." But how do we go beyond the naming and locating of our colonial injuries? Going beyond colonial injury is a struggle to claim and reclaim power, our voice, histories, and humanity. For racialized/oppressed/minoritized bodies it requires that to effectively respond to the questions of "who, how, why our project of reclamation" which requires that speak from our racialized, gendered, sexualized, classed, abled and dis-abled embodiments.

Our story has pointed to several important lessons for the critical teacher about violence, difference, and how our lives are about interstices. Here, we must speak about the intersections of race and disability, class, gender, and sexuality. From the discussion of our story, we must engage the colonizer/white male dominant body/oppressor's story and, moreover, allegation that a defilement of the space, hence the pretense of urination, was the issue at hand, requiring the means of punishment. To consider what the story of a Black bodies' urination on the landscape represents, we are forced to unpack the meanings that come to create the world, in which the problematic derives its significance and thus reason for being. Following disability scholarship, many like Tanya Titchkosky (2008), suggest common sensibilities around disability implicate it as "rare, but also nothing, but limit and lack, unexpected and undesirable , or simply, "trouble" (Abberley 1998;McRuer 2006; Michalko 2008)" (p. 48). Tichkosky's (2008) conceptualization of the disabled mark on bodies in popular common sense, parallels the naturalized degeneracy associated with raced bodies, and in particular the difference associated with bodies, diffused within the demoralization associated with Blackness as the precedent of "trouble". In this way, we must read the constructions around disability within the reductionist model that satiates the western imagination that hails the antecedent of value through the Black body, and the unimaginable existence in what Titchkosky says about disabled bodies as "a type, [which] do[es] not belong and so can never really be present;[and] if present, "They" are only questionably so" (2008; pp. 47).

When Titchkosky (2008) describes the dilemma of urination in her work *"To Pee or Not to Pee": Ordinary Talk About Extraordinary Exclusions,* it is articulated from the confining context of the university space, as one characterized by the privilege of ability, only occurring upon the exclusion of those unable to access the space as unexpected Others'. Here, we point to the intersections of race and disability, as the "unspeakability" of difference, which disposes it into Otherness', and exclusion in spaces marked by the respectability associated with Whitness, a construction which finds legs only by a myth of racial degeneracy. The disability afforded to Blackness serves at once to reify and negate the space for disabled bodies, and/or bodies marked by difference, as those of an "imagined type." Fanon teaches us the ways that the colonizer's grip hones tightly on a difference, enveloped by a myth of racial difference and, with such a charge of impurity, to create multiple meanings of degeneracy, in order to dispose the rightful meanings of our rightful ontological and epistemological origins. Thus we must recognize that race nearly always intersects with disability ideologically and thus materially, though different, but through a resulting treatment. And with such, we must see its insidious implications when speaking to the lived experience of colonial violence as a"dis-abilizing mechanism that creates pathology through its exclusionary practice and praxes." Thus Titchkosky (2008) is right when she says that "exclusion is made normal because dis-ability is made not normal," under the Western pathologization of difference, centering racial difference, undergirded by the exclusion of Others', is an emblem too closely associated with the mythologized embodiment of the White dominant subject.. We, therefore, must always bear in mind the implications of the colonial direction toward and for the colonizing space, whether it be in the classroom, university setting, or the great outdoors, confiscated by the material conditions, induced into the Western framework of capital that follows the "lawful" occupation of the bodies it contains along the praxis of race, ability, gender, sexuality, and class, among Others.

IMPLICATIONS FOR CRITICAL EDUCATION

The foregoing discussion has significant implications for learners today. Our classrooms and institutional settings are on [un]settled lands where the sanction of authority envelops in the violent occupation of White domination. Who gets to learn, or more importantly who gets to learn what? What are the implications of difference, particularly in the classroom, when we situate the violence cascaded along the intersections of race, disability, class, gender, and sexuality? Who gets to normalize space and police spaces? What gets constituted as a public domain policed with the sanctity of Whiteness? We would point out that intersectionality requires one to speak from where one is, from one's lived experience and history. There is a particular saliency and urgency to our lived experiences. The idea of saliency and urgency are not just about what one is but also what one does and the meanings we embody as multiplicate beings. The critical educator, as teacher in a school system undergirded by White heteronormative male domination, could recognize the noncooperation of one's position as both Whiteness/teacher and criticality, in order to bring forth cooperation. This could be done in terms of reframing one's humanity first through self in such Whitened positions, and second, as a self that flows through the humanity of the community of learners, hence, students/community stakeholders among many notable others. With such it is important to note the significance placed on pedagogy as both one's scholarship in relation to practice. If we do not align practice with theory and praxis, our pedagogy is as lethal as that of the oppressor, and at worst a reformulation of oppressive relations, penetrating the whole.

We can extrapolate Fanon's writing further to speak about difference, differently. An imposed fixed duality is about a contradiction and negation. Our task as colonized beings is to fight back. Too often retreating appears destined as this is the very site for colonial domination to steal our values and belief systems to turn them against the possessed, in order to make and sustain what becomes an oppressed population. Fanon's pedagogy calls us to fight because our existence is made to be under a state of ideological, metaphysical, and material siege. Fanon (1963) tells us that the colonized is their truth and we see too many oppressed people and "their communities made to die on their knees rather than to live on their feet" (p. 39) through the ongoing colonial project put in place, underpinning the irrational practice and theoretical adherence to racism and anti-difference. Not until the cleansing occurs and the colonial lie sheds away, so as to allow the native to reclaim their history and humanity, to no longer give the colonizer the attention and life force they require to suffice its ambiguous ontological position and domination in our space and place, we risk the continuous reorganizing of the wretchedness of the colonial encounter. In effect, we must locate sexuality, gender, and disability and other differences in Fanon's call for solidarity in the antiracist, anticolonial struggle.

In revisioning Fanon's pedagogy on violence we argue that the delineation between violence and nonviolence requires us to revisit and situate such dichotomous understandings in what Fanon describes as that hopeless Manichean divide. Thus it is important to reframe our understanding of violence to a more multiplicate understanding for us to locate violence in nuanced ways that precisely explain the social world and its complexities at present. For example, Presbey (1996) notes comparatively the violent and nonviolent approach Fanon and Gandhi implore, to serve as indications of their ontology of practice in medicinal knowledge basis. Though Presby (1996) revisits the complexity of violence, and finds common ground between them, she falls yet into the Manichean divide in her categorical analysis of both Fanon and Gandhi as exclusive to one another in their approaches, although she notes their similar ambitions. Presby nevertheless fails to account for the deliberate colonial divide and the context, overlooking not only to the wretched demands of the colonial situation, but moreover the wretchedness it imposes onto the lived realities of both the oppressed and oppressor both materially and immaterially. We must revisit to revision Fanon's pedagogy of violence, in order to account for the lived realties that are predicated on scarcity, and, in such conditions, grounded within a violence that at once is structural and symbolic, which no one is immune to without the Other.

Fanon's prescription is for embodied action which is at once healing and self-redeeming. Fanon tells us:

> Colonialism is not a thinking machine, nor a body endowed with reasoning faculties. It is violence in its natural state, and it will only yield when confronted with greater violence. (1963, p. 61)

We must then recognize that greater violence is not one that matches the colonizer's violence, for that would only come to be "violence for others" to fuel the colonizer and justify his violence against the colonized and their continued oppression. As Fanon says, "The Manicheism of the settler produces a Manicheism of the native"; we must recognize this as violence in the wretched encounter between colonized and colonizer (1963, p. 93). It is imperative we understand the dimensions of violence, as one that exists on a continuum, similar to the way that energy is understood to occupy many different wavelengths, and might we say strengths. In this way, what can be made of Fanon's conceptualization of greater violence is similar to what can be understood as emotive, but closer to Spiritual violence, one which is a violence that subverts the colonizers' gaze from the colonized and returns it honestly to the colonizer. As described in our story, when the White dominant male body's phallus intuitively became the object of interrogation, distance grew between the Black-White bodies. In addition, the dissonance the questioning and interrogation returned remained with the White dominant body yet needed release even to the detriment of the White dominant body. It is our intention to assert that through softening one can unleash the violence of subversion. When the colonizer attacks, softening ourselves to the ways in which we are vulnerable returns us to our rightful power in the surrender foremost to ourselves, which is the path to the reclaimation of our rightful humanity. The oppressor/settler has no retreat and no course of action, but to a multiplicity of myths, and/or to the consciousness that is not ours, but was always theirs. As Fanon has said, it is important "when understanding the colonial world" to understand "the phenomena of the dance and possession" (1963, p. 57). We must not fail to remember that the co-relational relationship of the colonial situation is at once an intimate and structural relation. We must recognize the power of subversion to understand more deeply its instrumental implications and applications against the co-relational relation of the colonial encounter, and the stake we all have in doing such work.

To follow the logic of subversion put forth as it speaks to pedagogical implications, it becomes imperative that we have a transformative pedagogy that locates and inserts spirituality in educational praxis. To change what we teach and how we teach so as not to become a standard to legitimate the status quo, but rather follows the needs of the individual as a multiplicate being which flows and thus has a stake in the health and sustenance of the community. This means rethinking humanity and with such its role in the larger ecological community. It requires reworking of our values to which we usher through and upon to come to exist in the world in a place of dominion over it, rather than in our rightful coexistence, webbed in its ecological health that must be recognized as a function of our own holistic well-being.

REFERENCES

Abberley, P. (1998). The spectre at the feast: Disabled people and social theory. In T. Shakespeare (Ed.), *The disability reader: Social science perspectives* (pp. 79–93). London: Cassell Academic.

Austin, D. (2006). Frantz Fanon's diagnosis: Fanon did not prescribe violence; he diagnosed it. *Toronto Star*, October 23.

Azar, M. (2000). *In the name of Algeria: Frantz Fanon and the Algerian revolution.* http://www.eurozine.com/pdf/2000–12–06-azar-en.pdf.

Biko, S. (1978). *I write what I like: Selected writings.* San Francisco: Harper & Row.

Cherki, A. (2006). *Frantz Fanon: A portrait.* Ithaca, NY: Cornell University Press.

Fanon, F. (1963). *The wretched of the earth.* New York: Grove Press.

Fanon, F. (1967). *Black skin, white masks.* New York: Grove Press.

Fanon, F. (1988). *A dying colonialism.* New York: Grove Press.

Fanon, F. (2004). *Black skin, white masks.* (new ed.). New York: Grove Press.

Geismar, P. (1971). New biography of Fanon. *African Studies Review, 14* (3): 510–513.

Hansen. E. (1997). Frantz Fanon: Portrait of a revolutionary intellectual. *Transition, 46*, 25–36. In Nigel Gibson (Ed.), Rethinking Fanon: A critical anthology on aspects Frantz Fanon Thought. Atlantic Highlands, NJ: Humanities Press.

Macey, D. (1996). "Frantz Fanon, 1925–1961". *History of Psychiatry.* 7(28):489–497.

Madan, A. (2012). State-sanctioned violence and mental health: Implications for learning and treatment: A dissertation proposal. Department of Humanities, Social Sciences and Social Justice Education, Ontario Institute for Studies in Education of the University of Toronto.

Gordimer, N. (2003). Foreward. In A. Memmi. *The Colonizer and the Colonized* (p.26-44). Boston, Beacon Press.

McRuer, R. (2006). *Crip theory: Cultural signs of queerness and disability.*
New York: New York University Press.

Mercer, K. (1996). Decolonization and disappointment: Reading Fanon's sexual politics. In Alan Reed (Ed.), *The fact of blackness: Fanon and visual representation.* Seattle: Bay Press.

Michalko, R. (2008). *Double trouble: Disability and disability studies.* Manuscript under review.

Presbey, G. M. (1996). Fanon on the role of violence in liberation: A comparison with Gandhi and Mandela. In Lewis R. Gordon, T. Denean Sharpley-Whiting, and Renee. T. White (Eds.), *Fanon: Critical reader* (pp. 283–296). Oxford: Blackwell Critical Readers Series.

Samuel, J. J. (1997). Ignoring the role of violence in Fanon: Playing with the bones of a hero. *Fuse Magazine.* May.

Titchkosky, T. (2008). "To pee or not to pee?" Ordinary talk about extraordinary exclusion in a university environment. *Canadian Journal of Sociology C33* (1): 37–60.

Wright M. F. (1975). Frantz Fanon: His work in historical perspective. *Black Scholar*, 6 (10): 19–29.

Wyrick, D. (1997). *Fanon for beginners.* New York: Writers and Readers.

3 Colonialism and Neoliberalism: Twins of Inequities

A Conversation with Vijay Prashad

Professor Prashad, please would you begin by telling me a little about yourself?

I was born in Calcutta, India. I lived in many different places in India, including during my years in boarding school in Dehra Dun, and in Delhi. My family was well-off, largely because of the efforts of my father. The roots of my family, however, are in the intellectual world and in the state bureaucracy. My paternal grandfather ran the Indian Museum in Calcutta, was a zoologist, a pioneer in marine biology in India, and remarkably spent his evenings translating old books from Persian, Turkish, and Arabic. My world was widened by these sorts of influences. My grandmother lived in England. My grandmother and grandfather went to England in 1947 to live and work at the new Indian embassy because India had just won independence. My grandfather died some years later and my grandmother stayed in England and ran a boarding house for Indian women who were working for the airlines or the British consulate, something of that sort. She also wrote the first Indian cookbook published in England by Indians after 1947 (her coauthor was Attia Hossain, the writer). I used to spend time with her in England. It had a large influence on my life. It showed me the intimate connection between England and India. There were so many Indians there and there have always been so many similarities between India and England. Colonialism had this mutual impact. It is true that England leached India of wealth, but India was also able to derive mischievously certain things from England, including England's bad bureaucratic management. England had to take some things from India that it may not have wanted like, for instance, Indian people and cultural practices, which became embedded into British culture. These two societies are intertwined, so I was lucky I had that experience. It taught me a great deal about the complexity of cultural life.

How would you define or characterize the colonial relationship between India and the UK?

There's no one description because it has phases. The British first came to India in the 1500s and 1600s as traders. They were astonished by what they saw. For example, they found that Dhaka, which is now the capital of Bangladesh, was one of the most advanced cities in the world, more advanced than London. They also found that the rulers of Northern India looked at the English as irritating mosquitos. For the Mughals, overseas trade was not important. They saw ownership and control of land as important. Initially, the English remained on the margins, trading, bringing a few things into the Indian market, trying to get access to Indian goods with a dwindling supply of gold and silver. The English were therefore in a subordinate position in a peculiar way. This changed after 1757 when the English established themselves in the *diwani* in Bengal and began to re-create Bengal's economy in the interest of an emerging British colonial economy. Bengal was to be central in the triangular trade. It was here that the British harvested land revenue and opium to pay for what the British needed more than anything: Chinese tea. India became Britain's plantation, not so different from the plantation colonies in the Caribbean. A drain of wealth ensues, to finance the industrial revolution. This was the colonial phase, and it ran for about a hundred years. As these examples illustrate, there were different phases in the colonial relationship between India and Great Britain. One has to be acute to these phases. Otherwise, they would all look the same. History is not all the same. After 1858 the crown dominated India. So for a hundred years it was a company, the English East India Company, in command. In 1858 the British crown took charge of India after the big uprising of 1857–58. They started a whole new regime of control. This was also the period in Europe of high imperial power where a new culture of empire was developed as well as new forms of exploitation of Indian labor. From the gaps in English colonialism emerged Indian industry, the roots of Indian working class. And from that emerged the Indian freedom struggle. So England's relationship with India and India's relationship with England is very complicated. It's hard to have a sort of cartoon image of it.

Could you share how your experience has been in the U.S. academy and beyond?

My experience has been good partly because I have been a part of the vaunted model minority, which I have written a lot about. Asians were barred from entering the United States from 1924 to 1965. During this very long period of about forty-one years, no Asians could come in legally. Some came in as professors. But typically there was no mass migration. In 1965 Asians were finally allowed to enter the United States again. This was at the same time as the Civil Rights Movement had its major victory with the Civil Rights Act and the Voting Rights Act. Asians became part of the ideological reconfiguration of racism. The idea that was put out culturally was to look at these Asians as *making it*. The questions that have arisen from this were: The Indians are so smart; why do Black people, why do Hispanic people need welfare? Why do they need state support? Why can't they be like the model minority? So in that sense Indian people had to suffer some forms of discrimination while at the same time enjoyed the fruits of being treated as a model minority. Now the model minority is a bogus narrative because after all we were not brought in on slave ships. We were chosen, that is, people with high advanced degrees were chosen to come into the United States. So to compare a state selected population with a randomly selected population that was captured and brought to the country is incredibly disingenuous. The model minority thesis is a garbage thesis. But that doesn't mean it doesn't have real effects. The real effect it has had on me is that people look at me and say, "You are Indian, you are safe, you work hard, and you are smart." So in that sense I have not had an adverse experience in the American academy. Now I've had an adverse experience in that I see how other colleagues are treated, and that gives me pain. But I don't want to collapse my experience with everybody of color because I think that's also disingenuous.

Do you think being seen as the model minority has put a lot of pressure on you? If so, how have you dealt with that pressure?

I mean, there's pressure—you're right. That's a very good question because the question assumes that the model minority keeps succeeding and that failure is not allowed. Therefore, your production rate must be higher or should be higher than other people. To be perfectly frank, I haven't felt that a lot. I personally feel like the pressures come in a different way, the gentle pressure that all faculty produce under, which is the whole tenure process, as well as the bad jobs market that we have all experienced. So I think there are some general pressures which have to do with the structural organization of academic life. Some appalling pressure that people are put under is a seven-year probationary period where essentially you are treated as an indentured servant. If you annunciate any sort of adverse kind of position, you can be penalized. Or if you don't wear deodorant, they don't like you. It's ridiculous. The whole structure is ridiculous. Certain faculty members are presumed to fail. Specifically, there is always a presumption that Black and Hispanic faculty might fail. There's that. For women faculty, there's always a presumption that they'll have children and therefore fail. For a man from South Asia there are huge privileges in this. I don't suffer the consequences of the worry that I'm going to have a child and may not obtain maternity leave. Also, there's no worry that I'm going to fail, stumble and fall. So yes, there are pressures with people expecting you to do more than what other people will do. I agree. But to put it in context, the demand that I face to write hundreds of articles is such a low demand compared to being expected to fail. Of course there are pressures, of course there are problems, but not pressures compared with those that other people face.

The one pressure that is universal regardless is the political pressure. Radicals in the academy are tolerated, but not embraced. And if you tread too closely to certain issues (justice for Palestinians, conditions of work at the college itself) you are going to run into the limits of tolerance. I feel like the most difficult political problem on college campuses is to have an honest discussion about the role of Israel in U.S. foreign policy and Israel's war on the Palestinians, as well as on the role of the colleges itself on the declining towns that house them.

What has it been like moving from a colonized land, India, to the imperialist land, the United States?

Well, while I was growing up in India, it wasn't quite a colonized country anymore. India had become quite a powerful country; its armies and its police forces had been dealing with local minorities with so-called secessionist areas. So India itself didn't feel quite like the India, say, of maybe the 1840s. India felt like a powerhouse. I left India around the time of the great massacre of Sikhs in Delhi, where 3,000 people were killed essentially on a weekend. The state concluded that one of the largest blots on the Indian body politic was that killing in 1984, after the assassination of Indira Gandhi. I never felt that India was a colonized country alone. I felt that India was in an unequal relationship with the West but it was no longer a colonial country. It had an advanced capitalist sector. It had an armed force that was very powerful. So when I came to the United States I didn't feel the disjuncture enormously. While I was in college in the United States, I got very involved with two movements: The antiapartheid movement and the solidarity committee with the people in El Salvador.

What year are you talking about?

This was in 1984, 85, 86, 87. During that period, my America, if I can put it like that, was not the America of Wall Street. My America was activists fighting against apartheid, universities that disinvest from South Africa. My America was El Salvadorian refugees who were fighting against the U.S. inclusion with the death squads in El Salvador. So when I came to the United States, I didn't come from a country that had recently been colonized. I came into a country that was an imperial power. I left the country when it was getting aggressive with its own power, and I entered a country where the America I saw was not money and weapons. But my America was activists and strugglers fighting for social justice here and abroad. So I had a very interesting take for myself on this country. It has always been a complicated beast. I had no illusion early on about its greatness. Nor did I see it as monolithic. I always saw it filled with people who are dissatisfied with its policies.

Could you share what has inspired you to dedicate your professional life to explore post colonial and neoliberal issues. Where did you get that inspiration from?

What else do you do when the world is sinking? If you have an ounce of rationality you'll have to see that the *why not* question is the essential question. It has, of course, been like that for you, for me, and for so many people. Honestly, I'm so unselfconscious about why this is important to me. I don't have a story. I don't have an incident. Obviously, I don't have my own experiences. I have my experiences of growing up in India seeing how people in my background in India wanted very much for India to become like America. Also, I've had experience coming to the United States and seeing how working-class people, people of some kind of social vision wanted America to be something other than what it was. I appreciate both kinds of experiences. I appreciate the nationalist dream, the "Third World" nationalist dream, which was to re-create world affairs. I found inspiration very much in the South African struggle for liberation and in Central Americans against immense odds fighting in Nicaragua and in El Salvador to make a different world. I have gotten my inspiration in people fighting against incredible odds, like the Haitians slaves who made a revolution. They then had to decide: What do you do when you win the revolution? Do I give it back to the French? Or do I try something different? Those are difficult decisions. You don't necessarily win when you have a Western power wanting to put its knee right into your gut. These stories are monumental. So, what I think pushes me is the idea that what is available to people is so pathetic. There has to be a different story. There has to be a different solution. It seems enough to say, "Let's all donate money and send a basket of goodies to a famine victim in Ethiopia." To me, that is an extraordinarily limited reaction to international catastrophe. There's no one incident; there's no one story.

So to what degree do you feel that your work has contributed to a sound understanding of socioeconomic and political issues that people in the Third World and the West have been facing?

It's hard for me to assess that.

Okay. What have you hoped your work would contribute to in terms of socioeconomic and political issues people around the world have faced?

I can answer that. Well, I have maybe two different projects that have been with me. The first project that has been with me is about the nature of race, culture, and economics in the contemporary West, broadly speaking. So I wrote a book called *The Karma of Brown Folk*, where I talked about how immigrants are pitted against previous immigrants, how mainly African Americans are pitted against Asians in the United States. That book told a story of South Asians. I tried to create for myself a sort of method that links cultural analysis with political and economic analysis because I felt that in the 1980s–90s these roads were beginning to diverge between those who work in cultural things and those who work in political and economic things. And they were seen as two different approaches. The next one I wrote was *Everybody Was Kung Fu Fighting*, which was about trying to create a different grammar around the issues of multiculturalism seen as cultural discourse. I wanted our narrative to be fully aware of the socio-economic and political impact of multiculturalism. I wanted to create a kind of framework that analyzed multiculturalism without just seeing it as a cultural policy but also the political, the economic, and the social impact of it. So that's one project that I have, which is about the questions of race, culture in the political economy of the West.

The other project that I've had, which I'm working on now, is a project to rethink the politics of the Third World and the question of the global South. I've been working on a very long history of the countries of the South, which goes back from the 1920s to the present and beyond. The first volume, *The Darker Nations*, about the Third World as a project, as a deliberate attempt of countries of Asia, Africa, Latin America, and Yugoslavia to enter a debate about interstate relations, about intercontinental relations, and to suggest a different part than that offered by the advanced industrial states of the Atlantic world and the industrial states of the Soviet block. So that was the first part of that project. And that project essentially is to reframe 20th-century history away from the cold war in the north to considerations of the South being at the center.

The second volume of that is called *The Poorer Nations*. It will be history of the global South that is taking the story forward from the 80s into the future. The goal is to reconsider parts that were not taken in the 1980s, things that the states could not have done. And what if they have done them? How would international relations have been different? How would intercontinental relations have been different? And so this second project is the thing that's really interesting now. And I'm going to say it in a crazy way. I want to rewrite 20th-century history. No longer should Accra be seen via London. I want people to see London via Accra. Accra should be the starting point. They should see Accra via London not London via Accra. What I'm saying is the following: Let's look at England from Ghana. Let's look at the United States from Mexico. We're always looking at things from above. So that's part of the project.

It seems with this project you are pushing for a shift in the Western socio-economic and political paradigm with regard to the current social, political, and economic state of developing countries. Is that a fair statement?

I don't want to say it's a paradigm. Paradigm is a huge thing. I don't know if it's a paradigm. You cannot really grasp the history of, say, India only as a history of the Indian state after 1947. The best way to understand this country is on multiple levels. And the level that's been well written about countries like India, Ghana, or Nigeria is that they are state histories. We have really good narratives of nation-state histories. What we don't have is a narrative of all these countries coming together to create a project to challenge Washington, London, Paris, and Moscow. So we don't have that kind of platform written in history books. So the project I'm working on now is not a paradigm shift. Rather, it is gestures towards taking seriously intercontinental politics, an attempt to reframe the planet's relations not just bilaterally but on a much bigger scale.

Western neoliberalism has had a significant impact on the world. So what is your assessment of the Western neoliberal agenda?

I mean the Western neoliberal agenda has a long history. It opens in a small town in Switzerland, *Mt. Pelerin*, where a host of economists and other intellectuals met in the late 1940s. They came up with a theory that the modern welfare state is too powerful and that the state needs to be cut back, so on and so forth. Von Hayke and Friedman were there. At this meeting they came up with a platform but they were nowhere near being in a position of authority. Why? Because they were politically subordinate to European social democracy, American welfarism, Soviet Communism, and the Third World Project. When European social democracy collapsed in the 1970s, so did American welfarism; when Soviet Communism went into a downfall in the late 70s and when the Third World Project fell apart because of the debt crisis. The bottle opens and neoliberalism emerges with a new set of ideas. That's one narrative.

The second narrative is that in the postcolonial states the generation that fought for independence in the late 40s, 50s, 60s, 70s, and early 1980s no longer wanted to be controlled by the independence struggle. They no longer wanted to be attached patriotically to the working class and peasantry. They wanted to free themselves so opportunistically from this class. From this new emerging class emerge neoliberal ideas. And in the West, one sees the morbid symptoms of capitalism in crisis: Stagflation caused the elite to move to a new globalized production, a new geography of production, a new accumulation strategy on a global scale. There is no longer interest on ideas of national economy. They had a different scale. These new social developments ended the great ideologies of the 20th century. Out of this emerges the new elite in the South, and a fledgling global elite in the global cities. They become the agents of change. Reagan gives Van Hayek the U.S. Medal of Freedom. This ideology is elevated, no longer suppressed. David Harvey and others see neoliberalism emerging out of the North. I don't see it like that. I see neoliberalism emerging out of the North and the South. They see neoliberalism as emerging out of the United States and then it's exported through the IMF. I think it's the wrong approach. I think neoliberalism emerges in New York and in Port-au-Prince, and in New Delhi.

This is an interesting way of looking at the emergence of neoliberalism. Would you give more concrete examples to illustrate such an approach? In other words, how do you substantiate your argument in concrete terms?

Well, the elite in those societies say that they no longer want to be responsible for the lazy urban settlers. The rich should prevail. We work hard, so we should get the fruits of our living. Why do we have to pay high taxes to keep drunks going; they're impatient with society. Just as Margaret Thatcher once said, "There is no society, there's only individuals elites in Delhi, in Accra, there is no society, they are only individuals." I work hard, so I should be able to keep my money in the Swiss bank. I should be able to build a big house. I should not feel embarrassed about being rich. In the colonial era we fought as freedom fighters. Then the first generation felt embarrassed being rich because they didn't want to be independently rich. They wanted society to advance. You could track these changes in the new kinds of architecture in the South, or in the new urban planning: these are good examples, but so too is the graphic cutback in agrarian subsidies and the emergence of a deep-seated agrarian crisis in the entire South.

So I don't accept the view that neoliberalism starts in New York and gets exported to the Third World countries through the World Bank and IMF. I see it as a class question. Neoliberalism emerges in these places almost simultaneously. After the collapse of European social democracy, the collapse of Soviet Communism, and the collapse of the Third World Project, new elites emerge. If you go to the world economic foreign meeting, it's not at all a White meeting. You will see Africans that are totally confident, people from Latin America, and from Asia. They are not in a subordinate position.

Now it's true there is still an unequal balance in the world. Of course some countries are more powerful than others. It doesn't mean that when a Malaysian capitalist shows up at this meeting, they say he or she is lesser than an American capitalist. They are friendly with each other; they exchange business cards; and they go skiing together. I think that element of neoliberalism has been suppressed. That is the culpability of the elite in the countries of Africa, Asia, and Latin America.

There have been many arguments made about neoliberalism and its colossal negative effects on the poor. Is it fair to argue that neoliberalism is a new form of colonialism disguised with a different mask?

Not at all. I don't think it's a new form of colonialism. I think it's a different form of domination because in a straight form of colonialism the domestic bourgeoisie was suppressed. They had a feeling of suffocation and therefore they allied with working-class people and peasants against the imperial power. Today, the domestic bourgeoisie do not feel suffocated. They do not feel suppressed. They are confident. They are happily joining forces, in partnership with transnational corporations. They're not collaborating.

That language is not useful anymore. They are willingly, happily in partnership with the centers of imperialism. They will happily come to the United Nations and vote on this, that. No, there is still imperialism. But it's not colonialism. They are colluding openly, and colluding is again the wrong word. They are partners in imperialism. Indian government buys arms. Enormous amounts, 50 billion dollars of arms from the United States. It has it's own regional ambitions, of course. It's helping stabilize the American economy. Indian government buys half of Israel's arms production. So we're not talking about societies that are under the thumb of London, Washington, etc. We're talking about elites who have made concessions. So it's not that there is no imperialism. I see imperialism as the way the politics and economics are structured on the international scale. There are great disparities, great unevenness. There are geographies of domination. But the bourgeoisie in most societies is powerful enough not to be suffocated by the bourgeoisie elsewhere. And I think that is where the colonial question comes. The bourgeoisie is not necessarily allied in the struggle against international imperialism.

You stated that neoliberalism emerges both from the South and the North simultaneously. But who has dictated the rules of the neoliberal games? Whose decisions resulting from the neoliberal agenda have had the major impact on Third World countries? Would you expand and clarify what you stated earlier about neoliberalism?

It's not the North. Here's the interesting thing: In the second volume of the book I'm writing, entitled *The Poorer Nations*, the second chapter is on the South Commission. In 1986, in Kuala Lumpur, Malaysian Prime Minister Mahatir Mohamad of Malaysia announced the formation of the South Commission, and he picked as the chairperson Julius Nyerere, formerly President of Tanzania. And Nyerere went on and selected commissioners from different parts of the world, including Carlos Andres Perez of Venezuela. What did they do? They deliberated from 1987 to 1990. And when they published a report in 1990, such a report was essentially a neoliberal report, with some differences from the North. Great differences. For instance, the report essentially argued that the debt on the South is odious because it doesn't allow growth. Can these countries use their resources to grow an industrial sector? They're not talking about starvation, poverty, etc. They wanted every country in the South to become an export-processing zone. Now who pressured them to do this? Nobody pressured them directly. They were committed to the neoliberal project as well. What I'm saying is we are in a position now where some class realities have emerged, where a certain class has a very strong commitment to neoliberalism and it doesn't take orders from Washington.

The other interesting thing is the disagreement of the South Commission with the North. The North says you can't have your debts forgiven.

That's a power play. The South says we cannot be properly neoliberal unless the debts go. There's no radical critique anywhere here at that level. The North is saying you have to pay back your debts and be neoliberal. The South is saying we want you to forgive our debts, so that we can be neoliberal. So I'm not clear that the South is a homogenous entity. That is, they're under the thumb of the North. I'm not clear that these are allies for justice. I think these are people who very much believe in the similar kind of pathway as the North.

So now let's talk about the effect of the Western neoliberal agenda on people, especially the poor.

Why are you saying Western neoliberalism?

It is important to name it for what it is. Isn't it?

Okay. The new world agenda doesn't impact only the poor but also the so-called middle class. But let's now focus on the neoliberal agenda. How do you understand its effect on the most marginalized groups both in the Third World and in the West? Some people assume that the neoliberal agenda only affects people in the Third World but people in the West are also affected by it. You don't only theorize about these things but you also have to be grounded in activism. I don't see neoliberalism as Western neoliberalism. I see it for its flexibility. In other words, the mechanisms of subordination in France or in the United States are increasingly similar to mechanisms of subordination in Brazil, Russia, India, and China. There are some countries like Mali where the question of survival is still the central question, not subordination. There are hierarchies of countries in the South that we need to engage with as well. But both in the United States and in India, I think, processes are under way where the state has shifted its responsibility from a state with some sort of democratic commitments to a state of security, where the state principal energy is to produce a kind of security zone. At the same time both in India and the United States there's a different understanding of working class. That is to say, large numbers of people are now considered actively helpless. It is a kind of helpless humanity. They're disposable. I wrote a book years ago called *Keeping up With the Dow Jones*, which is about the American shift in class structure where the shift landed America in a position where you get rid of welfare and you have to expand the police state. Even if you don't put people in jail, the neighborhoods become jails. So what happened in the slums of America was similar to what happened in the slums of India. There are informal ways in which people survive. They are heavily garrisoned. But they become relatively helpless for the accumulation of capital on the global scale. That's why I don't see neoliberalism as a hydraulic thing coming from North to the South. I see neoliberalism as a class phenomenon. It is essentially a class policy of resubordinating populations that had exerted themselves in the period of the great capitalist boom. Working class in the North exerted itself. Different classes of peasantry are in the South. And with the neo-liberal dispensation these classes have to be resubordinated not as workers necessarily but as helpless. So they are garrisoned. And the garrisoning happens in very similar ways. You call it the war on terror. You call it the war on drugs. Whatever you call it, it's garrisoning.

As you know, many institutions, such as universities and colleges, have been following a corporate model of education. Consequently, professors who bring more grant money to the institution where they are working often get acknowledged more than those who do not or bring less grant money. Also, corporations that have given money to certain universities have had a great influence on these universities. Where do you stand on these issues?

This is exactly the consequence of neoliberalism. You're going to have places of higher education collapsing and losing their ability to survive. Consequently, you're going to have to internalize the neoliberal model. You're going to have to figure out how to better deliver their own budgets. If they don't get people's money as tax money, they have to increase fees. Essentially, all those are consequences of the neoliberal class attack. There's very little that differentiates the corporatization of the university from the fact that old people don't get somebody to come into their house and read to them. This is all the same thing. I don't see this corporatization of the university as separate from the end of welfare. They are all part of the same process. If you see it differently then you think universities are special. But they are not. They are just like the little kids who no longer have breakfast at school in the morning.

Thus far we have identified the problems that come with neoliberalism. We know that neoliberalism has caused social inequality in so many ways. In your opinion, what should be the solution to all of the problems neoliberalism has caused?

I mean there is one solution. That solution is class power of the elites has to be overthrown. That's the ultimate solution. But I don't live on Mars. I'm not a juvenile. I understand that's not a simple solution because that solution is a final goal, as it were. Until that point we have to have a program of struggles, so that we understand that the small struggles we conduct now lead somewhere. They're shifting class power on a global scale. We have to have a program. We need build on smaller fights to head towards bigger fights. Immediate fights, for instance, in the United States should be against militarism. It's a big fight. Militarized border, militarized cities. Militarized budget. The fight against the military inside the United States is a principal fight. I oppose how much money of the state budget goes into the military. I oppose the militarization of the border. These elements should be the first instance of a program. We have to fight against that. And if the current political system cannot deal with those, we then need to challenge our neighbors, friends, and people here to think about a different kind of political dispensation. But to do this, you have to have a program. I know what the eventual solution is: the transfer of class power. Again, to get there you need a program. There has got to be a program to lead us there. And that program is a program that derives from political struggle. There can be no first element of a program in the United States which doesn't entail fighting against militarism because militarism of cities, of borders, is really sucking the life, the blood out of the population.

Would you agree that neoliberalism has a lot to do with the history of slavery and colonialism?

Neoliberalism has nothing to do with slavery directly. Slavery and indentured colonialism have produced the unequal conditions in the world. Simply put, neoliberalism was an ideology that emerged in the 1940s in a way that does not consider differences in the world. It doesn't consider the inequalities of history. The neoliberal idea is to make those inequalities natural. Neoliberalism is not a product of slavery or colonialism. By blinding itself about the disadvantages of history, neoliberalism makes inequalities appear natural. Therefore, if somebody fails in a neoliberal dispensation it's not because they were disadvantaged by history, but rather because they were inadequate. So neoliberalism feasts on history even though it denies it, but in itself it's the product of that history.

You stated that neoliberalism is not a system of oppression. It's an ideology. Isn't it fair to say that it's an ideology that is translated into the oppression of the "other"?

Of many others. But in a sense neoliberalism is an equal-opportunity oppressor because it will squeeze the middle class in America, the White middle class, and therefore create the resentment that leads to the Tea Party. Understand? It doesn't care whom it squeezes. It will foreclose houses on anybody. That's the beast of neoliberalism. Slavery has produced unequal conditions. Neoliberalism operates equally against everybody. It's Martin Luther's great line what Anatole France said, which is that "The law in it's majestic equality says that nobody can sleep under the bridge." But it's an unequal law because only the homeless sleep under the bridge. So it's a law that targets the homeless. It's not a majestic equality. Neoliberalism is saying that we want enterprise to be rewarded, okay. It looks at life without gender, race, or history. But because it has to operate on the conditions of history, on the terrain produced by history, it operates unequally.

You say that neoliberalism squeezes everyone. But who are mostly affected by it?

The poor, women. They're affected because of the conditions produced by colonialism and slavery. Neoliberalism is racist in its consequences. But it's not racist in its ideology. That's why neoliberalism appeals to people of all backgrounds.

Well, it gives them the illusion that they can benefit from it. But the reality is that the ones that benefit from neoliberalism are the ones on the top.

Of course, but the ones on the top who are going to be African, Latin American, or Asians, etc., can tolerate neoliberalism, whereas they could not tolerate apartheid, because apartheid affected them directly and neoliberalism very smartly is a solvent ideology. It's an ideology that claims to be outside race. It's like merit color blindness. But because it must operate on social conditions that are produced unequally it has unequal results. It's not neoliberalism that's producing the unequal conditions. It's colonialism, slavery that produces the unequal conditions. Neoliberalism operating on those unequal conditions has unequal results. And the reason I insist upon that point is it's the only way we can understand how African, Latin American, East Asian, etc., elites find neoliberalism appealing, because they are succeeding; they have benefitted from the fifty years between colonialism and neoliberalism. They live in the gated communities in Lagos, Rio de Janeiro, Bombay, and in Nairobi, for example, and they are benefitting from neoliberalism.

That's what makes the ideology behind neoliberalism a very dangerous ideology, right?

Yes, precisely.

The illusion is that race doesn't really matter, but it does matter.

It matters because of social conditions.

Is it only because of social conditions? The ones that are mostly affected by liberalism are mostly the poor dark- skinned Haitians. Those who are benefitting from it are the Haitian mulattos and a very few rich dark-skinned Haitians. So skin color and race play a fundamental role in the way neoliberal profits are made and distributed.

You need to travel to Africa. You will see very dark-skin Africans embracing neoliberalism who are doing extremely well.

But how many? Are they the major neoliberal players?

A degree of kind and quality. This is not important to me. I'm not sure that this is essential. I think neoliberalism itself should be separated from the social conditions in which it operates. The reason I insist on that is that it's an important distinction. It's like saying the idea of merit is not a racist ideology. Which is why it's appealing to people even though the ideology of merit, as it hits the ground, has racist effects. Somebody has to decide what is merit in an unequal society. Those who do well are therefore prepared to exercise merit. But merit itself is a very appealing thing. It's a bizarre way in which even working-class people can buy into neoliberal ideas of merit, believing if you work hard you can succeed. If you don't it is because you didn't study hard enough. That's why I insist on their separation. That is the social conditions of slavery that are there. If you don't have ideology that recognizes those conditions, those differences, you then build equality out of difference. You will end up reproducing difference. So neoliberalism says history has ended. I believe history is with us.

From what you just stated, it can be inferred that you do not agree with the statement that was made earlier. That is, neoliberalism is a new form of colonialism disguised with a different mask.

I don't agree with your statement. I don't agree with it at all because now there is a presence of a mature bourgeoisie in these societies that no longer feels suffocated. That's why I even said when I talked about India you have to look at phases. You have to look at shifts. You have to look at emergence of different classes. If you collapse everything onto everything, then you might as well just read ancient history or psychology. History happens because different classes emerge and history changes. Context changes. Categories have to change. Now I'm not an apologist for today. I'm a critic of today, of the present. But I don't want to be a critic of today, believing today is today. I want to study history to explain why today is like it is. But I don't want to believe when I look out the window I just see Charles Dickens walking by because he's dead. The times of Dickens have changed. We live in different times.

It seems that you are arguing that neoliberalism is more like a class issue than it is a race and class issue. Race also plays a major part in the neoliberal agenda, so it is not only a class issue.

I keep this analytically separate. Neoliberalism is a class attack on the population of the planet. Don't collapse these two things analytically. The ideology is here. Its social effects on the social conditions are here. If you collapse the two you won't get a read of either. Neoliberalism to me is a class assault. It is not a racial assault. It is not a gender assault. It believes that everybody can succeed. But it doesn't acknowledge the social conditions to make only certain people succeed. The idea of merit is not a racist idea. But when the idea of merit strikes the word, it is racist.

Factors such as class, gender, and race often prevent many from having access to resources that would enable them to succeed. Would you agree with this assertion?

I'm not arguing with you about this. I'm just analytically separating two pieces. When you say merit, it's the ideology of merit, which is not racist. Then there is the experience of merit in the world, which is racist. If we don't keep these two things analytically separate, you don't understand why young Black children want to succeed. Otherwise, you're just saying, "Well, everybody knows that the game is rigged. So why should they even try? Why should anybody with dark skin study?" But that's absurd. The world doesn't work like that. People try because ideology is raw. When the iron strikes the world, it has differential effects. That has to be analytically separate. Otherwise, I cannot understand how the world works.

4 Countering the Colonizing Allure of (Pseudo)-Scientific Discourses in Education Research and Policy

Myriam N. Torres

INTRODUCTION

Postmodernists and poststructuralists place language at the center of social relations, identity, knowledge, and research. This move is often called the *linguistic turn* of human and social sciences, and it is mostly considered a premise of poststructuralism. Derrida (1974) argues that language is everything. Nevertheless, before anybody started talking about poststructuralism, the Bakhtin Circle (Bakhtin, 1986a, 1986b; Voloshinov, 1973) in the 1920s were discussing and writing about how language—the link of all socially organized human activity—is constitutive of ideology. In other words, according to the Circle, we cannot appropriately study and understand human activity, power, and ideology without acknowledging the role of language, which functions not only as a means but intimately constitutes and is constituted by them. The focus of the Circle was the language in use, including all the semiotic components of regular human activities which define discourse.

It's important to note here that by bringing up the role of discourse as constituted by and constituting power and ideology, it is not to say that "language is everything," as Derrida (1974) maintains. There are components of social practices and social structures which are not of linguistic nature, yet they are dialectically interrelated with the linguistic elements. Fairclough (2003, 2010) developed theoretical and methodological frameworks for demonstrating such dialectical interrelationship through critical discourse analysis. In the same vein, Rikowski and McLaren (2002) point out that postmodernists' excessive reliance on "discourse" and its limitless games results in not giving enough attention to the structural constraints set by capitalism and its social relations.

By and large, Western science is anchored in the idea of language as transparent and devoid of values. Thus, scientific discourse is just a means to convey "valid" knowledge about the nature of natural, social, and human phenomena. In this framework, it's easy to create not only the myth of neutrality of scientific knowledge and science at large, but also a reverent attitude toward them. Based on this cultural phenomenon of Western science, in the United States, education policymakers came up with the No Child Left Behind (NCLB) Act of 2002. Specifically, in the section devoted to literacy—Reading First Initiative—the phrase "scientifically based research" is repeated many times (some have counted more than 120 times in that document) to create a halo of irrefutable truth. This mantra is trumpeted to teachers and the general public, and they accept it at face value without questioning its truthfulness. It has played out as a mechanism of control not only mental and psychological but also in a policing manner specifically applied to the teaching practice.

Actually, the way scientific discourse is used in NCLB is not science but *scientism* given that it is presented as irrefutable truth. Susan Neuman (2002) from the U.S. Department of Education at the working group conference held on February 6, 2002, argued that "scientifically based research" is "indisputable." However, according to the canons of logical positivism—as theorized by well-known philosophers of the science such as Karl Popper (1972) and Hans Reichenbach (1961)—scientific knowledge and scientific research have a basic distinctive principle: to be disputable or liable to be empirically refutable by testing alternative hypotheses. This is opposed to the dogmatic creed preached in the NCLB policy on literacy teaching. We may think that NCLB is already past policy, but as Krashen (2010, January) attests, Obama's policy on teaching literacy called the LEARN Act (Literacy Education for ALL, Results for the Nation, 2011) is "Reading First on steroids." This "new" policy allocates "$2.35 billion for comprehensive literacy programs, to support local school-based literacy programs (birth to grade twelve)." It also includes "Providing high-quality, research-based professional development opportunities" and "Supporting promising and innovative practices to improve literacy and writing, especially for students reading and writing below grade level" (from the policy summary). Krashen is right in comparing it to the failed Reading First Initiative because the LEARN Act expands dramatically the population that will suffer its impact, from kindergarten back to birth, and from 3rd grade all the way to 12th, but the approach to literacy is the same, as well as the discourse of scientism. Nonetheless, two things are new and good in the LEARN Act: writing is included as part of literacy, and the policy refers to literacy, not just reading. But, in general, those responsible for this "new" policy still seemed to be under the lure of scientism and/or were trapped by the special-interest groups.

The allure of scientism is referred to in this chapter as the reverential attitude toward the scientific discourse as a way to impose the target measures and preempt the possibility of those affected to question the appropriateness of policies such as Reading First. Freire (1998) rejects *scientism* because of its myopic view of the process of knowing as exclusively intellectual. In his view, we know with our entire being, including our emotions, intentions, and experiences. Lather (2008) refuses "to concede to scientism" since it is actually a move to the "repositivization" (her term) of scientific research in education. Harding (2006) and L. T. Smith (1999) go on to question the goal to colonize minds and maintain inequality: Eurocentrism, male ways of knowing and thinking, racism, heterosexism, and classism. The value-free premise of scientific research is actually self-serving. For Harding, Western science's denial of the influence of researchers' interests in the research process is ludicrous because they are part and parcel of the research process, at least at the unconscious level. Along the same line, Lynd (1939) argues that denial of the influence of interests in research results leaves the back door open to the uncritical acceptance of values of the status quo.

The purpose of this chapter is twofold: 1) examine and demonstrate the allure of pseudoscientific discourses in education research and its colonizing effect on the public, including parents, educators, and researchers; 2) Describe concrete cases of how to counter such colonization by using critical discourse analysis (CDA) as a tool of analysis and a framework for unveiling the intended meaning of those discourses, and by engaging concerned educators and other people interested in actions to defend public education and democratic schooling.

THE ALLURE OF SCIENTISM OR PSEUDOSCIENTIFIC DISCOURSE

I claim that the allure of pseudoscientific discourse has been used in education research, policy, and practice as a mechanism of control for imposing top-down education reform promoted and controlled by the business community. This purported reform has eroded democratic practices and concern for the whole child and her/his well-being. It is a path for corporate control of the most fundamental activities in the schools: curriculum development, pedagogical practices, and assessment of students. It permits the "education industrial complex" to become even more ubiquitous, included testing, textbooks and materials, teacher training, school commercialization, tutoring, and many more school services.

This is not to say that the allure of pseudoscientific discourse is the only factor in this takeover of education, but it has helped to discourage debate and discredit the resistance of conscientious teachers, administrators, parents, and students, and sedates the general public and even serious researchers. As Susan Neuman (2002) claims, when she refers to the validity of the skill-based phonics approach to teaching literacy of the Reading First Initiative: the scientific basis of it is "undisputable." In the same vein, the legislature of the state of New Mexico has recently introduced bills (HB 70a, HB 74, 2011) to make what the sponsors call the "scientific teaching of reading" a state mandate and require colleges of education to prepare teachers in the skill-based phonics approach to teaching literacy.

The legislation on literacy of the NCLB Reading First Initiative was the enactment of the National Reading Panel's (NRP) report. However, as Coles (2003) and Yatvin (2002) document, the claims of a scientific basis for the NRP and hence the NCLB Reading First mandate are bogus. The whole process has been a scam, disseminated and maintained through propaganda (Rendall, 2005). As Yatvin, the only teacher member of the panel, describes, there were many questionable things that made that report everything else but scientific: the choice of panelists; obvious preagreement by most members on the "hierarchy-of-skills model"; the actual number of studies examined (a minuscule number in contrast to the hundred thousand alleged by then Secretary of Education Ron Page); uncorrected, undeliberated, and unapproved subcommittee reports; dismissal of the "minority report"; and the fact that a public relations company wrote the report presented to the government and to the public. Thus has been spun this mantra of "scientific-based research" over an approach which actually has no scientific basis. However, all the problematic implications of the policy have yet to dawn on the public and even most educators.

Unfortunately, these maneuvers in policymaking do not constitute an isolated event. They are part of a large conservative-neoliberal agenda circulating in the United States for more than four decades, with an overarching focus on rolling back the progressive achievements of the social movements of the 1950s–1970s. This agenda covers all institutional and social affairs, is extremely well funded, and has as one of its goals to dismantle the welfare state and public services, including public education and consequently the profession of teaching. According to Demarrais (2006), who tracks the trajectory of this conservative agenda by "following the money," it was found that the conservative agenda has four pillars: 1) Develop a cadre of young people on college campuses to organize and voice their views of education and society and confront "radical" students and teachers; 2) Prepare scholars able to produce research (apparently ideologically neutral) that supports the conservative agenda; 3) Establish a network of conservative regional and state policy centers (called "think tanks") to promote their views and write education legislation; and 4) Establish conservative media networks (even those with a liberal reputation) to carry their message and agenda (p. 201). The success of this agenda is undeniable as we look at its progress in the last four decades. As Kumashiro (2008), in his book *Seduction of Common Sense,* points out, "The Right has been successful at addressing multiple issues and framing its initiative in ways that mask its intentions, divide and conquer the Left, and bring many from the middle on board" (p. 97).

We can appreciate some of those strategies and strategists at work by considering Newt Gingrich's pamphlet *Language: A Key Mechanism of Control* (1996). He points out the importance of saying the "right" words at the right time. Of course it's a "language game" of simplicity and clarity, yet words can actually mean something very different from what most people think they mean. He compiled a long list of words to describe himself and his party as well as a list for describing liberals and Democrats.

Today, mainstream media are mostly owned or controlled by the conservative establishment which, rather than checking for facts or contradictions, go crazily spinning those statements or judgments using the "resonance effect" (Torres & Mercado, 2006, 2007) with no accountability. Small lies and, especially, "big lies" go unquestioned. This propaganda technique of Nazi Germany has become commonplace in the media in the United States: When a lie is big enough, and is repeated over and over again, it becomes an unquestionable truth for the general public. Now we have the aid of big money supporting big lies, and the impunity is even more blatant. The National Reading Panel and hence the NCLB are undoubtedly good examples of this "big-lie" propaganda strategy.

The conservative agenda is not as simple as it may appear. Apple (2006) has been studying the "right turn" in the United States, its modernization through broad-based alliances, as well as its complex impact on education policy and practice. In his book *Educating the 'Right' Way,* he describes four distinct groups: *neoconservatives, neoliberals, autocratic populists,* and a *professional managerial group.* Briefly, the *neoliberals* consider the market as the organizing principle and neutral regulator of all social, economic, and political affairs, under the assumption that markets regulate themselves. *Neoconservatives* are concerned with high standards, excellence, accountability, "back to basics," or the teaching of "real" knowledge. Actually, they are for a strongly interventionist state so that "only legitimate content and methods are taught" (p. 43). The *autocratic populist* or Christian Right conservative group pushes Christian fundamentalist values for schooling: creationism instead of evolution, gender roles and "family values." For the *professional and managerial new middle class,* the mantra is high-stakes testing: the more and more often, the better. They also support the privatization (or corporatization) of schools, which opens venues for alliances with neoliberal and neoconservative groups.

The alliance of these various groups and their influence on the government and on all institutions and society in general are overwhelming. Andharati Roy (2003) calls the takeover of governments by elites and corporations an "outrageous, promiscuous crosspollination." For her, neoliberalism has taken over the mechanisms of democracy such as checks and balances, public spheres, media, schools, an independent judicial system, and free elections. Nowadays we don't have democracy but plutocracy, or government of the elites. As Giroux (2004, 2008) put it bluntly, the neoliberal doctrine is free-market fundamentalism, which has created the "common sense" that social services and the welfare state are bad, and so they promote their dismantling based on a big lie. This started in President Reagan's times with the infamous report *A Nation at Risk* (National Commission on Excellence in Education, 1983). However, at the same time, neoliberals and their allies fight furiously to keep the welfare program for corporations, as George (1999) notes.

In education, we have a very grave problem with idly conceived education reforms promoted by pseudo-educators. For Hursh (2008), standards, standardization, and accountability with high-stakes testing have been the main contributors to the real crisis of education in the United States. Arrogance, false assumptions, antidemocratic and inhumane educational practices are at the core of the new educational policy, its overwhelming control of teaching and learning, and its devaluation of the profession of teaching. The situation is even worse, as Hursh notes, given that this neoliberal doctrine has become completely embedded in political, economic, educational, and discourse practices. In this context it is difficult to talk about democratic values, focus on the whole child, respect academic freedom, and recognize that teachers should control curriculum, pedagogy, and assessment.

The previous description is undoubtedly a grim picture of the state of affairs of education and society at large. Nonetheless, as George (1999) argues against the neoliberal undertaking, "We have the numbers on our side, because there are far more losers than winners in the neo-liberal game. We have the ideas, whereas theirs are finally coming into question because of repeated crises. . . . The threat is clearly transnational so the response must also be transnational."

Of course, our task is overwhelming; it requires solidarity, funding, organization, and a broad base of coordinated struggles covering many fronts and short-, middle-, and long-term goals. One of the fronts we need to cover is the disentangling of pseudoscientific discourses, countering them in the context of democratic and critical research and action. How? This is the subject of the following section.

COUNTERING THE COLONIZING EFFECT OF PSEUDOSCIENTIFIC DISCOURSES IN EDUCATION

MacLure (2003) highlights the need of what she calls *discursive literacy* in education research. This consists of disarticulating the textual components of educational realities to understand the construction of identities, values, and the workings of power. She defines *discursive literacy* as "a matter of learning or choosing to 'read' educational events and situations as texts" (p. 8). The theoretical and methodological frameworks of critical discourse analysis (CDA), as developed by one of its pioneers, Norman Fairclough (2001, 2003, 2010), can help us to expose the hidden agendas and strategies of the promoters of those pseudoscientific discourses in education research and practice.

Fairclough (1989, 1992, 1995, 2001, 2003, 2010) developed a sociocritical theory of language. For him, discourse is language in use, working in synchrony with other semiotic modalities. Discourse is a social practice or mode of action situated culturally, socially, and historically. Discourses shape and are shaped by institutions and social structures. Fairclough stresses the dialectical dynamic between discourses as social practices and social structures; thus, he opens the door to consider a two-way impact between them. This creates the possibility of changing social structures, because we are able to change discourses by developing and endorsing counterhegemonic discourses. He is careful, unlike most poststructuralists (e.g., Derrida, 1974), in making explicit that there is more than discourse and semiotic modalities in human activity and societal affairs; that is, there are nonsemiotic components of social structures. Hence, Fairclough uses CDA to expose or make more obvious to most people not only the workings of power and the prevalence of ideologies and their agendas, but also to track the path between the transformation of discourses and changes in social structures, and vice versa. In other words, he aims to make transparent the mechanisms between the semiotic and nonsemiotic elements of social structures and institutions, as well as to demonstrate how they affect the daily life of individuals. In other words, he wants to expose how ideologies and power constitute and are constituted through language, and how we can change them by changing discourses about the issue at hand.

In accordance with his theory of discourse, Fairclough (1992, 2003, 2010) develops a methodological framework of critical discourse analysis, which includes linguistic and other semiotic tools, as well as an interdisciplinary approach that mediates text and social analyses. Why CDA? It allows us to display how social wrongs are produced and maintained, as well as techniques of resistance and possibilities of change for the common good. The first step is to construct the object of research by identifying a social wrong, which often is an interdisciplinary issue, and the obstacles we might find in attempting to right the wrong. In the process of identifying a social wrong, we start by examining the social order, identifying and selecting relevant texts, and defining the categories for analysis. Then, we need to examine the semiotic aspects of the obstacles and track their dynamic interaction with nonsemiotic aspects in social practices, institutions, and social structures. CDA, as developed by Fairclough (2010), includes a transformative process for changing discourses, given that radical changes start by changing the discourse. This includes an action plan on how obstacles could be overcome.

Below, I briefly go through this process with a specific example. First of all, the social and educational wrong is the use of pseudoscientific discourse to control the teaching and learning process at schools. This is first of all an educational problem, but it is also a social, political, language, and mass media problem. Hence, pseudoscientific discourse as a mechanism of control of teachers and schools is an interdisciplinary subject and should be studied as such. The relevant texts selected are: 1) a pamphlet *What Is Scientifically Based Research: A Guide for Teachers,* created by the National Institute for Literacy; and 2) the critical sections of HB 70a and HB 74 of the 2011 New Mexico Legislature. The semiotic analysis includes the linguistic and nonlinguistic components of the texts.

The first text, the pamphlet *What Is Scientifically Based Research: A Guide for Teachers,* has images and contextual text that frame its scientific (natural sciences) character. The front cover has a picture of a beautiful five- or six-year-old African American girl who is completely absorbed looking at or reading a book. The title of the picture is "Using Research and Reason in Education." The inside of the front cover is a picture of the solar system and a story about a person called Sizi, who criticized Galileo's discovery of planets, alleging that it was not possible. Sizi based his statement on beliefs and opinions, not the knowledge achieved using the scientific inquiry and methods. The inside back cover is a picture of a galaxy. What are these pictures telling us? Clearly, they are making a case for the "scientific method" of teaching literacy as the rational and only valid way to do so, in order to be at the level of the "hard" sciences such as astronomy. For critics of the "soft" character of educational research, the solution is to emulate the natural sciences and their "hard" methods of research. The Reading First initiative (No Child Left Behind Act, 2002) started at a time when the federal government and the states curtailed the diversity of paradigms and modes of inquiry and knowing, and went on to mandate the reductionist positivist scientific method as the most desirable and therefore fundable way of doing research in education.

The pamphlet contains many authoritatively phrased and patronizing statements about what is scientifically based research, built upon the federal perspective on this subject. It starts with the title "Becoming a wise consumer of education research." The federal government mandates, especially in the case of Reading First, that all the instructional teaching methods of literacy should be "proven effective" with "systematic empirical methods that draw on observations or experiment," and "rigorous data analysis," by "a peer reviewed journal or a panel of independent experts through a comparatively rigorous, objective, and scientific review" (p. 1). The scientific experts' specification of proven effective methods is what counts as valid, so teachers' own research, experiences, perspective, and philosophy of teaching and commitments have no role in teaching literacy. They are discarded from the outset:

> More than ever, educators are expected to make decisions that guarantee quality instruction. As knowledge emerges, so do philosophies, opinions, and rhetoric about definitions of instructional excellence. From policy makers to classroom teachers, educators need ways to separate misinformation from *genuine knowledge* and to distinguish scientific research from poorly supported claims. (p. 1, italics added)

Labaree (2011) confirms the trend toward hypervaluing the discourse of *scientism* for claims of validity. He refers specifically to the lure of statistics, given the perceived low and *ad hoc* status of education research, researchers and policymakers are looking for data that "look authoritative and scientific and that present a certain face validity" (p. 628).

The pamphlet also includes explanations of the role of "independent peer review" which "provides a baseline of quality control" (p. 2) and the "replication of results by other scientists," because it says "*True scientific knowledge* is public and open to challenge . . . subject to change based on contrary evidence" (p. 3). By understanding these notions, teachers will become more acute in "recognizing effective research" (p. 2). This sounds fair: recognition of the openness of scientific research by replication to confirm or refute prior results. However, the federal perspective on SBR, as set forth in the NCLB Act, does not include this distinctive feature of constant renewal of the approaches to teaching literacy. The federal Reading First mandate, the New Mexico version of Reading First, and many other government documents and mandates trumpet *scientifically based research* to teachers and school administrators as *the* only scientific way of teaching literacy. However, those teachers, administrators, and other educators do not have the opportunity to question this "scientific" truth (actually pseudoscientific discourse) about the teaching of literacy. Thus, it becomes doctrine, not science. Karl Popper (1963, 1972), a proponent of the positivist quantitative methods in the 20th century, came up with the principle of "falsifiability" or refutability as the most distinctive feature of science. In other words, for him all knowledge is provisional or hypothetical. The only conclusive knowledge arises when a theory is refuted. Consequently, we can counter, following the same principles of positivism, that Reading First's alleged science is not conceded to be refutable, so it's not science.

In New Mexico, the Public Education Department took the federal Reading First policy, added some context corresponding to the state demographics, and started pushing this policy aggressively in schools and colleges of education. During the 2011 New Mexico legislative session, two bills were passed imposing extremely controlling and threatening measures to ensure that teacher preparation programs in colleges of education focus on the "science of teaching reading." The first one, NM HB 70a, states:

> HB 70 would enact a new section of statute to:
>
> - *require* that, to qualify for state funding, a college of education or teacher preparation program at a public postsecondary institution must instruct students in how to teach reading in courses that:
>   - are based on *current scientifically based reading research* and the *science of reading*;
>   - are aligned with Public Education Department (PED)-adopted reading standards; and
>   - include strategies and assessment measures to ensure that beginning teachers are proficient in teaching reading (p. 1)
> - *prohibit* distribution of an appropriation for a public postsecondary institution to a college of education or teacher preparation program that does not provide such instruction; and

- *require* the Higher Education Department (HED) to certify that a college or program meets the requirements of the section. (italics added)

The authoritative nature of the policy can be identified by the use of terms at the beginning of each main paragraph: *require, prohibit, require,* as well as the conditioning of funding to compliance with this mandate. The specific mandate concerns the teaching of reading courses that "are based on *current scientifically based reading research* and *the science of reading*" (italics added). In this authoritative sentence, the determinant *the* in "the science of reading" carries a great deal of power and restrictions for those who need to comply with this policy.

Actually, the elected officials are determining for college faculty *what* to teach in reading courses for prospective teachers, and are thus trampling on their academic freedom and the local control of curriculum. By the domino effect, through this policy the state legislature is also determining for new teachers *what* and *how* to teach reading to children. Elected officials are trampling on local control of curriculum and pedagogy and the academic freedom of teachers and students as well.

To complete the demands of HB 70, the New Mexico Legislature passed unanimously the bill HB 74 of 2011 to require that all teacher candidates take a standardized state examination on the "science of teaching reading" for elementary education licensure.

> HB 74 amends the *School Personnel Act* to require that, as of July 1, 2012 [it was amended on January 1, 2013], the New Mexico teacher assessment examination that candidates must pass for standard or alternative Level 1 elementary teacher licensure must include a *rigorous* assessment of a candidate's knowledge of the *science of teaching reading.* (italics added)

The repetition of clauses such as "the science of teaching reading" gives the reader a sense of consensus and cohesiveness between the texts of the two bills. Again, the use of the determinant *the* in "the science of . . ." conveys tremendous power to exclude other approaches to teaching reading under the threat to put at risk prospective teachers' passing of the state exam, and consequently a loss of funding for the teacher preparation program of the respective college or school of education.

What is incredible about these policies is that the first sponsor of the bill HB 74 is a Democrat and a retired educator, and the legislature of New Mexico is majority Democratic. It's clear that the sponsor—-the education committee and the rest of the legislators—did not do their homework concerning the (pseudo)-scientific character of the "science" of teaching reading, which originated in the National Reading Panel debacle. Undoubtedly the lure of "scientism" had something to do with preventing legislators from informing themselves about the multiple approaches to teaching literacy as well as the dynamics and richness of the field. To start with, they would have found serious studies, testimonies, and well-documented articles and books concerning the shortcomings of the National Reading Panel report (the basis of Reading First) (Coles, 2003; Metcalf, 2002; Yatvin, 2002). They would have found that, according to data from the National Assessment for Education Progress (NAEP), when comparing four years of reading scores and the net gains (for fourth and eighth graders nationwide) before NCLB (1998–2002) with those obtained during seven years of NCLB implementation (2003–2009), fourth graders gained four points before and three points during the seven years of NCLB, while eighth graders gained zero points before and one point during the implementation of this policy. What's clear is that Reading First is not working despite extending the time of instruction, all the preparation for tests, tutoring, and many more measures such as reducing or eliminating recess.

Unfortunately the politicians, and the media that serve their interests, do not talk about studies that show how this policy is not making any difference in terms of the revered scores in standardized tests. A study was conducted by the National Center for Education Evaluation and the Institute of Education Sciences (2008), the latter being the culprit of "scientific research" in education, under purview of the Department of Education and aimed at learning about the impact of Reading First (NCLB) on reading comprehension (measured by the subtest from the Stanford Achievement Test during three years of data collection). The most important result was that "Reading First did NOT produce a statistically significant impact on student reading comprehension test scores in grades one, two or three" (highlights added) and on "student engagement with print." However, the report includes several significant statistical tests showing changes in classroom practices and professional development. Of course, those changes should have happened, if the teachers were implementing the Reading First mandated curriculum, pedagogy, and professional development. They should have done all those things for improving reading, which is what matters, according to the model of achievement of this frenzied policy. So, yes, teachers are doing what was mandated, but the mandated approach to teaching literacy was bluntly ineffective.

Of course, this failing was predicted from the onset by educators who know and have taught children to read and write using holistic, sociocultural, functional sociolinguistics, or critical literacy. Now the problem is why, despite the failure, the Obama administration continues on the same path with the LEARN (Literacy Education for All, Results for the Nation) Act, which is no less than an extension of the testing frenzy and the same phonics approach, from birth to twelfth grade. Krashen (2010, January) considers this "new" policy as NCLB on steroids. So the situation is, if the federal Department of Education really continues with the same policy, so will many states.

Another major issue, under the lure of scientism—which effectively covers up the vested interests' agendas—is the reduction of "scientific" research in literacy to nothing but quantitative randomized experiments. Thus, numerous and diverse other types of research are dismissed or rendered inappropriate. These are often more culturally sensitive to the local literacies and ways of learning to read, based on the reading of the world that children in different places are familiar with. The already harmful consequence of this exclusionary policy is that funding has been wiped out if the prospective research proposal is not quantitative and directly related to the phonics approach to literacy.

"The lure of statistics for educational researchers," as Labaree (2011) puts it, is "a mechanism to shore up their credibility, enhance their scholarly standing, and increase their influence in the realm of educational policy" (p. 621). The basic assumption here is that measuring is the best way to represent the educational state of affairs and its changes—an assumption that is highly contested on practical, theoretical, and philosophical grounds. For Hostetler (2010) the *experimentalist evidence-based* turn of education research leads us to "(mis)understanding human beings: theory, value and progress in education." Indeed, it is the path to regressive change, Hostetler maintains. On the other hand, I agree with Labaree that quantitative research in education has a place, but for "narrow purposes" such as demographic information and broad trends. Teaching literacy as a social practice demands that we consider its highly contextualized, culturally bounded, and complex processes; its nature and practices cannot be represented fully and appropriately with just *quantitative* data. R. Smith (2011) introduces the term "metricophilia" to refer to the obsession with and reverence for measurement and statistics as the hallmarks of scientific research. He contests the often-stated argument that the progress of society is a consequence of the progress of science, alleging that even while this statement carries some truth, it "does not justify scientism, and the colonizing of science or any other form of thought, and the assumption that whatever problem we have, the solution will inevitably be a scientific one" (p. 633).

The challenge for all conscientious educators is that in our current political climate of plutocracy and "mediacracy"—corporate media–style democracy—what matters in a policy like Reading First is how well it serves the vested interests of the corporations that have taken over education, not if the policy is ineffective, if it causes harm to children, teachers, and the profession of teaching, or even if it jeopardizes the future of the nation. The bottom line is to make public education look bad despite all the money "thrown" to improve it, as too many people echo this mantra. So what's to be done?

Following Fairclough's (1992, 2001, 2003, 2010) methodological framework for doing CDA, once the texts are analyzed to make transparent the workings of power in and through language, and to explain them in the context of institutional discourse practices (e.g., legislatures) and at the macrolevel of social forces (e.g., the conservative agenda), we need to move toward changing those discourses. In other words, we need to take action based on what we now know about the social wrong in using pseudoscientific discourse of literacy teaching as a smoke screen to advance the conservative agenda of dismantling public education.

"Don't tell me about problems without talking of their solutions." I have often heard this admonition by my students who are mostly teachers and/or prospective teachers. Although this request often implies a "quick fix" of the problem, it ultimately demands that one close the gap—the "division of labor" between studying the problem and working on its solution—which contributes to diffusing responsibility and letting the problem grow bigger. In the academic world, this gap has been institutionalized by separating scholarship/research from action. Bridging this gap demands that academics embed the role of scholar with that of activist. For instance, CDA of the texts of literacy mandates provides concrete and persuasive evidence to convince some of us that just doing research, giving presentations, writing, and publishing have little or no impact on diversifying, democratizing, and/or humanizing the teaching and learning of literacy in the schools. We need to change strategy if we want to see these urgent changes happen.

My humble suggestions for moving into a more activist strategy are framed along two dimensions: time (short and long term) and coverage (from modest to more ambitious projects, on as many coordinated fronts as possible). Unlike the conservative agenda that is comprehensive, coordinated, and well funded, active progressives, liberals, leftists have numerous, yet uncoordinated, projects and activities, with a chronic lack of funding. One large difference is that mainstream media networks are either owned or controlled by conservatives. They have reached this goal as part of their agenda beginning in the 1970s. I'm going to indicate some short- and long-term and interconnected action projects that might help change the discourses and practices in literacy teaching in schools from pseudoscientific to more open, multicultural, multilingual, holistic, and/or critical, indicating why these projects are important in such pursuit. We need to be conscious that countering a big lie, as the literacy hoax is, will need a great deal of solidarity, persistence, organization, coordination, and coverage.

Project 'Educate'

Starting with those who are directly dealing with the literacy mandates policy—teachers, administrators, parents, students, and others—we need to educate them about how exclusionary, antidemocratic, and completely ineffective it is, presenting them documentation showing that this *Scientific Teaching of Reading* originated in a hoax. We will provide information and models concerning alternative theories, research approaches, strategies, and practices, making people aware of the intentionally misleading use of the term "scientific" to justify the top-down, undemocratic, and highly authoritative policies of control which discourage resistance or even debate. The reduction of the term "scientific" to the single, and usually infeasible, method of randomized groups is also in fact of itself unethical. There are other types of research that are more culturally sensitive to the local literacies and ways of learning to read, and based on the reading of the world children are familiar with. This "Educate" project needs to be taken to professional educational organizations by bringing up this literacy hoax in presentations, forums, listservs, and workshops, as well as in publications. Politicians, especially legislators, need to be educated as well. We need to make this literacy issue political by requiring their commitment to change their rhetorical discourses and the respective policies.

Organizing Project

Educating people about this literacy issue should create opportunities to do something about it. Some colleagues and I are starting an organizing project called LEON (Literacy Educators Organizing Network) as part of our participation in a literacy conference in our institution. The preliminary exploration on the viability of the project has shown us how uninformed are our colleagues about this matter and also how hesitant they are to get involved in countering this problem. We need to join synergies with other organizations working on similar or larger issues, including unions. Social media, such as blogs, Web pages, listservs, Facebook, Twitter, and so on, could be of great help to reach out and organize a great number of people. We could also use more traditional media such as letter campaigns and op-eds.

Mass Media Project

In order for these projects to work on a large scale, we need mass media working for the public interest. This type of media should be accessible to anyone regardless of his/her social consciousness levels and access to the Internet. These media should become identified as those that work for the public interest: a) to give truthful information; b) to facilitate democratic debate on issues that matter to all people; c) to promote organization around those issues; d) to conduct in-depth investigative reporting on issues affecting the public interest; e) to make elected officials accountable to the public for what they promised, say, and do. In brief, we must look for the type of media that are the watchdogs of the public interest, that reach all classes of people, not just those who are already highly conscientious and able to access alternative media, which are mostly on the Internet. Part of this media project should be that of rescuing the public media from the tentacles of the oil corporations, conservative groups, and foundations, to serve the public interest, which has been their mission since the creation of the Corporation for Public Broadcasting in the 1960s. I know that this media project seems like *Mission: Impossible*. However, achievements in media democracy happening in other countries, and in the United States as well, make this media project more reachable today than it was ten years ago. One encouraging example is Argentina's media law, which is called *"Ley de servicios de comunicación audiovisual"* (Helson, 2011). This law divides the media space and airways in thirds: one-third public interest media, one-third private media, and one-third associated media. It's important to note that the title of the law includes "services," which stresses the social function of the media to serve, not just to make money. This law hopefully pays back the "debt of democracy," as Ardouin-Elias (2009) calls the various decades of military rule, suppressing anyone or any medium dissenting from the official doctrine of the dictatorship of the ruling class. Several countries are following in the footsteps of Argentina's media law.

Clean Elections Project

"The solution to *Citizens United* that no one is talking about," wisely warns Frances M. Lappé (2012). She refers to *clean elections*, which means running for public office with public funds and no contributions from any private donors. This is not just an ideal but already a timid practice in a handful of states (e.g., Maine, Arizona, California). In a "Clean Money Initiative Fundraiser" event (funds for the campaign itself) hosted by Ted Williams in Los Angeles, California (Democracy University Series, 2005), the lemma was: "The reform that makes possible other reforms." I can't agree more with Lappé's observation. I understand why corporate media, elites, conservative and corporate politicians are silent about this possibility, but it's hard to understand why progressives and leftists, and even alternative radical media, are not talking about this promising possibility to change discourses and institutions from the bottom up. This initiative is not esoteric, it's possible for anybody who wants to get involved, and it opens up a whole range of possible reforms aimed at righting the social wrongs which are widely prevalent today.

I know that these are ambitious projects, but as educators and scholar-activists, we cannot continue working just in our little niches. The conservative and neoliberal agendas are nonstop, comprehensive, and entrenched in every dimension of society. Countering their arrogant power demands from us a great deal of organization and solidarity. Susan George (1999) points to these needs:

> We have the numbers on our side, because there are far more losers than winners in the neo-liberal game. . . . What we lack, so far, is the organization and the unity which in this age of advanced technology we can overcome. . . . Solidarity no longer means aid, or not just aid,

> but finding the hidden synergies in each other's struggles so that our numerical force and the power of our ideas become overwhelming.

No doubt the occupy movement, among other things, is creating all sorts of synergies, and building the solidarity necessary for embracing real democratic reforms. We also need high hopes and social responsibility. In this regard, Freire (2003) is inspiring: "We must envision our work with a sense of perspective and history. Our struggle of today does not mean that we necessarily accomplish changes but without this fight, today, the future generations may have to struggle a great deal more" (p. 10).

REFERENCES

Apple, M. (2006). *Educating the "Right" way* (2nd ed.). New York: Routledge.

Ardouin-Elias, D. (2009, October 9). Debt of democracy: Mass media law in Argentina *Dispatches News*. Retrieved from http://www.dinews.org/index.php?option=com_content&view=article&id=52:diego1&catid=43:argentina&Itemid=61.

Bakhtin, M. M. (1986a). The problem of speech genres (V. W. McGee, Trans.). In C. Emerson & M. Holquist (Eds.), *M. M. Bakhtin: Speech genres and other late essays* (pp. 60–102). Austin: University of Texas Press.

Bakhtin, M. M. (1986b). Toward a methodology for the human sciences (V. W. McGee, Trans.). In C. Emerson & M. Holquist (Eds.), *M. M. Bakhtin: Speech genres and other late essays* (pp. 158–172). Austin, TX: University of Texas Press.

Coles, G. (2003). *Reading the naked truth: Literacy, legislation, and lies*. Portsmouth, NH: Heinemann.

Demarrais, K. (2006). "The haves and the have mores": Fueling a conservative ideological war on public education. *Educational Studies, 39*(3), 201–240.

Democracy University Series. (2005, October 18). Clean Money Initiative on *Take Back the House* [DVD]. Los Angeles, CA: Justice Vision.

Derrida, J. (1974). *Of grammatology* (G. B. Spivak, Trans.). Baltimore, MD: Johns Hopkins University Press.

Fairclough, N. (1989). *Language and Power*. London & New York: Longman.

Fairclough, N. (1992). *Discourse and social change*. Cambridge, UK: Polity Press.

Fairclough, N. (1995). *Critical discourse analysis: The critical study of language*. London: Longman.

Fairclough, N. (2001). Critical discourse analysis as a method in social scientific research. In R. Wodak & M. Meyer (Eds.), *Methods of critical discourse analysis*. London: Longman.

Fairclough, N. (2003). *Analyzing discourse: Textual analysis for social research*. London: Routledge.

Fairclough, N. (2010). *Critical discourse analysis: The critical study of language* (2nd ed.). London: Longman.

Freire, P. (1998). *Teachers as cultural workers: Letters to those who dare teach* (D. Macedo & A. Oliveira, Trans.). Boulder, CO: Westview.

Freire, P. (2003). *El grito manso [The gentle shout]*. Buenos Aires: Siglo XXI Editores.

George, S. (1999, March 24–26). *A short history of neoliberalism*. Paper presented at the Conference on Economic Sovereignty in a Globalising World.

Gingrich, N. (1996). Language: A key mechanism of control. *GOP Action Committee.* Washington, D.C., Retrieved January 21, 2012 from: http://www.informationclearinghouse.info/article4443.htm

Giroux, H. (2004). Neoliberalism and the demise of democracy: Resurrecting hope in dark times. *Dissident Voice. Available at* www.dissidentvoice.org/Aug04/Giroux0807.htm.

Giroux, H. (2008). *Against the terror of neoliberalism: Politics beyond the age of greed.* Boulder, CO: Paradigm Publishers.

Harding, S. (2006). *Science and social inequality: Feminist and postcolonial issues.* Urbana & Chicago: University of Illinois Press.

Helson, B. (2011, March 25). Argentina's take on guaranteeing media plurality. *Social European Journalism.* Retrieved *from* http://socialeuropeanjournalism.com/2011/03/25/argentinas-take-on-guaranteeing-media-plurality/.

Hostetler, K. (2010). (Mis)understanding human beings: Theory, value, and progress in education research. *Educational Studies, 46*, 400–415.

Hursh, D. (2008). *High-stakes testing and the decline of teaching and learning: The real crisis of education.* Lanham, MD: Rowman & Littlefield.

Krashen, S. D. (2010, January). Comments on the LEARN Act. Retrieved from www.sdkrashen.com.

Kumashiro, K. (2008). *The seduction of common sense: How the Right has framed the debate on America's schools.* New York, NY: Teachers College Press.

Labaree, D. F. (2011). The lure of statistics for educational researchers [essay]. *Educational Theory, 61*(6), 621–632.

Lappé, F. M. (2012, July 30). The solution to *Citizens United* that no one is talking about. *Common Dreams.* http://www.commondreams.org/view/2012/07/30.

Lather, P. (2008). New wave utilization research: (Re)imagining the research/policy nexus. *Educational Researcher, 37*(6), 361–364.

Literacy Education for All, Results for the Nation (LEARN) Act 929, U. S. C. (2011)

Lynd, R. (1939). *Knowledge for what?* Princeton, NJ: Princeton University Press.

MacLure, M. (2003). *Discourse in education and social research.* Philadelphia, PA: Open University Press.

Metcalf, S. (2002, January 28). Reading between the lines. *The Nation,* 1–7.

National Center for Education Evaluation and Regional Assistance, & Institute of Education Sciences. (2008). *Reading First impact study: Final report* (evaluation report). Washington, DC: U.S. Department of Education.

National Commission on Excellence in Education. (1983). *A nation at risk: The imperatives for education reform.* Washingto,n DC: U.S. Department of Education.

No Child Left Behind Act of 2002, Pub. L. No. 107–110, part B, 115 Stat. 1535 (2002)

Neuman, S. (2002). Scientific-based evidence. Retrieved February 27, 2002, from http://www.ed.gov/nclb/research/reyna.html.

New Mexico Legislature (2011, March 4). No Funds for Certain School Education Programs. *183647.1*, HB 70a.

Popper, K. (1963). *Conjectures and refutations: The growth of scientific knowledge.* London: Routledge.

Popper, K. (1972). *Objective knowledge: An evolutionary approach.* Oxford, UK: Clarendon Press.

Rendall, S. (Writer). (2005). FAIR on Bush administration funding of Armstrong Williams: "The government is running a domestic propaganda operation secretly targeting the American people." In S. A. Kouddous (Producer), *Democracy Now.* Pacifica Radio, Free Speech Channel.

Reichenbach, H. (1961). *Modern philosophy of science: Selected essays*: Greenwood Press.
Rikowski, G., & McLaren, P. (2002). Postmodernism in education theory. In D. Hill, P. McLaren, M. Cole, & G. Rokowsk (Eds.), *Marxism against postmodernism in educational theory* (pp. 3–115). Lanham, MD: Lexington Books.
Roy, A. (2003). *Instant-mix imperial democracy: Buy one, get one free.* Unpublished manuscript. New York, NY: Riverside Church.
Smith, L. T. (1999). *Decolonizing methodologies: Research and indigenous peoples.* London: Zed Books.
Smith, R. (2011). Beneath the skin: Statistics, trust, and status. *Educational Theory, 61*(6), 636–645.
Torres, M. N., & Mercado, M. (2006). The need of critical media literacy in the teacher education core curriculum. *Educational Studies 39*(3), 260–282.
Torres, M. N., & Mercado, M. (2007). The need of critical media literacy in the teacher education core curriculum. In D. Macedo & S. Steinberg (Eds.), *Media Literacy: A reader* (pp. 537–558). New York, NY: Peter Lang.
Voloshinov, V. N. (1973). *Marxism and the philosophy of language* (L. Matejka & I. R. Titunik, Trans.). Cambridge, MA: Harvard University Press.
Yatvin, J. (2002). Babes in the woods: The wanderings of the National Reading Panel. *Phi Delta Kappan, 83*(5), 364–369.

5 Courageous Voices Against Neocolonialism and White Supremacy

Sandy Grande and Pierre Orelus in Dialogue

Orelus: *As an indigenous woman, what has been your journey in academia and beyond?*

Grande: I think for the most part my academic journey has been accidental. When I left for graduate school in Ohio I didn't really understand what graduate school was all about. After spending about eight years there, I was ready to go east to be closer to my family. The closest job I could find was in Maine, which was about a four and a half hour drive from my family's home. That's essentially the only reason I took the job. Soon after I got to Maine, my mom became ill and I found myself commuting fairly regularly to help take care of her. While on my pretenure sabbatical I noticed a job at Connecticut College which is forty-five minutes from home. So even though I wasn't really "on the market" I applied for the job. As it turns out, I got it and that's where I am now.

As a student, I had such a difficult time in school. I think that I've always had kind of an activist identity due to the way I was raised. We've been active in the community, whether it's our home community or other communities in which we live. My parents, especially my mother, have always worked for change in some way. I definitely took up that spirit as a student in college, graduate school, and then as a professor in the academy. Currently, I serve as chair of my department. I found myself doing administrative work also not because I seek it out but because at the time, I was the only person eligible to serve.

Orelus: *What are some of the challenges you have been facing as the chair of your department?*

Grande: As a chair, when I go to meetings, it's mostly White men and some White women. Now that I think about it, I don't think there's another faculty member of color who is chair of any department. There have been others that rotate through, but at this particular moment I think I am the only one. This makes it more challenging. If I speak up, for example, in a chairs meeting on issues of race or diversity, I am always heard as speaking from a place of self-interest; White faculty are the only ones afforded "objectivity." So I don't think its "voice" or being "silenced" that is the issue, but rather it's the challenge of legitimacy.

In terms of being an indigenous person, again I am the only faculty or staff member on campus. Therefore, I don't advocate for a greater indigenous student presence because they don't have the capacity to serve students, so it could only be a kind of tokenism. If they're not going to be committed to hiring faculty, then I will not participate in recruiting students. Within this landscape I also do very limited "programming" since without a foundational commitment at the structural level it can only be about consumption, commodification, and the (White) "gaze." So in my role at the college, I am just chair of an education department and teacher certification program. In my courses I always center the history and contemporary struggles of indigenous peoples, but I don't teach any "Native American" courses.

Orelus: *You said there are some female chairs at your institution. Do you feel a sense of solidarity between you and them?*

Grande: Not really. I have to say within the context of the academy my personal experience is that I have been more supported by White men and men of color than by White women. While I support Gender and Women's Studies (and on my campus they are an important political force), as an indigenous woman, I remain just as much on the constitutive outside of the feminist project as I do from the general "democratic" project. For some reason, it seems more difficult for other women to understand this. So no, I've never formed any particular solidarity with the other female chairs.

Orelus: *So how would you characterize your research? In other words, what is the focus of your research?*

Grande: It's primarily theoretical. I use the frames of critical pedagogy, Marxist theory, Marxist feminist theory, queer theory, among others, to theorize indigeneity, to articulate "the colonial difference" and the colonial present. My choice to do theory as opposed to research with human subjects stems from my discomfort with the long history of "research" being enacted upon indigenous peoples and communities. Just the vernacular of "human subjects" is disturbing to me. So I make the choice to do theoretical work and not to write about my own or anyone else's community. I would never want my connection to my home community and family to be part of my research. I know other people make that choice, and I am fine with it. I think everybody has their own reasons for how or whether they work with native communities. Whether to connect your professional career to your home is a very difficult choice for indigenous scholars. It's a personal choice that no one can make but themselves.

Orelus: *You said you simply theorize about Native Americans. If you don't actually go into the community to have a better sense of how they live their lives, how does your theoretical work reflect their daily struggles?*

Grande: I'm in communities all the time, so I do have a very good sense of daily life. But I just don't write or research about those connections in the manner that is recognized as typical qualitative or quantitative research. For example, in a few days I am going to Oregon and Montana to work with some reservation schools, so I'll hear firsthand what their particular struggles are. I will engage in whatever work the communities may ask of me. While I will talk with many people about the challenges they face in their schools, I won't "interview" them and I won't write about what they share with me.

My experiences with communities certainly inform my work, how I think about broad constructs, and what the indigenous struggle is really about: settler colonialism. I also write about how our particular struggle as colonized peoples is connected to other contemporary struggles, anticapitalist, environmental, or whatever, and theorize the relationships.

Orelus: *Can you explain further why you choose not to do this type of work?*

Grande: I think because different communities have different histories. But in general I think it's something that began a little bit unconsciously. At the time I was formulating a research agenda, all I knew was that I was not comfortable with doing research in my own or anyone else's community. I am starting to think more deeply about it and realize that I also mistrust the process of opening up information for public consumption, especially if I am not a member of that community.

There are native scholars who have done good work within communities that has really served the project of self-determination. The challenge is that you don't have any control over how work gets consumed on the outside. That's troublesome enough to me that I just choose not to do that kind of work. Again, I certainly have nothing against other indigenous scholars conducting this type of research. In fact, I rely on their work to a large degree to inform my own work. But I just haven't been able to sit down at my computer and write about people's day-to-day life.

I think similarly about research in urban and other underresourced schools. A lot of work is done in such communities and much of it is very valuable. But there's also a lot of other work that isn't, and that can be problematic. It all contributes to some kind of broader public discourse that is usually not very positive. It's not a discourse that privileges the voices of people living inside communities. So for me it's a difficult line to negotiate, and I am glad that some people take on that challenge. But I am more comfortable with keeping the work that I do with communities as part of my private life and not my public professional life.

Orelus: *You said you have been involved in your community. So can you share with me some of the challenges that you have witnessed people in your community face in terms of racism, classism, and sexism?*

Grande: I would say the primary pressure is definitely capitalism. I think everything else kind of falls from that. Race plays a role. Clearly, there is still the racial discourse where "Indios" are at the bottom of the hierarchy and have minimal rights as compared to other marginalized peoples. But I see the primary pressure being capitalism and an ongoing colonization of which I think capitalism is a part. In the last fifteen years or so, there's been a drastic change in my community where you have five-star resorts and restaurants, something you would never have imagined previously. So the whole tourist industry has a huge impact on the community. For example, traditional artists used to weave in a traditional manner, which takes time and high levels of skill. There are particular colors that you can only achieve through natural dyes that come from particular plants. The process of weaving was both an artistic and spiritual process. Now there's all this access to synthetic yarn that is already bleached in whatever colors. It's cheaper and faster to weave with this yarn and there is now a market of tourists looking to consume "native" goods. In a monetized culture there is tremendous pressure to buy and sell, and, with the depletion of land, it is the only way many peoples can support their families. But this also means that the traditional handmade craft is not getting passed on to younger generations.

I was with a friend of mine, and this guy from a neighboring community went up to an older gentleman who was selling the kind of prefabricated machine woven hat for about ten dollars. He had on his own head a hat he wove himself in the traditional style. The gentleman asked: "Why don't you make these anymore?" He said, "It takes too much time to make them." He replied, "These are very rare now and there aren't many of them. You should continue to practice this craft and pass it on to the younger generation." The man replied that he needed to sell goods to help his family. My friend replied, "Well, if you need to sell you could sell one traditional hat to collectors or museums for thousands of dollars versus selling a hundred of these things that you make in one day to all these tourists." He couldn't convince the man that it was better to continue to practice a traditional craft. And the older gentleman couldn't articulate the pressures of daily living and the seduction of capitalism. It was heartbreaking.

Racism has also affected the Native community. The estimates are anywhere from 55,000 to over 100,000 indigenous people who were killed, relocated, and dislocated through the mid-1980s. Yet, the issue of genocide doesn't get talked about much. Meanwhile, all the effects of genocide are now present in the community due to post-traumatic stress, alcohol, drug abuse, and fractured families. People are being dislocated and have to live in places where they weren't initially raised and where they have no traditional ties. There's a certain age group of men that is essentially disappeared; it's eerie to walk in certain communities and realize that men of a particular age group are absent. It's devastating.

Orelus: *How would you explain the invisibility of indigenous men in their own community?*

Grande: They were killed. I mean they were just wiped out. Literally, it's a genocide. They conscripted these men to be soldiers, and if they didn't comply to orders, they were killed. Most people assume that if they are missing, then they were murdered. I don't think people would be in a city somewhere and not be in contact with their family.

Orelus: *Did that happen in all indigenous communities or in certain indigenous communities?*

Grande: Mostly in certain communities in the Sierra near Ayacucho, the ostensible home of the Shining Path, where their leader Abimael Guzman was a professor at the University of Ayacucho.

Orelus: *In terms of having access to quality education, how do you think indigenous people have been doing in the U.S. school system?*

Grande: Obviously, in the U.S. there's a long and devastating history of native peoples and education beginning with boarding-school experiments. Native children were essentially stolen from their communities and sent to off-reservation boarding schools, where they were not only miseducated but subject to cultural genocide. It wasn't until in the 1970s where Indian education moved into an era of greater self-determination.

Now it really depends on which community you are talking about. In general, I think access to a native-centered education is still limited because schools and resources are still to a large degree under the control of the federal government. I should say there are also a vast number of native students who don't live in reservation communities and attend public, mainly urban, schools. So to the same degree that any student in an urban school lacks access to quality education, native kids do too. In the traditional school curriculum there is very little content on indigenous peoples other than superficial treatment around Thanksgiving or Columbus Day. Basically, I would say we only appear in the broader school curriculum until the early 1900s. It is as if our people just don't exist anymore after that. That's not only troublesome for native kids but all students who are being miseducated about the history and contemporary struggles of the United States.

There are challenges to native sovereignty all the time when it comes to schooling. Right now one of the major battlegrounds is Arizona and the banning of "ethnic studies."

Orelus: *In the indigenous community, how do you think sexism affects indigenous women?*

Grande: I think that's really community specific as well. But in some communities, including my own, women have a great deal of power. In other communities, due to the history of colonization in particular, women really have lost their status. So gender relations play out in indigenous communities the way it plays out in broader society. But again I think it really depends on which community you are talking about.

Orelus: *When you said that women in some indigenous communities have power, what kind of power are you talking about?*

Grande: Again, I would say it depends on the community. I can speak about my own community. Women are deeply embedded in the whole cosmology of what it means to be Quechua. Traditionally, women are not only part of the whole spiritual cosmos but also the political arrangements in society.

Traditionally among the Quechua, family names are passed through women. Women own land to the degree anybody "owns" land and it gets passed through the woman's family. They are cultural and spiritual leaders within community for a lack of a better word; they have that status. One interesting notation about the Shining Path is that the organization was very male centered and patriarchal. So when they were terrorizing communities, they took all the men, thinking that would make the community weak. They left behind women who were actually quite powerful. So what happened was that women started organizing, and basically it was indigenous women who helped bring the Shining Path to their knees. It wasn't the military; it wasn't anybody else; it was basically the organizing of these women that people totally underestimated because they didn't understand how much power and leadership they already had in their communities.

So to go back to your question, I would say it depends on the history of the particular community and whether women have always played important roles. In these communities, there's very much a balance between male and female roles. I think that's true in a lot of communities. It's just the degree to which communities have been able to live by their traditional ways or not. I think in less colonized and patriarchal communities you see more of a balance among gender.

Orelus: *In your book* Red Pedagogy, *you use a term that I found very interesting and profound. Instead of using the word "mainstream," you used the word "Whitestream." What exactly do you mean by that?*

Grande: That's actually a term that Claude Denis, a Canadian journalist, used. Basically, it's similar to feminists' use of the word male-stream to indicate that what people talk about as the "mainstream" as being really defined by an underlying patriarchy. For me, when people talk about the mainstream, it isn't simply patriarchy. It's settler colonialism, a system in which White women are also privileged.

Orelus: *How do you see the continued effect of colonization on your own community? And how does the legacy of colonization influence your work and impact your subjectivity?*

Grande: I think about it today mostly in terms of varying forms of dispossession. When you talk about dispossession, it goes beyond any kind of particular identity politics. I think the experience of literally being dispossessed of land, of spirituality, or whatever shapes how people see the world and how the world sees them. Centering dispossession as opposed to oppression also creates a very different political project. I think experience of colonization not only influences the way I see the world but also impacts everything and everyone, including those who benefit from the capitalist system—the colonizers. I think we are getting closer and closer to a time where everybody is basically paying the price for the ongoing colonization of minds, bodies, and souls. Unless we really do a lot of work to change that, the world will succumb to the capitalist nightmare of consumption; it will cannibalize itself. .

Orelus: *How do you see the link between slavery, colonization, capitalism, and racism?*

Grande: I see colonization as the overall umbrella construct of which race and capital interest and a certain kind of religious fundamentalism get played out. To me, these colonial projects were designed, for example, to Christianize Indians, to dispossess them from their lands, and to basically register the supremacy of the White race over Indians.

So again the overarching concept construct is colonization of which class and capitalism fall under. Marxism, for example, is a Western paradigm. It's very much infused with a certain kind of anthropocentrism situating human beings at the center of a linear progression through history. I think it is a very useful and informative paradigm but I can only center my work in indigenous paradigms.

Orelus: *Now we have a Black president. Are you hopeful that Obama will contribute to some kind of change in the indigenous community?*

Grande: I would say I am hopeful. But I don't know if I would say I am confident. I think the defining characteristics of Barack Obama is that he's always been a moderate. If you follow his own particular political path since the time he was a graduate student at Harvard, he has always been a moderate, somebody in the middle. So I never expected him to go in and try to be this radical president. He has somewhat shifted away from the radical neoliberalism of the Bush administration in some respects. His agenda as far as education goes is an abomination. That is one area in which he is extending the neoliberal paradigm and he has continued the all-out assault on public education.

In terms of native peoples, he has already engaged communities in a way that has been unprecedented in terms of his campaign, his election, and certain kinds of structural changes in his cabinet. But what's unclear is whether or not that's just a kind of window dressing to "include" native people. I think he's been more involved than any other president, at least in my lifetime. So I am hopeful. But I wouldn't say I am overly optimistic.

6 Surviving Language as a Refugee

Marisol Ruiz

ACTIVIST SCHOLAR

What does it mean to be an activist scholar? For me, speaking from the positionality of a person whose first-language fluency is other than English, it means standing for something, in this case changing the views we might have of Standard English (SE). Continuing in this vein, because an activist informs the community how we must stand against hegemonic ideologies, my activism is to resist the educational policies that insist on top-down acquisition of English. As Janks (2010) has said, to acquire a language is to acquire its ideology, that is, its hegemonic energy, or, speaking more generally, the ideology of capitalism, which in other words can be the me! me! me! world of consumerism.

Janks (2010) has also asserted that, as more and more people are required to learn English and with it the hegemony of English, the English language is being transformed. She elaborated this concept, describing how monolingual English speakers have difficulty understanding English speakers who have acquired it as their second language. One of the reasons for this is because as we (learners of English as a second language) speak and write English, we transform it by making it our own. This phenomenon has triggered an entire movement to demand English-only and a push for a specific kind of fluency as one of the standards of literacy. Advocating English-only is, in and of itself, racist and xenophobic, assuming as it does there is only one way to speak and write English and that there is, therefore, a privileged group of speakers. Nevertheless, English has been and continues to be changed in the United States by Chicanos. There is even a Chicano dictionary, as English words have changed to follow more a Chicano style and accommodate their culture and experience with English.

In the movement to push for multilingualism and multilingual ways of speaking English and de-standardizing the English language, we have not told the counterstory of refugees living in the United States. Thus, the activist scholar must begin to write the counternarratives of these not-yet-told stories, and at the same time construct the knowledge not yet heard through these voices. As an activist scholar, I view my voice as, if anything, the only weapon I possess to deconstruct "power knowledge" and to create new knowledge with others through counternarrative storytelling. The voice is a tool to fight the fabrication of knowledge that stereotypes speakers of languages other than English and pigeonholes us into little boxes—a people's voice is their tool for freedom.

IDENTITY AND LANGUAGE

James Paul Gee (2000) described identity as an "important analytical tool for understanding schools and society" (p. 99). Identity is always a unique yet common experience. Identity is crucial in understanding pieces of the puzzle on the development of language of refugee students in the United States. Some of the experiences we have as refugees are similar; memories of witnessing death, or memories of the feeling that your life will be taken away at any moment, are common experiences of a refugee from any country, but each experience in our respective Latin American, African, or Asian countries is unique. A common experience among Latin Americans is curfew, *toque de queda* (a time set by the government, and no one can come out of their houses after that time and if one does one can be killed). By understanding how our identities shape our language, one can continue to understand a little more of what it is to be a refugee student in California. Through our unique experiences we have commonality of experiences. Our experiences are little pieces of the puzzles that educators can read to understand refugee students.

Refugee students are also shaped by their experiences in the country they come to live in. For me, it was living as a refugee in San Francisco; my experience living in an inner city shaped my language. My experience in inner-city schools was not unique, but a common experience of many children of color attending schools that ill-prepare us, as Gilyard (1991) has seen with the African American students he teaches (p. 11). As Latino refugees living in the inner city we definitely do not speak SE, and it costs bloody sweats to write SE, which is never good enough. Unlike Gilyard, who was able to write SE at an early age, I still struggle with writing; someone or other is always saying something about how I write and express myself.

Refugee students have their own language, a language of flashbacks, Spanglish, nonverbal communication—a language of poverty, of inner-city youth. The language we have developed is not part of the canon; the canon wants us to scratch off our identity and assimilate to its way of speaking and writing something. This has been difficult for me to do; the canon does not register in my brain. I believe that personal narratives are legitimate for the study of language development because they are accurate historical accounts (Gilyard, 1991, p. 12). Personal narratives help to understand how the language one speaks is part of one's identity, the identity that many do not want to lose—yet under many present circumstances if one does not want to lose it, then one will not have access to resources or social mobility. But some of us consciously refuse to speak only SE so as not to lose our community or family—we learn to code-switch even as adults.

LANGUAGE AS A SOCIAL DEVELOPMENT

Language is part of the social development of an individual, but this development is influenced by the politics of a society. We are societal beings and indirectly or directly we are affected by the politics of a country, because a country's politics targets specific groups in our society, such as the poor, women, people of color, gays and lesbians, and others. We also develop language skills within our families who influence the literacy we receive. Language is created politically, culturally, racially, in the family, and communally.

I developed language as a refugee in a diverse community in San Francisco. The politics of the country affected the way I developed language. There I learned verbal and nonverbal communication. When I remember everything my community and I went through, tears are brought to my eyes and I ask the question, "How can this racist society put children of color and Third World children through so much misery and pain?" Children were not born with the awareness of, or ability to deal with, racism, poverty, and imperialism. Only by growing older and wiser can one begin to cope with discrimination and unfair treatment in the United States' unequal society and world. I am not saying poor and youth of color in the United States. and Third World countries are not happy children; we are, but one can say that the innocence and protected sheltered happiness were ripped away from us the minute we were born. All over the world we want children to be filled with happiness. Youth of color and Third World children, the minute they open their eyes to the world, learn the language of oppression and power.

Words take on different meanings for different people depending on what they have lived through and experienced. In my experience words develop into new words as one grows older. Words are accompanied by experience and change. Your unique experience teaches you to deal with words that once filled your heart with pain and hate, and now fill it with love, for those words have changed their meaning to hope. As one grows older, experiences teach us new things; words develop into memories and reflections of the world one understands a little better today. I developed language in Chile when Salvador Allende was overthrown by the U.S. CIA-backed coup and the red scare began. I also developed language as a refugee coming to this country and living in a predominantly poor-people-of-color neighborhood. I developed language with the beginning of the busing system in which youth of color were bused in an attempt to desegregate schools. However, desegregation did not work because there was White flight; therefore, I also developed language in a San Francisco public school which was composed predominantly of poor youth of color.

YANKEE IMPERIALISM/*IMPERIALISMO YANKEE*

Yankee Imperialism/*Imperialismo Yankee* are some of the first words I remember learning. To me, this short series of sounds, *Imperialismo Yankee*, meant those who killed my family, who tortured my dad, who did not—do not—allow freedom of speech, who killed you for thinking and speaking differently from them, those who—even though my dad got out alive—still killed his soul and spirit. My dad would snap from time to time, and it was scary. Only now do I understand so well that torture makes you distort reality and memory. His screams made me shiver. I felt as though I could feel him being tortured. His memories of being tortured did not let him live in peace.

FEAR/*MIEDO*

Fear/*Miedo* is a word that penetrated my veins. It meant: having to hide, so the children of the supposed communist will not be killed. It meant: The minute we see a policeman, we tremble and our hearts beat as loud as drums, but we are always hoping these policemen will not hear it, and so will not stop you for being a "communist." Fear of not being able to live to see tomorrow. Fear of *allenamiento*/search of your home and the military finding something they did not like or declared communist. I helped my mother burn all of the books: Pablo Neruda, Victor Jara, Violeta Parra, Marxismo/Leninismo, and Gabriela Mistral. Libraries of books. Fear of reading or being caught with a book, cassette tape, or record, even a red bandana, was considered to be communist propaganda.

Miedo. When I think of this word I remember my sister and I walking by a policeman. My sister was eleven and I was twelve, and I told her I was going to scream *asesino*/murderer! and I would throw a rock at him and then we would run. My sister started to shiver, she turned pale, and told me to please not do anything stupid. I told her not to fear the beast. I would protect her! But her fear constrained me from doing something that really was stupid. I mean, really, what is an unarmed twelve-year-old girl going to do to an armed man?

However, many times my anger did not let me be afraid, and because I did not fear I committed many *locuras*/crazy actions that could have gotten everyone killed, such as throwing rocks at cops and screaming at how evil they were and then I would start running. Fear. *Miedo*. That word means so much to me. It makes me remember my experiences with the military in Chile. I associate the word with my life in Chile.

CURFEW/*TOQUE DE QUEDA*

Toque de queda/curfew, such a scary word. When it was *toque de queda*, you better stop what you are doing and run home because if the cops see you on the streets they just shoot you. When I hear *toque de queda* I remember Victor Jara's song:

Correle Correle Correrla	*Run Run Run*
Correle que te van a matar	*Run that they are going to kill you*
Correle Correle Correla	*Run Run Run*
Por aqui por aca por alla	*Over here over there*
Correle Correle Correla	*Run Run Run*

To run: This is exactly what one needed to do when time was running out and you thought you might not make it home on time. I still remember looking out the window in Chile and seeing a man on his bike pedaling as fast as he could to get home and he was shot. I saw him fall from his bike and die. I can't get this image out of my mind. When I saw the man falling off his bike being killed I was only three or four years old. I even thought I was imagining things, but my mother says it was true because she saw it too. She told me, "and he supported Pinochet," so that told me that *toque de queda* meant everyone would be killed if they disobeyed. Disobeying was a subversive act, so one should be killed is what the military regime believed. As soon as I hear the words *toque de queda*, I remember the man on his bike pedaling furiously homeward and then falling dead. Words have meaning and for children living in a war-torn country, words have images that are sometimes not erasable. When children are made to live these experiences, you kill their spirit, their love for life; they do not see the beauty of

life, but only the ugliness and therefore the first words they develop in their minds are negative ones, words that are full of pain, and words of surviving to live without chains.

REFUGEE

Refugee is who I am. I came to this country when I was five, fleeing persecution from Pinochet's dictatorship. I went to school in inner-city San Francisco. I do not remember learning English; I just felt like I always knew it; it was easy. I do not remember struggling to know it. In my school there were many like me, refugees from Vietnam, Cambodia, El Salvador, Nicaragua, and Mexico. Even though we were the kids who were bused in the desegregation effort, I do not remember seeing White children in my school. I do not remember seeing Anglos until I got to college, where I received a culture shock. I had been with poor people of color all of my life and to go to school with more affluent students was, to say the least, a trip, a cultural disconnect in ideology and thinking.

Refugee meant being angry; everyone in my school was angry. It meant having bad dreams when the memory of your home country came to mind. The anger one feels, as a student of mine who was from Cambodia who saw his uncle blown up because of the land mines the United States and Soviet Union left in his country. When he told me this he hugged me real tight, crying, he could not erase the memory from his mind. When I remember his name I still feel his hands around my back and his tears wetting my shoulder. He had a hard time adjusting to school; he hated the teachers. He felt they would never understand what it was like being a refugee. Teachers had little patience with his "don't-give-a-fuck attitude." But how can anyone "give a fuck" when death and violence is your normal, what you are surrounded with? How can you "give a fuck" when the memory of your people being killed is so deeply etched in your consciousness? How can you make sense of lily-White literature and history when they never speak of U.S. imperialism with what you know to be true, for you were the one, not them, who saw the streets of your country filled with the innocent blood of so many of your people? What teachers should know is that it is very hard to adjust after you have seen so much violence. We are thrown into classrooms as though nothing has ever happened. No one wants to deal with our issues, with our pain, with our memories, so we must cope on our own. This is what it means to be a refugee. Refugee is synonymous with anger, with a "don't-give-a-fuck attitude" about life, about our own life, and that is synonymous with being the fearlessness that creates suicidal actions.

NONVERBAL COMMUNICATION

One of the things I remember learning in the United States was nonverbal communication. My first lesson was *Do not stare at anyone if you don't want to fight.* If someone stared you up and down, that meant they wanted to fight. Once someone stares you up and down you respond, "What the hell are you looking at?" The person staring would respond with something smart like, "Not at your ugly face!" Or, "At your monkey face!" That said, you proceeded to slap them silly and then the fighting began. Another lesson was *You better fight or you will be called a chicken.* You will be harassed and disrespected. So inner-city schools taught me nonverbal communication skills and how to be a goddamn good fighter, because once you are a good fighter people fear you a little and don't mess with you so much. I was not only getting A's academically, but also in street fighting. I was surviving inner-city schools. I fought boys and girls; my anger and fearlessness did not allow me to discriminate.

RESPECT/RESPETO

Living in the inner city meant that you developed another word, respect. Every time there was a fight someone always said: "Who do you think you are, disrespecting me?" Or, "I don't know where you came from, but you better respect me!" So one knew that the reason the fight broke out was because someone disrespected someone else; it could have been an accidental push or a look or a word. Once again the refugee is exposed to violence, different in nature, but violence nevertheless. No one was being killed, but one always had to be ready to fight to prove that one was not a chicken and would fight anyone to be respected. I think it was because we were so disrespected by adults that everyone felt they were not going to allow anyone, especially a youngster, to disrespect them.

Not everyone went through what I went through in inner-city schools. My sister did not get into any fights. She was all about peace. When people harassed her she stayed quiet and walked away. This is how she dealt with the violence in those schools, but I, on the other hand, responded with a fist or whatever I held in my hand. I was fearless, suicidal at times. When you do not fear for your life you commit many suicidal actions.

COP/MILICO/POLICIA/LA CHOTA

Many people in this country, when they think of a cop, associate the word with an image of a person who serves and protects people. People living in inner-city poor neighborhoods really do not believe this to be true. We see them as licensed murderers. Rodney King just validated how we felt about cops. This isn't the only reason we mistrust cops; we have lived with police harassment in our neighborhoods or while driving. I remember my friends and I, heading to a camping trip in Sonoma, we decide to camp by a lake. While we are sleeping, four police cars surround us. I freak out. I think we all do, some of us being refugees from Chile, El Salvador, Guatemala, Mexico, we really believe these are milico who will kill us and just dump us somewhere and who could know? The thought flashes through my mind. These white cops just confirm our mistrust of them. We speak to each other in Spanish and this big white woman pulls out her gun, aims it at our heads and orders us to stop speaking that "Spanish shit." The cops search our cars, saying a liquor store had been held up and that the storeowners had said the thieves were "spics" wearing Oakland Raiders jackets. These cops, so racist and violent, they are pointing guns at our heads and they make us kneel on the ground, side by side, keeping us like this until they discover all of us are U.S. citizens and do not have records, and some of us are college students, others honest workers.

Our experience with these racist cops only confirmed our belief that cops will harass and violate the rights of Latino youth. Today, my own students confirm this belief, because they are constantly being harassed by cops and being accused of gang affiliation, their homes are raided because someone may have said it was a drug house, showing to them as I saw years ago that cops have no intention to protect the human rights of Latinos. These experiences just confirm to me the meaning of the word "cop": to harass and violate the rights of youth of color.

SOCIAL CHANGE/ACTIVISM/RESISTANCE

These experiences confirmed in me that to resist social injustice one must be a social activist. Social activism to me means to fight to change the conditions of people of color living in the Bay Area to more humane ones. Social activism is not just a movement in the United States but a fight in worldwide solidarity to change the conditions of people. I was trained at the Center for Third World Organizing in Oakland, California. From this experience we began to fight against the landowners who were refusing to remove old lead from the buildings where poor people of color lived. I joined the fight against environmental racism, fighting for unions in low-income jobs, and then, finally, fighting for youth of color to be respected and given a good education in poor inner-city schools in the Bay Area. I have been an advocate with teachers and administrators for them to have patience with children who lose their tempers. Many times educators do not want to deal with very vocal youth, choosing to just kick them out of school instead of finding ways to help them. I have fought vigorously for school officials to understand youth of color and for them to be given a good education, not merely provided with a No Child Left Behind curricula guaranteed to impoverish our children's minds and schools.

Social activism, for me, means the fight that we must all join to stop oppression all over the world. Social activism, this one phrase when I think of it or say it, sparks up other words such as fight, oppression, and disillusionment. When I was younger I thought we were going to change the world with our activism, but as I see us going backwards I feel disillusioned, which at the same time cannot stop us from continuing to fight against oppression.

ANGER VERSUS LOVE

As I grew older and was able to deal with my anger and I understood my anger, I developed the word "love" for my community in inner-city schools and for Third World countries that were victims of U.S. imperialism. Through love one can make change. Love for me means patience, because even when we are faced with setbacks and become frustrated, our love must not be transformed into anger or violence towards each other. Love for me means faith in a better world, a world in which children are no longer exposed to violence. I know it is ironic to say this when children around the world continue to be victims of so much bloodshed, but I have faith that one day oppression will not exist and if it does, I guess my love for others will move me to fight to the end of my days.

CONCLUSION

This is a long story, too long for this present chapter, telling how I developed language and key words that became part of my consciousness, with memories, some painful, some happy. I could write a book on how language is sociocentric, key to a child's experience with the world. As you saw in my chapter, one is constantly reflecting on the words one says or uses in conversation. These words were key in developing meaning in my world and reality, which is a shared reality of refugee children living in the United States. As children we develop negative painful meanings for words that we learn in a civil war, in an invaded country like Chile was or Vietnam was. We develop negative language living in poor cities in the United States.

Throughout our lives we learn to survive violence; we learn the other side of life, the beauty of living, even in an oppressive world. As we get older we learn to deal with our reality positively through activism and education. As activist scholars we begin to voice our counternarrative, which constructs new knowledge in a world filled with fabricated knowledge. These narratives based on experience help future teachers reflect on the ways we teach and interact with refugees. Our voices are our freedom vehicles.

REFERENCES

Gee, J. (2000). "Identity as an analytic lens for research in education." Madison, WI. http://www.jamespaulgee.com/publications.

Gilyard, K. (1991). *Voices of the self: A study of language competence*. Detroit, MI: Wayne State University Press.

Janks, H. (2010). *Literacy and power*. New York: Routledge.

7 Unfair Comparisons

Monolingual Norms and Language Discrimination Against Nonnative English-Speaking Students at U.S. Colleges and Universities

John Katunich

Recently, a writing tutor at the institution where I work relayed the following conversation between her and an ESL student she was tutoring. At the end of the session, the tutor, with the intent to reassure the student that his work on the assignment was strong, complemented the ESL student, saying, "Your English is very good." The ESL replied, "Not compared to yours." Wishing to recognize the amount of time and work that the ESL student had spent in learning academic English, the tutor answered by saying, "That's not a fair comparison." "But that is how I am being compared everyday," the student replied. That ESL student's reply gave the tutor pause, and caused her to reflect on the institutional climate that ESL and international students experience at our university, and should prompt those of us working with international students in U.S. higher education to a deeper investigation of how these "unfair comparisons" and tacit norms of monolingual English impact the learning and academic identities of international and nonnative English-speaking students in U.S. universities.

At the institution in which the above conversation occurred, a small liberal-arts university in the Northeast United States, we have a small but growing population of international students (5–10% of entering class). Overall, our student population is predominately white (85% of entering class), and our campus is located in a rural area of our state, in very predominantly White and English-speaking small town. The large majority of the international students who come here speak English as a second or third language have attained a high level of proficiency in a standard variety of English required for English. Even as the university seeks to diversify its student population by increasing international enrollment to 10% of every entering class, the institution is in a position to be selective of the international applicant pool, and generally does not admit students who fail to meet minimum test score cutoffs. International students are not placed into developmental English-language courses (either ESL or so-called "mainstream" developmental courses), not only because of their level, but because such courses do not exist here. Even so, once at the institution, most international students perform well here academically and complete their degrees in four years.

One might ask what exactly is the problem here. Terms like "linguistic apartheid" or "linguistic discrimination" might seem improbably used to describe our institutional context or that of other institutions of higher education in the United States, given that U.S. universities in fact attract and retain considerable numbers of international students (Hanassab, 2006).

Yet, oppression and oppressive relations often occlude themselves and work invisibly, and the goal of this chapter is to bring to light some of the systemic patterns of discrimination that impact nonnative speakers of English at U.S. institutions of higher education, in an era when ever-increasing numbers of nonnative speakers of English are attaining an education in these institutions whose fundamental monolingualism positions nonnative speakers of English and other language minorities on the margin.

The monolingual norm of U.S. higher education is one such modality of discrimination that is pervasive enough to be taken for granted. For example, until 2011, the institution mentioned above has had no formal requirement for foreign language study. As a U.S. institution of higher education, it is not alone, and this lack of requirement signifies a broader and more pernicious attitude not about the role of English at a university (i.e., the primary language of learning here) but about lack of any standing for languages other than English (cf. Trimbur 2006). Here, and in a great many other institutions, the native speaker is the default, "ideal" student at whom classes, curricula, and instruction are directed (Matsuda, 2006). This "taken-for-grantedness" of monolingual English obscures the reality of language bias that operates in our own institution and in society at large. It is important to uncover and name these biases not only as an ethical duty (for having recruiting linguistically diverse students as a part of fulfilling a diversity mission) but as a pedagogical responsibility. Simply because students do come to our institution in part to acquire a higher level of Standard English, this does not mean that ignoring the reality of language bias for students is pedagogically appropriate. By acknowledging, naming, and responding to language bias, as an institution as well as in individual classrooms, students' performance (linguistically and academically in general) will benefit.

In this chapter, I wish to raise the question of how language discrimination, in the particular form of monolingual, native English-speaking norms, impacts students' academic identity and performance at U.S. universities. While using my own institution as a contextual starting point, this inquiry is more broadly concerned about monolingual biases in the larger landscape of U.S. higher education. By looking at this monolingual norm of U.S. higher education, I aim to decenter commonsense notions of how and why English is deployed hegemonically in these settings. Moving beyond that, I look at evidence of language bias in the literature, in particular negative stereotypes of international and/or nonnative speakers of English, and connect the reality of these negative stereotypes to likely impacts on students' academic identities.

THE MONOLINGUAL UNIVERSITY

In the United States the institution of the university is intimately associated with standard, monolingual English (Horner & Trimbur, 2002; Tardy, 2011; Trimbur, 2006). This linguistic inertia remains despite increasing numbers of nonnative English-speaking students coming to U.S. universities to study, and multilingual realities of U.S. higher education classrooms (Matsuda, 2006). International students from nonnative English-speaking backgrounds have grown in total numbers in U.S. higher education, doubling in the last twenty years to nearly 750,000 international students in 2010/2011, and comprising around 3.5% of the total enrollment in U.S. higher education. Some 40% of these students are in STEM (science, technology, engineering, and math) fields, and just under half are enrolled in graduate programs. The majority of non-U.S. resident students (i.e., international students) come from largely nonnative English-speaking countries, with China, South Korea, Taiwan, and Saudi Arabia the leading countries of origin for nonnative English-speaking students in U.S. universities (Institute of International Education, 2012). Furthermore, nonnative English-speaking students also include significant numbers of U.S. nationals and residents. There are 55 million U.S. residents who speak a language other than English at home (nearly 1 in 5 Americans), an increase of 140% over the last three decades (Shin & Kominski, 2010).

A vigorous defense of linguistic diversity in U.S. higher education has rarely been made. Language policies in U.S. higher education have been almost exclusively unstated policies, an effect of the historical *laissez-faire* approaches to language policy and practice in the United States (Crawford, 1989). These unstated policies operate through the reproduction of taken-for-granted practices around monolingual language use in U.S. higher education (Tardy, 2011). Given the tacit policies of "English-only" that predominate in U.S. higher-education context, it is important to understand how those assumptions impact the experience of multilingual students in this monolingual, Standard English environment, and form their linguistic, academic, and personal identities. Specifically, as nonnative speakers of English in a monolingual, Standard English environment, nonnative speakers of English are "othered" in the context of the university, and we need to understand the processes by which these negative stereotypes, as realized in their status as nonnative English speakers, may lead to disengagement, underperformance, and ultimately exclusion from full participation in the academic community that they had chosen (and been invited) to join.

There is some evidence, albeit anecdotal, that as the international student population grows, more nonnative English-speaking students are experiencing exclusion, self-segregation , lack of engagement, and, in some cases, academic underperformance (Bartlett & Fischer, 2011). International students are recruited to many universities under the auspices of campus diversification, putting these students in the classic "model minority" double bind (Cargile, Maeda, Rodriguez, & Rich, 2010). As campuses recruit international students as a means to diversify their campus population, many universities may not be ensuring that these international students are sufficiently supported for their success.

Ironically, the gap between *access* to higher education and *conditions for success* in higher education has been observed for the racial, ethnic, and gender minorities during the latter half of the 20th century, in which more equal access to higher education has not ensured equal *success* within these institutions. A persistent gap in achievement between White and non-White students in U.S. higher education has been well-documented (cf. Steele, 1997). Thus, since the mid-1990s, there has been a growing body of research that has striven to explain why, after the lifting of institutional barriers for minorities' participation in higher education, there remains a gap in achievement. One particularly robust area of investigation in the fields of psychology and sociology has identified the phenomenon of "stereotype threat," a particularly pernicious process in which minority students who operate within environments in which the majority holds negative stereotypes about their innate intelligence or aptitude in specific fields are negatively affected by the cognitive and social demands required to not confirm such negative stereotypes, leading to negative impacts on these students' performance, learning, and academic identities (Good, Aronson, & Harder, 2008; Keller, 2002; Kellow & Jones, 2008; Nguyen & Ryan, 2008; Spencer, Steele, & Quinn, 1999; Steele,1997, 2011; Steele & Aronson, 1995; Taylor & Walton, 2011).

STEREOTYPING LANGUAGE IN THE MONOLINGUAL UNIVERSITY

Despite the fact that in U.S. institutions of higher education, international students. as a collective, are perhaps the most heterogeneous groupings in a university (Hanassab, 2006; Institute for International Education, 2011; Spencer-Rodgers, 2001), international students as a whole are subject to stereotypes, both negative and positive, held by noninternational students (Spencer-Rodgers 2001). The negative stereotypes that are most likely to impact students' linguistic, academic, and personal identities are stereotypes of being "different" (Spencer-Rodgers, 2001), "socially maladjusted," or "unsociable" (Spencer-Rodgers, 2001; Spencer-Rodgers & McGovern, 2002), or "not speak[ing] English well" (Spencer-Rodgers, 2001; Spencer-Rodgers & McGovern, 2002).

Research has shown that native speakers in the United States listening to nonnative varieties of English may classify these varieties (and the speakers of these varieties) in highly negative terms (Gluszek & Dovidio, 2010b) even without being able to correctly identify the origin or type of accent (Lindemann, 2003). When asked to evaluate different types of English based solely on a category (e.g., "Chinese" or "Mexican" English), native speakers had consistently negative associations toward the nonnative varieties (Lindemann, 2005).

Frequently documented stereotypes based on language variety include these speakers being less intelligent (Lindemann, 2003), less attractive (Bresnahan et al., 2002), or lazy (Gluszek & Dovedio, 2010a, 2010b; Lindemann, 2003). In the specific context of higher education, nonnative English-speaking students have reported being viewed on the basis of their language variety as less successful, less creative, and having poor critical thinking skills (Ryan & Viete, 2009).

One of the most frequently stereotyped features of language is accent, that is, a consistent phonological variation from a native-speaking norm (Bresnahan et al., 2002; Gluzsek and Dovidio, 2010a, 2010b; Lindemann, 2003, 2005). Nonnative speakers of English with an accent often experience stigma of their accent (Gluszek & Dovidio, 2010a), which motivates them to try to completely eliminate nonnative accents (Derwing, 2003), which is, for a variety of biological, social, and psychological reasons, probably unrealistic for many nonnative speakers. In fact, one of the earliest studies on attitudes toward language accents, Ryan, Carranza, and Moffie (1977), showed how native English-speaking listeners were able to distinguish even very fine differences in language accent, attributing lower evaluation and stigma to more progressively accented varieties of Spanish varieties of English.

Stereotypes based on language accent is also dependent on the perceived status of a nonnative English speaker's first language, with accented varieties of English by Western Europeans (e.g., Italian-accented English) much more positively evaluated than other, less-valued varieties, which were described as "broken," "poor" (describing Chinese accents of English; Lindemann, 2005, p. 200), or "sloppy" (describing Mexican accents of English; Lindemann, 2005, pp. 202–203). Negative stereotypes of accents are influenced by the assumptions that native speakers have about the nature of accents as mutable or changeable; native speakers who believe accents are mutable features of a second language are more likely to view speakers of English with a nonnative accent as "lazy" (Gluszek & Dovidio, 2010a).

Students need not directly experience discrimination based on their language variety in order to feel threatened by a stereotype. A "threat is the air" (Steele, 1997) when nonnative English-speaking international students hear native-speaking students express doubt about the capacity of nonnative English-speaking instructors and teaching assistants to communicate and teach because of their nonnative accents (Fox & Gay, 1994; Gluszek & Dovidio, 2010a; Kavas & Kavas, 2008; Marvasti, 2005; Rubin, Ainsworth, Cho, Turk, & Winn, 1999).

Negative stereotypes and stigma of one's own language variety or accent are often internalized by nonnative speakers of English. Hu and Lindemann (2009) demonstrate how speakers of Cantonese varieties of English are likely to negatively evaluate the features of their own variety as compared to perceived native speakers, whereas Tokumoto and Shibata (2011) identify similar patterns for speakers of Japanese and Korean varieties of English, suggesting that the social context for learning (i.e., the presence of a monolingual or multicultural social context as well as social and pedagogical norms about "correct" versions of English) can explain this internalized stigma of one's own nonnative language variety.

Kang and Rubin (2009) identify a separate mode of stereotyping that may occur in the context of heterogeneous settings (such as universities) as "reverse linguistic discrimination," where it is the knowledge of a speaker's status (international or not) that disposes the listener to hear the accent in a certain way and respond accordingly. In a similar vein, Lindemann (2003) demonstrates the need that native speakers feel to resolve uncertainty about "foreignness" in order to properly evaluate the speaker's speech as competent or not. It is this kind of subtle cue, the ostensibly harmless question of "Where are you from?" (Derwing, 2003), that can index these negative stereotypes, precisely because it is marked as a question to be directed at a "foreign" speaker (Lippi-Green, 1997).

THE EFFECTS OF NEGATIVE STEREOTYPING

In their seminal 1995 study, Steele and Aronson suggested academic environments are rife with subtle or overt cues about belonging (or more specifically *not* belonging), and minority students experience the majority group stereotypes of their group (in the case of Steele & Aronson, 1995, this was African American students) as either less innately intelligent or less competent in a specific field. The perception of these stereotypes can trigger a threat to one's identity and raise stakes for these students that they may be confirming negative stereotypes held about their group. Under these conditions, which Steele and Aronson (1995) termed *stereotype threat*, the effects of an additional cognitive load, anxiety, or disengagement have been shown to impact performance, learning, and academic identity (Good, Aronson, & Harder, 2008; Keller, 2002; Nguyen & Ryan, 2008; Spencer, Steele, & Quinn, 1999; Steele, 1997, 2011; Steele & Aronson, 1995; Taylor & Walton, 2011).

When working on difficult academic tasks, the effects of stereotype threat are more pronounced, due in part because success on easier tasks disarms some negative stereotype threat, whereas difficult tasks will cause higher rates of error (or uncertainty), which triggers the stereotype threat (Spencer et al., 1999). Just as increased difficulty increases the effects of stereotype threat, the higher the stakes for a task, the more marked the effect of stereotype threat (Kellow & Jones, 2008). In addition, those who identify strongly with the domain of the task are more negatively affected by activation of perceived negative stereotypes (Lasko & Corpus, 2006).

The experience of stereotype threat triggers several psychological or social processes that impair cognitive function (Schmader 2010). Under the conditions of stereotype threat, individuals are highly vigilant against the possibly confirming a negative stereotype of their group, which ironically imposes a "cost" on one's cognitive processing, leading to marked decrease in working memory, which in turn negatively impacts performance on a specific, high-stakes task, such as a high-stakes test (Schmader, 2010; Schmader & Johns, 2003). Individuals who are vigilant against confirming a negative stereotype are also much more sensitive to any errors that are produced, leading to heightened anxiety (Schmader, 2010), which is itself subject to a heightened awareness of negative internal states, under stereotype threat, and an increased likelihood of viewing anxiety as a form of self-doubt. As the circular psychological processes drain cognitive resources precisely when these resources are needed the most, there is evidence of disassociation from the task, an avoidance of help-seeking activities, or severe "overefforting" that can lead to so-called "John Henryism" (Steele, 2011) in which long periods of psychological stress negatively impacts long-term health.

It is important to note that any group can feel the effects of stereotype threat, if they are performing in a context in which their group may be negatively stereotyped vis-à-vis another group. For example, while women may experience stereotype threat (and thus underperform on a math task), if they are told they are being compared with men, White men will similarly underperform if they are told they are being negatively compared with Asian men. (Aronson et al., 1999; Steele 2011)

How, then, might nonnative speakers of English living and studying in a monolingual institution be impacted by these processes of stereotype threat? Keller (2002) describes one of the conditions for stereotype threat to be cases "when ability is submitted to evaluative scrutiny" (p. 194). For nonnative speakers of English in a tacitly monolingual institution of higher education, those cases of evaluative scrutiny are ubiquitous. Accented utterances or nonconventional modes of writing may be evaluated as deficient (rather than different) and may prime language-minority students in the university to experience stereotype threat.

Models of stereotype threat link heightened cognitive loads and subsequent underperformance on high-stakes tasks to the increased effort and attention to avoiding mistakes or errors that might confirm negative stereotypes of their groups. However, for many nonnative speakers of English, pedagogical approaches to developing proficiency in academic English may focus on raising awareness of errors in the writing and speech of nonnative English speakers in the academy. Similarly, the underlying assumption of a deficiency model of language learning (cf. Ryan and Viete, 2009) can contribute to the sense of a threat in the air that triggers negative processes of stereotype threat. For example, Wang and Li (2011) suggest that modes of feedback from research supervisors to international doctoral students which focus on grammatical errors or other forms of correctness, rather than more holistic support, are more likely to trigger emotional responses that lead to frustration, self-doubt, and ultimately academic disengagement in the form of passivity and dependency in their doctoral research. Conversely, international doctoral students who perceived that their research supervisors viewed them as colleagues (or emerging colleagues) expressed confidence and authority in their work. We can see how "evaluative scrutiny" of grammatical errors marks a group membership, distinguishing them from a "mainstream" norm who may be less likely (or perceived to be less likely) to receive this kind of scrutiny, and links that distinction (tacitly in the vast majority of cases) to negative stereotypes about their innate ability.

By and large, international students are choosing to study in a U.S. institution for four or more years of their life, and this choice, along with the reality that these students have been very high achievers in English (as evidenced in my institution by average TOEFL scores in the 80th percentile), indicates that nonnative English-speaking international students in U.S. universities do exhibit a high identification with the domain of English. In an ironic twist of the stereotype threat effect, however, high identification makes an individual more susceptible to these effects (Lasko & Corpus, 2006). In particular, Lasko and Corpus identify high identifiers under stereotype threat (in their case women taking a math test) to be more likely to discount the validity of the task. In other words, under these conditions, students under stereotype threat respond to all negative evaluation as invalid, thus limiting their ability to uptake new knowledge. This may seriously limit nonnative speakers of English, from whom it is a goal to continue developing an academic variety of English at the university.

Another bitter irony of the research on stereotype threat has been the impact it has shown on performance in high-stakes tasks. For nonnative speakers of English, where class discussions or written assignments are done under the shadow of "evaluative scrutiny" of language skills, the additional cognitive burden imposed by stereotype threat can negatively impact performance on those very tasks.

All of this is not to say that nonnative speakers of English are merely passive recipients of the negative stereotypes around them, and are helpless to resist their effects. Rather, many individuals operating under conditions of stereotype threat find productive and meaningful strategies to work through or around negative stereotypes. McGee and Martin (2011) describe some of the stereotype management strategies deployed by academically successful

African American math and students in U.S. universities. Whereas stereotype management strategies for nonnative speakers of English at U.S. universities are likely to be dramatically different from those in the sample of McGee and Martin (2011), it is almost certain that, given the academic success experienced by nonnative speakers of English, many of them have innovated a variety of strategies to succeed in spite of (rather than because of) stereotypes and hegemonic monolingualism of English.

ENVISIONING ALTERNATIVES TO HEGEMONIC MONOLINGUALISM

The research on the effects of stereotype threat largely describe the phenomenon as situational, that is to say, it impacts students in specific situations in which these negative stereotypes become salient (Keller, 2002; Spencer et al., 1999; Steele, 1997). The situationality of this effect allows us to envision ways in which our classrooms and institutions can operate that are not predicated upon the primary place of standard English, and the "un-belonging" of other languages and other varieties.

Pedagogies emerging out of recent work in composition studies have begun to explore ways in which English can be decentered as a hegemonic practice. Canagarajah (2006), Matsuda (2006), and Tardy (2011) are among those who are offering ways to reenvision the university as multilingual. These pedagogies make space for students' use of languages other than English or nonnative varieties of English when appropriate for the students' purpose or task. Canagarajah (2006) proposes rethinking in our pedagogy the divide between native (read: privileged) and nonnative (read: nonprivileged) varieties as the number of nonnative speakers increases not only on our campuses but in the global context as a whole. For Matsuda (2006), so-called English-only approaches not only preclude prospects of multilingualism in composition pedagogy (and, by extension, pedagogies across the university where students use language) but also render the nonnative speakers of English invisible, considering students at the university "native English speakers by default" (p. 637). This kind of invisibility and assumptions of linguistics homogeneity cannot hold in the 21st century, as it increasingly fails to meet students' needs, and those students are comprising a significant number of institutions' population. Tardy (2011) invites institutions, programs, and even individual classrooms to identify and articulate policies that affirm that multilingualism and linguistic diversity are valued.

Resistance to reenvisioning language practice in U.S. higher education runs deep. Monolingual English is positioned as natural, obvious, and the only possibility for organizing language practices in the university. By accepting this position on monolingual English, negative stereotypes around nonnative varieties of English (or non-English languages) are permitted to work in pernicious ways to undermine the learning and success of nonnative speakers of English. Practically speaking, for historical and social reasons, there will always be an important role for English to play in the university, and what is being suggested is not precluding or replacing English, but rather the subverting of the hegemonic monolingualism of English in the university, and the attendant assumptions of belonging and membership, which form the basis of negative stereotypes and the experience of stereotype threat.

We may not be able to replace monolingual English nor even be able to overturn (in the short term at least) the pervasive negative stereotypes of nonnative speakers and varieties of English. However, by opening up possibilities for multilingual ways of being in the university, we can begin to provide the appropriate conditions for academic success for the language minorities who *are* here, and who will continue to grow in number.

REFERENCES

Aronson, J., Lustina, M., Good, C., Keough, K., Steele, C., & Brown, J. (1999). When white men can't do math: Necessary and sufficient factors in stereotype threat. *Journal of Experimental Social Psychology, 35*, 29–46.

Bartlett, T., & Fischer, K. (2011). The China conundrum: American colleges find the Chinese-student boom a tricky fit. *Chronicle of Higher Education*, Nov. 3, 2011. http://chronicle.com/article/Chinese-Students-Prove-a/129628/. Accessed March 13, 2012.

Bresnahan, M., Ohashi, R., Nebashi, R., Liu, W., & Shearman, S. (2002). Attitudinal and affective response toward accented English. *Language and Communication, 22*, 171–185.

Canagarajah, S. (2006). The place of world Englishes in composition: Pluralization continued. *College Composition and Communication, 57*, 586–619.

Cargile, A., Maeda, E., Rodriguez, J., & Rich, M. (2010). "Oh you speak English so well!": US American listeners' perceptions of 'foreignness' among nonnative speakers. *Journal of Asian American Studies, 13*, 59–79.

Crawford, J. (1989). *Bilingual education: History, politics, theory, and practice.* Trenton, NJ: Crane.

Derwing, T. (2003). What do ESL students say about their accents? *Canadian Modern Language Review, 59*, 547–566.

Fox, W., & Gay, G. (1994). Functions and effects of international teaching assistants. *Review of Higher Education, 18*, 1–24.

Gluszek, A., & Dovidio, J. (2010a). The way they speak: A social psychological perspective on the stigma of nonnative accents in communication. *Personality and Social Psychology Review, 14*, 214–237.

Gluszek, A., & Dovidio, J. (2010b). Speaking with a nonnative accent: Perceptions of bias, communication difficulties, and belonging in the United States. *Journal of Language and Social Psychology, 29*, 224–234.

Good, C., Aronson, J., & Harder, J. (2008). Problems in the pipeline: Stereotype threat and women's achievement in high-level math courses. *Journal of Applied Developmental Psychology, 29*, 17–28.

Hanassab, S. (2006). Diversity, international students, and perceived discrimination: Implications for educators and counselors. *Journal of Studies in International Education, 10*, 157–172.

Horner, B., & Trimbur, J. (2002). English only and US composition. *College Composition and Communication, 53*, 594–630.
Hu, G., & Lindemann, S. (2009). Stereotypes of Cantonese English, apparent native/non-native status, and their effect on non-native English speakers' perception. *Journal of Multilingual and Multicultural Development, 30*, 253–269.
Institute of International Education. (2012). Open doors report. http://www.iie.org/en/Research-and-Publications/Open-Doors/Data/International-Students/Enrollment-Trends/. Accessed March 13, 2012.
Kang, O., & Rubin, D. (2009). Reverse linguistic stereotyping: Measuring the effect of listener expectations on speech evaluation. *Journal of Language and Social Psychology,* 28, 441–456.
Kavas, A., & Kavas, A. (2008). An exploratory study of undergraduate college students' perceptions and attitudes toward foreign accented faculty. *College Student Journal, 42*, 879–890.
Keller, J. (2002). Blatant stereotype threat and women's math performance: Self-handicapping as a strategic means to cope with obtrusive negative performance expectations. *Sex Roles, 47,* 193–198.
Kellow, J., & Jones, B. (2008). The effects of stereotypes on the achievement gap: Reexamining the academic performance of African American high school students. *Journal of Black Psychology, 34*, 94–120.
Lasko, A., & Corpus, J. (2006). Discounting the difficult: How high math-identified women respond to stereotype threat. *Sex Roles, 54*, 113–125.
Lindemann, S. (2003). Koreans, Chinese or Indians? Attitudes and ideologies about non-native English speakers in the United States. *Journal of Sociolinguistics, 7*, 348–364.
Lindemann, S. (2005). Who speaks "broken English"? US undergraduates' perceptions of non-native English. *International Journal of Applied Linguistics, 15*, 187–212.
Lippi-Green, R. (1997). *English with an accent.* London: Routledge.
Marvasti, A. (2005). US academic institutions and perceived effectiveness of foreign-born faculty. *Journal of Economic Issues, 39*, 151–176.
Matsuda, P. (2006). The myth of linguistic homogeneity in US college composition. *College English, 68*. 637–651.
McGee, E., & Martin, D. (2011). "You would not believe what I have to go through to prove my intellectual value!" Stereotype management among academically successful black mathematics and engineering students. *American Educational Research Journal, 48*, 1347–1389.
Nguyen, H., & Ryan, A. (2008). Does stereotype threat affect test performance of minorities and women? A meta-analysis of experimental evidence. *Journal of Applied Psychology, 93*, 1314–1334.
Rubin, D., Ainsworth, A., Cho, E., Turk, D., & Winn, L. (1999). Are Greek letter social organizations a factor in undergraduates' perceptions of international instructors? *International Journal of Intercultural Relations, 23*, 1–12.
Ryan, E., Carranza, M., & Moffie, R. (1977). Reactions toward varying degrees of accentedness in the speech of Spanish-English bilinguals. *Language and Speech, 20*, 267–273.
Ryan, J., & Viete, R. (2009). Respectful interactions: Learning with international students in the English-speaking academy. *Teaching in Higher Education, 14*, 303–314.
Schmader, T. (2010). Stereotype threat deconstructed. *Current Directions in Psychological Science, 19*, 14–18.
Schmader, T., & Johns, M. (2003). Converging evidence that stereotype threat reduces working memory capacity. *Journal of Personality and Social Psychology, 85*, 440–452.

Shin, H., & Kominski, R. (2010). *Language use in the United States: 2007.* American Community Survey Reports, ACS-12. Washington, DC: U.S. Census Bureau.

Spencer, S., Steele, C., & Quinn, D. (1999). Stereotype threat and women's math performance. *Journal of Experimental Social Psychology, 35*, 4–28.

Spencer-Rodgers, J. (2001). Consensual and individual stereotypic beliefs about international students among American host nationals. *International Journal of Intercultural Relations, 25*, 639–657.

Spencer-Rodgers, J., & McGovern, T. (2002). Attitudes toward the culturally different: The role of intercultural communication barriers, affective responses, consensual stereotypes, and perceived threat. *International Journal of Intercultural Relations, 26*, 609–631.

Steele, C. (1997). A threat in the air: How stereotypes shape intellectual identity and performance. *American Psychologist, 52*, 613–629.

Steele, C. (2011). *Whistling Vivaldi and other clues how stereotypes affect us.* New York: Norton.

Steele, C., & Aronson, J. (1995). Stereotype threat and the intellectual test performance of African Americans. *Journal of Personality and Social Psychology, 69*, 797–811.

Tardy, C. (2011). Enacting and transforming local language policies. *College Composition and Communication, 62*, 634–661.

Taylor, V., & Walton, G. (2011). Stereotype threat undermines academic learning. *Personality and Social Psychology Bulletin, 37*, 1055–1067.

Tokumoto, M., & Shibata, M. (2011). Asian varieties of English: Attitudes towards pronunciation. *World Englishes, 30*, 392–408.

Trimbur, J. (2006). Linguistic memory and the politics of US English. *College English, 68*, 575–588.

Wang, T., & Yi, L. (2011). "Tell me what to do" vs. "guide me through it": Feedback experiences of international doctoral students. *Active Learning in Higher Education, 12*, 101–112.

8 An *arabyyah-muslimah* Feminist Negotiating Gender/Nation/ Sexuality/Colonial Discourses

A Conversation with Manal Hamzeh

Please would you begin by saying a little bit about yourself?

I am currently an assistant professor in the sociology and Women's Studies Department at New Mexico State University. In 2007, I earned a PhD in critical pedagogy. Prior to this career in the academy, I was an educational audiologist for seventeen years in my native land, Jordan. As an educational audiologist, I worked mainly with children with hearing issues in schools, more in regular schools than the separate residential schools for the deaf. Within this period, I have pioneered projects in Gaza, Jordan, Egypt, and consulted on projects in the United Arab Emirates, Oman, and Syria. So, I have had experiences in the bigger *Arab* colonized and neocolonized contexts of the east Mediterranean region.

In the late sixties and seventies, I was educated in an all-girls school in Amman, the capital of Jordan. Established in 1926, this school was originally a British missionary school but was nationalized in the fifties. The school mission was to prepare Arab national women leaders enabled to build the nation resisting colonizing hegemonies. During that time, I lived the privileges of a middle-class family not only possessing formal education but also critical literacies necessary to survive in a deeply colonized context. Both my parents are educated with university degrees.

My father is a medical doctor and he has been a political and social activist and a writer throughout his life. My father and his siblings were imprisoned and/or exiled by the Hashemite royal regime in the sixties. My maternal grandfather established the first hospital in Jordan after he fled Palestine, resisting the British during the revolt of 1930s. Leaving Palestine, he was chased out to Lebanon, then to Syria, and he ended up in Jordan. That is, I grew up learning directly from the anticolonial and antiroyalist political experiences of my family that rooted me as a politicized intellectual and activist in this world.

I consider myself very Arab, and at the same time, I am multilingual or for that matter multiethnic (but this is a matter for another conversation). Though I am fluent in Arabic and English, I still consider Arabic my home language. With the university degrees I earned in the U.S., English has become the main tool with which I read and write in the academy. However, I am constantly reading Arabic literature and seeking Arabic sources that help my research. I am still doing the translation work necessary to teach and research but also to build and maintain relationships in the academy and beyond.

To complicate my positionalities or to show their complexities, I would also present myself as a queer feminist. I came out as gay or queer while doing my undergraduate and graduate studies in Washington, DC, in the eighties and continued to negotiate my sexuality during the years of building and sustaining my audiology career in Jordan from the mid-eighties to 2003. As a clinician, educational advisor to many schools and parents, and a public professional who was highly visible in the public media and in political events, I was constantly negotiating my sexuality, class, gender, ethnicity, or tribal and national affinity (my Jordanianness and Palestinianness).

Additionally, while living in Jordan and Palestine for seventeen years, I worked within the feminist and disability movements very much as a pioneer and had to negotiate my gender, sexuality, and nationality with the neocolonial regime in Jordan and the Israeli occupiers, west of the Jordan River. Now, I work in a public Hispanic-serving U.S.-border university as a faculty member in the department of sociology and women's studies. This is to say that throughout my life I have lived in many geographical places and crossed and negotiated several borders and hegemonic discourses. I am a hybrid *Arab-Muslim queer* feminist living constantly "out of place," as Edward Said (2000) put it.

So can you trace for me your journey from Jordan to the U.S.?

I made two distinct journeys between Jordan and the U.S. The first was to complete my undergraduate and graduate studies in Washington, DC (1979–1986). The second was to complete my doctoral studies here at New Mexico State University. For university studies, most of my high school peers were sent to Britain, especially if they had male siblings already there, or to Beirut in order to stay close to the monitoring of their families. I was the only one to head to the U.S. on my own.

I was able to negotiate early on with my family that I was not going to follow that expected trajectory of most of the girls in school at the time. I wanted to go to the U.S. mainly because at any price I wanted to get out of the British disciplinary educational system and be better educated in a more flexible and open system like the U.S. Additionally, I thought I would have more chances to enjoy sports in the U.S. since I was a national athlete with ambitions. Though I was accepted at several U.S. universities, I chose to go to Washington. DC. thinking that the location of the university will also add to my political education that I was also eager to cultivate.

Doing my undergraduate degree was not a journey without bumps. For one, I was not accepted on the George Washington University (GWU) varsity basketball team until I worked as a water/towel girl during my freshman year. In the next three years, though I was taken in formally on the team, I was never considered good enough, or shall I say not American enough, to play more than one or two minutes. Additionally, though I completed my undergraduate degree at GWU with a high GPA, all the graduate schools I applied for rejected me. Apparently, my GRE scores were not good enough to enter the audiology program of my choice in Gallaudet University. I was told in the letter of rejection that my English was not good enough to succeed. I challenged the decision, asking to be interviewed and be given the chance for one year as a special student under probation. In the meantime, I enrolled in another graduate program at GWU and completed the degree in one year instead of two and earned a GPA of 4.0. With this, I was accepted in Gallaudet's audiology program, and for two years I lived a unique eye-opening educational experience. I was the minority among a majority of deaf and hard-of-hearing people. So, I had to learn American Sign Language, make deaf friends, take courses in American deaf history, and engage in the deaf culture. This experience helped me become aware of at least my linguistic privilege and how hearing people colonized deaf people for centuries and the parallels with the hegemony of English in my school education and so on. My time in Gallaudet directly shaped my professional politics and sharpened my ethics of justice and equity. My main commitment in my audiology career work in Jordan and the Arab world was for/with deaf people. It was a constant battle to legitimize the local sign language and to make education and information accessible for the deaf.

So, the first stage of my education in the U.S. gave me the power of knowledge by earning three degrees, but more importantly it politicized me and prepared me to commit for the next seventeen years (1986–2003) toward endeavors of social justice mainly for/with the deaf and hard-of-hearing. As the second Arab audiologist (first woman), I mainly built my career in Jordan and Palestine. So, you can imagine the context at the time and how I had to politically negotiate my way to set the grounds for a new profession and to challenge those who for too long shunted the deaf out of inclusive and equitable schooling chances or covertly abused them in residential schools.

Having this in the backdrop, the first job I was offered upon my graduation in 1986 was to establish the first public hearing and language/speech service in Jordan. My father at the time was a minister of health and he opened the door for me to pioneer a national program and make it accessible and almost free of charge to all Jordanian children. Though my father's position at the time paved the way to huge and deep progress at least in health services provided for deaf Jordanians, the chance did not last long when he had to resign from the government for protesting the privatization pressures of the World Bank. From that point on, the challenges to make more strides in the audiological services within the health and educational public systems escalated and my job became harder and harder.

The gradual political changes or the suffocation of democracy in Jordan since the mid-1990s, the obvious reign of the neoliberal policies dominating Jordan by the end of the 1990s, and the escalation of militarism in coordination with the U.S.-led war on terror and the war on Iraq in 2003 not only presented me with more complex challenges but also robbed me the possibilities of change toward justice on all the fronts I was working. More importantly, these changes cultivated a context only benefiting the politically corrupt, neoliberal opportunists, and war profiteers, thereby shunting anyone calling and working for the long-term investment in education and well-being of all the citizens of Jordan. I could not tolerate being close to this way of being and I knew my time was up in Jordan.

By the time the former Israeli prime minister Ariel Sharon invaded the Dome of the Rock in September 2000 and instigated the so-called second Palestinian *intifada*, I knew that the spaces and chances of ethical and democratic work in Jordan would not come back in my lifetime. So, I had to leave my first home in Jerusalem and begin to close my audiology career in Jordan. With the consequences of the events of 9/11, i.e., the siding of Jordan with the "efforts in the war of terror," the invasion of the U.S. army first in Afghanistan in 2001 and then in Baghdad in March 2003, my life in Jordan came to an end. With these intense changes not only did I have to leave my second home, Amman, but I began to struggle with many questions of the injustices imposed on my life and more so on the lives of marginalized people with whom I have been working as an educational audiologist and activist in the disability and women's movement in Jordan. Moreover, by the end of 2002 when a friend of mine, a gay Jordanian artist, was murdered, I felt the subtle threat on my life as an out gay or queer, and was more convinced I had to move into exile.

In March 2003 when I left Jordan, I had almost no saving left. I began making a living on inconsistent and short consultations for the World Health Organization and other UN agencies in Europe and the U.S. I had no idea where I was heading in my life and I had by then more burning questions than I ever had in my life. When I left Jordan, I was like a refugee having to run between embassies getting my visas renewed and synchronized so I could stay away from Jordan longer until I figured out my next better move.

In February of 2004, while I was still in Europe with no end in sight about a job or a residency anywhere away from Jordan, the dean of the college of education, a friend and colleague since the time I worked in Gaza (1989–1991), called me and encouraged me to apply for the doctoral program in curriculum and instruction. As soon as I started writing the letter of intent for the application, I realized that through research about the critical pedagogy program, I would begin to answer some of the burning questions I left Jordan with and find an alternative career and resume a trajectory to contribute to a more just world.

How did this experience inform your current career?

This, I guess, brings me to the second part of my journey in the U.S., that is, first completing my doctoral degree here at NMSU and then my appointment as a faculty member in the program of women's studies. When the dean called me in early 2004 to convince me of the chances that would open to me earning a PhD, I was perplexed. I was asking myself how could I move to the U.S. now, the heart of the empire, when I just took off from the place in which its military might was re-anchoring. But I took the chance, trusting that my friend was seeing something beyond militarism and the empire that was of worth to me in some way.

Of course, I learned later or had the intelligence to realize that I am this empire's subject no matter where I am located. In saying this, I am emphasizing that a doctoral degree in critical pedagogy whether in the U.S. or elsewhere was something that I've been looking for but was not able to name and access. Doing it in the U.S. paradoxically opened to me a space where I am able to understand the injustice in the world and be hopeful and creative to teach and write to interrupt and challenge the status.

My experience both in Jordan and the U.S. between 2004 and 2008 made me realize that at this point of my life to challenge the injustices in this world, I would serve best as an educator and researcher/writer whether I am in the center of the empire or elsewhere—but as long as my physical safety is not in danger. Currently at NMSU, I am having the chance to teach and learn with graduate and undergraduate students who are related/affected like me, in one way or another, by unjust consequences of a closing society perpetuating and protecting the empire's wars. My scholarly status and my knowledge that come with my experience and position as *Arab-Muslim queer* feminist both bring me amazing opportunities academically and pedagogically. But so far working at NMSU in this border town, there are challenges that I face that need more of a collective and institutional support and more of justice-based milieu to negotiate. This is evident in how I had to negotiate my *Arabness* and/or my *Muslimness* with some military students or even colleagues who are running grants to save Afghani women, for instance, and to negotiate my *queerness* with the very few Muslim students at NMSU.

How do you do that? How is it different?

Remember the border towns of Las Cruces and El Paso have a high concentration of military personal. So, in 2008–2009, I had some military students in the introductory women's studies course. This course was harder to teach compared to my other courses. Most of them were very young, very ready to be deployed, to Iraq mainly, with minimal critical tools to question propaganda, and very much insisting on misconceptions about the war and Muslims and Arabs. So, in the classroom, most of these students coming from this specific mind-set, meeting a professor with an obvious Arabic name at least, present a challenge right at the beginning. I don't necessarily come out to them immediately saying that I'm Arab or Muslim, but slowly, as the course progresses and we tackle issues of racism, sexism, homophobia, then Arab racism and Islamophobia come up too, and I feel the tension rise in the discussion. Or when we start discussing the chapter on women, war and peace, and militarism, I always feel I am on the defensive right from the get-go.

For example, by identifying as an *Arabyyah-Muslimah* feminist, occasionally I feel silences or discomfort with many of my colleagues here around certain political events, like the Israeli war on Gaza in December 2008, and around certain topics like the U.S. spending on the obvious wars now and the budget cuts of higher-education institutes. If they are not colleagues of color, for example, and they do come from colonizing and neocolonizing contexts, I feel I have to be careful to whom I have these conversation and how. But, occasionally the space is open to have a more candid conversation about the empire and its effect on higher education and quality of life in the U.S., and on funding and chances to produce wise and critical knowledge more committed to issues of global sustainability and social justice. I find myself making connections and forging collaboration only with those colleagues who are committed to exposing and countering colonialism, racism, sexism, and homophobia, etc.

Juxtaposed to the above occasions of silence, I have been given the chance in the women's studies program to design and teach an upper-division unique course on *Arab-Muslim* feminisms. Teaching this course for the past two years is evidence of how NMSU and spaces in higher education are still very open to difference, especially at a time of anti-Arab and anti-Muslim racisms. This is also to say that negotiating my positionalities, as an *Arab-Muslim* antiracist postcolonial feminist scholar is not at all straightforward.

Having said this, NMSU is still not the environment for me as an *Arab-Muslim* queer feminist scholar. To grow as a scholar, I need to be in spaces where I can engage in dialogues that are more alive and more connected with political activism. Thus far, I am still looking for these spaces whether here at NMSU or outside it, such as the Special Interest Group at American Education Research Association (AERA), where I find myself approaching home with different kinds of colleagues who inhabit different academic spaces but are working with antiracist and anticolonial approaches whether in their teaching or research.

If you were to compare and contrast Jordan to the U.S., how would you do so? And how has your professional and personal trajectory been since you moved here?

Well, I think comparing as a method of understanding my very complex lived experiences is not so helpful. But I would say the two contexts, Jordan and the U.S., have parallels and connections that help make sense of my professional and personal trajectory. Living in Jordan, which was manufactured as a neocolonial regime in the beginning of the last century, I have gained survival skills that enabled me to maneuver within the very minimal spaces that such a regime left for people like me. The U.S. is different, of course, but has been acting domestically and in close proximity to my life the way the Jordanian regime has acted for so long towards the other and most importantly toward dissidents. From my grandfather's struggles as a rebel who had to leave Palestine, to my parents' struggles in the fifties and the sixties as nationalists, and then to my struggles in the eighties as a woman and out gay, I have lived injustices and oppressions and/or negotiated different kinds of otherness.

Growing up in Jordan, I was constantly on my toes negotiating my otherness whether as a girl in the beginning, as an athlete, as gay or queer, as a woman, then as an ambitious professional who worked in the public sector trying to change the health-care and educational system for the deaf. Now as an academic and an intellectual in the U.S., I am on my toes where Muslims and Arabs are the other. I negotiate my differences within the Muslim context here in the U.S. as my writing questions and challenges homophobic and patriarchal discourses within these contexts. At the same time, I am working my way within the margins of research and publications as my writing does not echo the neo-orientalist discourses constructing Arabs and Muslims as those others who are from cultures that are inferior and overly patriarchal. It seems that there are many connections between living in Jordan and the U.S. I am constantly negotiating my otherness or my strangeness in one dominant culture or another. I hope this shows how my trajectory between Jordan and the U.S. is interwoven.

What does it mean to be lesbian in Jordan compared to being lesbian in the U.S.?

Again comparing is not my tool to understanding my complex experiences as gay or queer, for example. Negotiating my sexuality in the eighties in the U.S. was hard because of where the LGBTQ movement was at the time. However, at the end of the eighties, I went back to Jordan and I was out immediately to all my friends, my family, and more or less to the public. Living my sexuality honestly and openly in Jordan, especially because I was a public figure, was not seamless. But for the most part I had covert and overt support and acceptance.

But to contextualize this, you need to know that in the eighties, fundamentalism was not that strong yet in Jordan. But it started to pick up after the Iranian revolution in seventy-nine and with the consequences of the imperial wars in the region—the so-called Iran-Iraq war, the first Gulf War, the sanctions on Iraq, the continuous ethnic cleansing of the Palestinians, etc. These wars created a good soil for fundamentalism in the nineties onward; however, cleverly King Hussein of Jordan temporarily contained the fundamentalists. Globally they were not yet that strong, so at this time my *queerness* was contested occasionally but not more than my gender.

I think I had more challenges negotiating my gender as an ambitious woman who was political and active in public life than my sexuality. Fundamentalism started to pick up by the end of the nineties. After the murder of one of my gay friends who was a national artist at the end of 2002 and the public humiliation of gay men in Egypt in the Queen Boat incident, I became aware that the Arab regimes are now using homosexuals to appease the fundamentalists (this is a whole other topic to discuss). With this and living my *queerness* honestly, I realized that I couldn't have the backup to protect my life in Jordan anymore.

Being gay or queer, I am not as at risk here in the U.S. as I would have ended up being in Jordan. While doing my dissertation with Muslim girls, I had to go to the mosque and work with the local Muslim community, which is religious. In the religious Muslim community, I would have had to negotiate my sexual status had I identified myself as such. Otherwise, I would have to hide it, which in a way I did while working with Muslim girls at the mosque.

How do you think you would be at risk because of your sexuality?

You mean being at risk here in proximity to the Muslim community because of my sexuality?

Yes.

For example, the publication of my dissertation of 2007 was delayed. That is, I made a request to NMSU's library to embargo it, i.e., not make it public until 2010. A big part of it was because I could not come out as a gay or queer to the Muslim community here. Describing myself as the researcher in the dissertation manuscript, I identify myself as woman, *Arabyyah*, and gay or queer. So, one of the reasons I didn't want the dissertation to be public until I have more time and more privilege in the academy is that in the event the Muslim community decides to differ with me they would be physical toward me.

Last semester I encountered two incidents of blatant homophobia from two Muslim students. At the time, I learned that institutionally there was no support for me or for the students for that matter. So, with some amazing colleagues we had to improvise to protect me and to alert those students to their responsibilities of engaging with difference on the basis of sexuality. And since then I have been thinking of integrating at least some content in my courses about sexualities and Islam, especially the *Arab-Muslim* feminisms course I teach every fall. Also, sexuality and Islam will be incorporated in the proposed LGBTQ minor we are proposing soon at the Department of Sociology and Women's Studies. Because of my sexual preference, the risks have been ongoing whether I was in Jordan or the U.S.

But personally and intellectually I have more resources now to tackle them. I think the more I am experienced and well published in the academy, I will be able to find safer heavens living my marginalized subjectivities in more and more places.

So what would happen if they knew that you were lesbian while conducting research with them?

So far, I have not had to negotiate my sexuality while conducting research. In the study of 2006–2007, which was focused on gender and patriarchal discourses in a Muslim context, my sexuality was not an issue. I had to negotiate with parents of the girls my *Muslimness* but not my sexuality. For example, not attending the local mosque, I was not *Muslim* like them. But they were gracious because somehow they trusted me in spite of this difference. They also trusted me because their girls were having a good time and learning something worthwhile with me. The girls were open with me too. So it was a balance between my ability to help their girls have a good time by engaging them in physical activities in the summer and by abiding by their parents' rules. But at the same time, I must say my *Arabness-Muslimness* or particularly my linguistic literacies allowed me to make that happen. Otherwise, I might have failed to walk the thin line of negotiating my sexuality successfully.

I think at some point my students or others in the academy will find out about my sexuality, but at this point, I feel I am more equipped to negotiate that as long as it's not violent, which is a probability. I've mentioned my friend who was killed in Jordan because he was gay. It is very possible that I would be victim of the same violence if I were not careful and not astute in certain contexts and if the institutional support here is not up to it yet. But perhaps because I'm a female and queer, the probability of being at risk is still lower than it is for a gay man in a dominantly Arab and/or Muslim contexts—so far.

Once I am in a confrontational situation and I need to verbally contest and argue homosexuality in Islam, I will be able to negotiate it as much as possible. But that doesn't mean that I don't experience the painful consequences of homophobia directed toward me from my own people, so to speak, whether it is subtle or blatant.

How do you see the intersectionality of race, gender, and class? How do you experience this intersectionality in your personal and professional life?

I'm very privileged just to have a PhD and to be a professor in a U.S. university. I am more or less middle class. I have also shifted in my class position many times. I think I am in the most privileged class right now not only because of the steady income, but also because of the availability of knowledge and spaces of producing knowledge in my life.

Negotiating my gender, class, and race is a constant struggle but it depends where I am, who I am with, and what I am doing. It's not within the academy itself that I only negotiate my intersecting positionalities, but also within bigger political context of, say, Las Cruces, New Mexico, and North America. Seeing and working within my intersecting positionalities on gender, race, and class are not separate from my positionality as a subject of a neocolonial, postcolonial, imperial power.

That is, being a woman is not separate from my *Arabness* and *Muslimness* in the context of a country waging war on my people. But, this is complicated. For example, I do not appreciate being called to advise on a marginal gender component for an NMSU USAID project. "Let's call Manal. She will help you out with Muslim-related issues here." I should not be representing all the Muslims and in this case, I would not want to be part of liberating Afghani women under the U.S. occupation. They are still looking at Muslim issues from a narrowed and racialized perspective.

I am not sure if I'm answering your question because it's hard to isolate class, gender, and race from my other positionalities. They are all interconnected. The way my positionalities become tested or negotiated depends on the context.

In 2005, as soon as I decided what my dissertation was going to be about, they were all interested and supportive. In some ways, I did not have to justify racially. People who were my professors in 2004 are now all my colleagues and close friends. They are invested in anarchist theories, neo-Marxist theories, critical feminist theories, and critical pedagogy. They were all interested in what I was doing, so they were engaged. They read some of my work. They were more than just, "Oh! We like you a little bit and we think you're exotic" writing about those "oppressed" Muslim girls. They were engaged, and many of them helped me out in the way I could develop and evolve in my work.

On the race issue, I'm not vividly a person of color or a minority, although I have an accent and most people can pick it up or maybe guess that I am an Arab. Also, identifying me as a scholar brings out my class for sure. When I book my flights, I add the prefix Dr. to make my class and status visible somehow in my travel records and hope to be less searched or humiliated in airports, for example.

But last year when I was traveling back to the U.S. on the U.S.-Canada border in Toronto airport I was not allowed back because I did not have a visa but I had a work permit. The officer inspecting my passport said, "Where's your visa? You are not allowed to enter the U.S." And I said, "I'm a professor and I have a work permit, so what do I need a visa for?" I continued, "I have students waiting at New Mexico State University and I am an employee of the state of New Mexico." He said, "So what?" I felt shame and humiliation surge in my blood. I responded, "Do you want to talk to the president of the university?" "Do you want to talk to the lawyer of the university?" But he refused. Suddenly, I was nobody. I was a criminal not a professor educating the young generation in New Mexico. I was a criminal and may not have the chance to prove myself otherwise. I was given by the officer three choices: "Go back to Canada because you have a visa to stay there, get detained for a hundred days, or get shipped to Jordan." I was in shock hearing these choices. This was anti-Arab racism in my face.

So, I went back to Toronto after they detained me. I then started communicating with my colleagues at the university so that they could find a way to get me back to the U.S. The senators of New Mexico started to work on this with the U.S. Embassy in Toronto to expedite my visa issue. It means that they had to re-scrutinize my records to see if I'm not a terrorist, though they have already done that four months ago when the university got me a work permit. It took so much out of me to survive this shock and the wait while keeping my sensibility and dignity. I pulled a lot of energy and grace from my students who reacted immediately by writing to their senators, representatives, writing to me, to the press, and the State Department.

This experience raised a lot of questions of how the academy or higher education in North America, specifically the U.S., is dealing with people who are able to contribute but have a different passport. However, because I was personally connected to the provost and the president at the time and more importantly to a friend who worked with one of the senior senators from NM, Senator Bingaman, I was basically not detained in a black hole and was able to come back to NM in five weeks instead of five months. In this case, my class worked for me by countering the racism I faced at the borders of this country. But, I must say that this experience scarred me pretty badly, being an *Arab-Muslim* at this time in the U.S. I think it is a good example of how the intersectionality of race and class sort of worked in my professional experience.

Since this incident, every time I cross a U.S. border, before I hand my passport, I almost pass as a White American. I don't look dark like you, Pierre! However, as soon as the officer reads my passport, some racist energy comes out. So, they rotate my passport in some panic—up and down, right and left. The print on my passport in Arabic—set from the right to the left, not from the left to the right—is the first visible marker to border officers about my race. That is, I am not American and I confuse them and scare them with my racial difference.

This is to say, my race never fades away. When I cross the border up north to Albuquerque with my partner, for example, we strategize how to cross that border because I am not White and I am not American. She is White with blue eyes and has a Canadian passport. She sits in the driver's seat and I sit in the passenger seat, and we hope that the officer who asks for the passport does not stoop down and say, "Let me see your passport." If they ask me, "Are you an American?" I answer their question saying I am not; they look at me and indirectly say, "Yah! You're not like us. Step aside." But my partner doesn't have to go through that because of her whiteness and her Canadian passport. When the officer says, "Are you American?" and she's in the driver's seat looking in his eyes and says, "No. I'm Canadian with a clear British accent." "Oh, welcome." That's their response.

A couple of times she said Canadians in plural and the officer said, "Please come in." Another time she said, "Canadian," and the officer looked down and said, "Ma'am, are you American?" I said, "No. Here's my passport." He looked at it and said, "Please step aside." I have to wait for them to check. A few times, they didn't check. They looked at the visa and said, "Please go in." During that moment, even though I was not in the head of that officer I could feel the tension building up. Even though I am aware of this kind of racism and know that it is coming at me, its toxicities build up in my stomach no matter what. Usually, after crossing any U.S. border, it takes me a couple of hours to detox from somebody looking at me and treating me as the scum of the earth.

You said that your accent is more like a marker than your racial identity. Can you say more about this?

No, it marks my racial or one may call it locally my tribal identity. For example, my last name is hard to pronounce, and I think that is the first visible marker of my racial identity. I don't look White. Some people think I'm Mediterranean or European. So, as soon as they see my name on, say, for the online classes or when they register online, they realize I am not Anglo. So, my last name is the first marker to who I am racially.

On the accent as a racial marker, I can't tell if my accent is obvious. Since I am more comfortable now in my department and have been in teaching for two years, I have asked my students about my accent. Most of them say, "We have no problem with your accent." Though I think my accent is subtle, my speech intelligibility is good, which means my accent does not affect the process of teaching and learning. So, I do not know how they perceive me. I assume that after a few weeks in class and with the way I teach, my accent stops being an issue or a marker of difference and the content of the course and the fun we have learning reigns.

So how have you seen your identity shifted?

I don't sit all the time in the margins, and I do see all of my subjectivities as fluid and not static. For example, as a professor, I'm in the center in some things and in the margins in others. With my work, for example, that critiques physical education research that racializes Muslim girls, I am not in the center. But by forging alliances with colleagues like you involved in the postcolonial Special Interest Group (SIG), looking into journals and publishers that would publish my work, has helped me close the gap I live between the margin and the center as a professor. But this move or shift is not my intention to be institutionalized but to bring my work, which I think is worthy, to a bigger audience, for which I am hopeful of. Being an *Arab-Muslim*, I feel now it is urgent to do so because I am not sure if the position I have now will last.

So what was it like living in Jordan? Was your racial identity ever an issue?

As noted earlier, I lived in a neocolonial context with the royal regime that was of course manufactured by the British and now maintained by the U.S. With the influx of Palestinian refugees in the forties and the establishment of the state of Israel in 1948, two distinct races/ethnicities emerged in Jordan: Palestinians and Jordanians. The regime had to make a clear distinction between the two. They used different mechanisms as a neocolonial regime would do, to make this distinction and ultimately to keep the people policed. This racializing project was in direct service of the Israeli state project ethnic cleansing of the Palestinians and the preservation of the Hashemite regime in power.

Not only were the Palestinians given clearly marked IDs and passports but also people like my family were forced to readopt their tribal name as their last name to show their distinctive Jordanianness and their alliance to the regime. In the addition of Al Smadi to my last name Hamzeh, I was reclassified as a Jordanian though I'm a mixture of Palestinian, Jordanian, Turkish, Syrian, and Kurdish. I was born in Jordan but my two grandfathers and one of my grandmothers were born in Palestine. So, in many ways I was privileged because of my tribal name. But because of what the regime was doing, I couldn't even show my Palestinian pride even when I wanted to do so.

So the government categorized people racially/ethnically, and this seemed to have worked in your favor.

In my favor, yes! But at the same time, it is not in my favor because fixating on one identity takes away from learning my history, my heritage, and thus my complexity with which comes also the richness of knowing oneself with many racial/ethnic identities. I was given something I didn't have to work for, that is, my Jordanian identity, and it was meant to make me feel and act superior to the Palestinians. So, in this case, I do not see it as a favor. Rather, it is a tool of the regime to close and silence the ways of being multiple and fluid, and thus to suppress dissidents.

I draw more on my *Arabness* than on my *Jordanianness*. A lot of my work is dependent on Arabic, my home language. I use Arabic words either in the Arabic script or in English letters in my writing, and I am challenging the sacred text of the Koran, which is also Arabic. So, my *Arabness* is very present in my writing and in my teaching too. Besides teaching an *Arab-Muslim* feminisms course, often I use Arabic words in my dialogues with students.

So do you plan on returning to Jordan or will you stay here as long as life allows you to?

Never say never! The context that I live in has to be a context that is respecting whatever I am doing and it is not silencing me in any way. I would just hope that I have the privilege to possess a legal document that would enable me to be more mobile in this bordered world without being scrutinized and demonized. With this, I will return to Jordan for family visits and maybe some field research. But, I don't think that Jordan is going to change so much in the near future in order for me to be valued or even to have chances to have a good job. It's a regime that is again neocolonial, antidemocratic.

It's a police state, hidden, invisible, of course, like this country to some extent. I wouldn't survive there because of my ideas and the hostile environment. In the short run, I don't want to live there. At the same time, I am not saying that I want to live here forever because I've been a nomad all my life. I think I will always be moving to places so that I can sustain my dignity and productivity. In both Jordan and the U.S., I have been productive even though I have to negotiate the hegemonic discourses all the time. I have maintained my position without being complicit with the regime in Jordan or for that matter with the New Empire's regime here.

9 Testimonios of Microaggressions on University and College Campuses

Marivel Oropeza

On today's college and university campuses, most students do not experience racism on the macro level, although that still exists. They do not usually see crosses burning on lawns. They do not daily see a noose hanging from a building, although in late February of 2010 such an incident did occur on the campus of the University of California, San Diego. A student admitted to hanging a noose from a campus library and was later suspended for that act. Daniels (2010) wrote about an incident at the University of Minnesota, Duluth in May, in which "Two first year students, self-described white girls, began a Facebook wall conversation after an African-American classmate entered the room where they were studying" (para. 2). What the students wrote was the following:

> ewww a obabacare (sic) is in the room, i feel dirty, and unsafe. keep a eye on all of your valuables and dont make direct eye contact. . . . i just threw up in my mouth right now . . . we're two white girls . . . she already has her (N-word) instinct to kill us and use us to her pleasure . . . (para. 3).

Those are obvious acts of racism, unquestionable, and although they also happen regularly, what occur daily are acts on the micro level, or microaggressions. Microaggressions can be defined as "incessant, subtle, yet stunning racial assaults" (Yosso, Smith, Ceja, & Solórzano, 2009). Unlike overt forms of racism, microaggressions are sometimes less obvious to observe or detect because they are so subtle and do occur often. What may be so difficult about dealing with microaggressions is the doubt with which victims are left in trying to decipher and understand the racist encounter he or she has just experienced. Sue, Capodilupo, Torino, Bucceri, Holder, Nadal, and Esquilin (2007) defined "Racial microaggressions as brief and commonplace daily verbal, behavioral, or environmental indignities, whether intentional or unintentional, that communicate hostile, derogatory, or negative racial slights and insults toward people of color" (p. 271). Sue et al. (2007) wrote about three types of microaggression messages. Those are the (1) microassault, (2) microinsult, and

(3) microinvalidation. Microassaults are obvious racial put-downs. For example, when someone calls you by a racial slur he or she is microassaulting you. The microinsult is when someone thinks she or he is complimenting you but instead she or he is insulting you. An example of this would be "You're so articulate" for a Latino/Black/Asian/Indian. The microinvalidation happens when a White person utters something you just said and all of a sudden it is "valid" when it was "not valid" when you said it originally. Microinvalidations happen daily and everywhere.

Directly tied to microaggressions is *racial battle fatigue*. Racial battle fatigue is the mental, emotional, and physical strain caused by microaggressions (Smith, 2004). Some of the symptoms associated with racial battle fatigue include: headaches, elevated blood pressure, anxiety, ulcers, insomnia or broken sleep, difficulty thinking or speaking coherently, emotional or social withdrawal, pounding heartbeat, rapid breathing, upset stomach, frequent diarrhea, and/or urination (Smith, 2004). Yosso, Smith, Ceja, and Solórzano (2009) found that some students even left campus altogether as a result of experiencing racial battle fatigue due to microaggressions.

This theoretical background is important in better understanding what transpires on college campuses nationwide on a daily basis. Students of color are confronted with incidents, experiences, messages, assaults, insults, and aggressions that are real. Those microaggressions do not just happen at University of California, San Diego, where the noose was hung in February, or at the University of Minnesota, Duluth, where the Facebook exchange between those first-year students occurred. Those microaggressions happen everywhere.

Testimonio or testimony is a qualitative method that draws upon identity and personal, spiritual, professional, and academic experiences to understand the present and create the future. Burciaga and Erbstein (2010) define testimonio as "similar to oral history, yet involves the participant in a critical theoretical reflection of personal, political, spiritual, and intellectual understandings of self and community . . . provides an epistemic lens to support an analytical inquiry of experiences within larger social contexts" (p. 5). The following are three testimonios of microaggressions that happened to me in higher-education settings.

Ditto

The room was full of students. The required research methods class always enrolled more students than for which there were chairs. Professor Williams's laugh was contagious; he was a funny man. He was nice. Professor Williams probably did not know that he was marginalizing me. He did not seem like a racist or like someone who would want to subjugate his students. However, instead of just listening, understanding what I was asking, and continuing with the class, he made a comment about a specific word that I had used in asking my question. "Ditto? How odd that you would use that anachronism. That's an archaic term. We have not used dittos since the 1980s. Surely you meant 'hand-out?'" Embarrassed, I just nodded and tried not to turn different shades of red. I had finally gotten the courage to speak up and ask a question about the previous week's assignment, asking if "the ditto that was handed out" had been another way to point out the differences in paleontological periods. That would be both the first and last time that I would raise my hand in that class.

Several reasons made Professor Williams's usage of the word "anachronism" an inaccurate and marginalizing act. Although in Professor Williams's world, ditto machines had not been used since the 1980s, in my community along the Rio Grande River in Texas, ditto machines were still in use, and widely so. Thus, what would otherwise make the word "ditto" an anachronism, using a word out of chronological or historical context, was not accurate for my community. Moreover, Professor Williams exhibited a form of linguicism by suggesting to others and me that my choice of one word was subservient to what he might otherwise use. Skutnabb-Kangas (1988) defined linguicism as "ideologies, structures and practices which are used to legitimate, effectuate and reproduce an unequal division of power and resources (material and immaterial) between groups which are defined on the basis of language" (p. 13).

I had several options for reacting to what Delgado and Stefancic (2001) would label a "microaggression." Delgado and Stefancic defined microaggressions as "sudden, stunning, or dispiriting transactions that mar the days of women and folks of color" (2001, p. 2). I could have taken this incident as a sign I needed to change, to blend more with the dominant group. The option could have led to severe circumstances, among them the resistance of self. Montoya (1994) described aspects of this resistance, "When we attempt to mask immutable characteristics . . . because historically they have been loathsome to the dominant culture, then the masks of acculturation can be experienced as self-hate" (p. 13). I had another option. I could have told my story. As Montoya (1994) pointed out, "Outsider storytelling is a discursive technique for resisting cultural and linguistic domination" (p. 1).

INTERNSHIP

The next experience happened while I was working at an office on campus, learning under the supervision of a campus administrator. I give the person under whom I worked much credit as this person allowed me different opportunities to observe processes and sit in on meetings. However, perhaps as a result of those observations, I was able to see that students of color were often excluded from that particular office's attention unless Latino and other students of color placed themselves on the agenda. On a particular day I was shown a brochure that would be used campus-wide to represent the university. I was asked for my opinion about the brochure. The content in the brochure was excellent and informative but what I was taken aback about was the picture on the front of the brochure. The picture was one of five White students. I asked myself, "Was this brochure for an all-White school?" Since I had been asked for my opinion, I provided it. I informed the administrator that if the brochure were to accurately depict this "Hispanic-serving institution" student body, the picture on the brochure would have to be changed, as the picture was not at least quantitatively accurate. Our university has 42% Latino students, 3% Black students, 3% American Indian students, and 1% Asian students. There are 9% of students for whom we do not know an ethnic or racial category.

However, we do not have a 100% White student body. I ask you, what is a microaggression if not an occurrence in which all populations of color are completely erased from the picture, literally? The message I took from the brochure, whether intentional or not, was "You are not wanted here. You do not belong here. This is our ideal population, our ideal student body. This is how we will recruit other students. This is how we will convince others to come here." Ironically, Yosso, Smith, Ceja, and Solórzano (2009) write, "Recruitment brochures would not advertise a campus climate wherein Whites enjoy a sense of entitlement" (p. 660). Yet that is exactly what this brochure would have done by completely eliminating all other students . . . or perhaps what it would have done would have to more honestly depict the realities of our institution; that some students enjoy certain privileges that others do not.

Two points do need clarification. First, part of the conversation that this administrator and I had was about phenotype. That is, the students' physical features. I did acknowledge to the administrator that I could not know for certain that the students on the cover of the brochure were not Latina/os or other students of color, simply by looking at them physically. Students of color certainly have blonde hair, fair skin, and blue eyes. Upon bringing up this point, this administrator seemed vindicated for just a moment, for having chosen that picture. However, I then explained that even though students of color, Latinos included, are diverse in many ways, including phenotypically, the great majority of our students of color do not have these White characteristics. Moreover, to only showcase White Latinos or White students of color would potentially highlight to students and families the same ideas as I had interpreted: the notions of non-White students not belonging, not being welcome, not being wanted here, than if we were to feature non-student of color, White students. The second point I should stress is that upon providing my opinion, the brochure was indeed changed, and a picture of a more diverse student body was included in the brochure. Although I credit the administrator for taking the feedback and making the change, I am left to wonder what would have happened had I not been an intern in that office in that given semester.

POLLOCK

Linguicism is powerful because it includes a vast array of issues of power and discrimination. Among these are discrimination based on accent, pronunciation, racist speech (Matsuda, Lawrence III, Delgado, & Krenshaw, 1993) and language deprivation through English-only policies (Deyhle & McCarty, 2007), among others. Nieto (2002) noted, "Linguicism has been particularly evident in racially and economically oppressed communities" (pp. 82–83). Linguicism is not just found in schools but can be found in government agencies, public housing, private companies, places of employment, among friends, between spouses, in public service areas. It is omnipresent.

This experience of linguicism occurred while working on a research project with a professor. This professor and I were working together and I mentioned that I had an article by a scholar. I showed the professor the book and said, "Oh, look, I found an article by Pollock." The professor's response was, "What?" I responded, "There's a great article here by Pollock." The professor proceeded to laugh. I turned to look at the professor and inquired about the laughter. The professor asked me to pronounce the author's name again. Pollock. Poll-Lock. P-O-L-L-O-C-K. POLLOCK. The professor laughed some more and then corrected me, "Pollock. You pronounce the name Paul-luck. You're hilarious." I turned and looked at the professor seriously, covering the OCK and said, "When I cover the OCK, all I see is POLL, "POLL," POLL, and when I cover the POL, all I see is "LOCK," so when I put it all together for me the word is POLLOCK. POLL-LOCK." The professor continued to chuckle as if this was all still so funny and my pronunciation was hilarious. The irony of the situation was that this professor and I were working on a manuscript about LINGUICISM. Stunning and crazy, yet that's the thing about racism, isn't it?

So, was there a power relationship there? Yes. Was I made to feel like I was worthless? Yes. Was I made to feel like an idiot and stupid? Yes. Was I made to feel as if I had to explain myself? Yes. I can go on and on, but the point I want to make is that there are many ways in which to correct our students, if we absolutely feel that we have to, with pronunciation. This professor could have said, "Oh, this article by Pollock is great. Let me take a long look at it." However, the point in knowing about linguicism, racism, and other forms of subjugation is that if we want to help our students, specifically our underrepresented students, is to embrace the richness, talents, wealth of culture with which they come to us. They may not come to the university with exact Polish pronunciations, but they come with so much more. We just need to be willing to open our eyes and look for it and appreciate it.

It is important to know that the ideas of race and racism do not exist in isolation to *Whiteness* and *White privilege.* Harris (1995) refers to

Whiteness as a form of property, where those with phenotypically visible whiteness can benefit from the breaks, leniencies, and differential treatment based on the ownership of White skin. Calderón (2006) provided a definition of Whiteness, "Whiteness represents . . . a flat epistemology in which the organization of knowledge is hierarchical, unidirectional, and reductive . . . totalizing, assuming a singular way of knowing . . . a flattened epistemology is one-dimensional because it is predetermined and disseminated in order to reproduce whiteness" (p. 75). Kendall (2006) defined White privilege:

> All of us who are white receive white privileges. They are bestowed on us impersonally and systemically, but they affect us personally. We can't not get them, and we can't give them back. . . . One of the primary privileges is having greater influence, power, and resources. White people make decisions that affect everyone without consulting anyone else. As white people, we keep ourselves central, thereby silencing others. We can include or exclude others at our whim. . . . We must be aware of how the power holders oppressed all people of color to shape the country as they wanted it. Racism is one of several systems of oppression. Others are class, sexism, heterosexism, the institutionalized primacy of Christianity, and able bodiedism. These systems work toward a common goal: to maintain power and control in the hands of wealthy, white, heterosexual, Christian, able-bodied men. (pp. 62–63)

The various forms of discrimination that people of color experience is the following: They are discriminated for being perceived to be culturally, linguistically, racially, ethnically, and in other ways inferior. However, that exists simultaneously with the idea that Whites are superior and privileged for their Whiteness. Thus, people of color face the dilemma of "being inferior" for that which they are, people of color, but also for that which they are not, White. Again, that relationship exists simultaneously and symbiotically.

Lastly, simply because you have not seen a phenomenon, experienced a phenomenon, lived it in one of its manifestations does not mean it does not exist. Simply because you do not fully or partly understand it does not mean you should not understand it. Simply because you do not agree with it does not mean you should not learn about it.

REFERENCES

Burciaga, R., & Erbstein, N. (2010). *Challenging assumptions, revealing community cultural wealth: Young adult wisdom on hope in hardship*. Healthy Youth/Healthy Regions Working Paper. Center for Regional Change, UC Davis.

Calderón, D. (2006). One-dimensionality and whiteness. *Policy Futures in Education*, *4*(1), 73–82.

Daniels, J. (May, 2010). Cyber racism on college campuses. Retrieved October 20, 2010, from Race-Talk website: http://www.race-talk.org/?p=4106.
Delgado, R., & Stefancic, J. (2001). *Critical race theory: An introduction*. New York: New York University Press.
Deyhle, D., & McCarty, T. L. (2007). Beatrice Medicine and the anthropology of education: Legacy and vision for critical race/critical language research and practice. *Anthropology & Education Quarterly, 38*(3), 209–220.
Harris, C. I. (1995). Whiteness as property. In K. Crenshaw, N. Gotanda, G. Peller, & K. Thomas (Eds.), *Critical race theory: The key writings that formed the movement* (pp. 276–291). New York: The New Press.
Kendall, F. E. (2006). *Understanding white privilege: Creating pathways to authentic relationships across race*. New York: Routledge.
Matsuda, M., Lawrence III, C. R., Delgado, R., & Crenshaw, K. W. (1993). *Words that wound: Critical race theory, assaultive speech, and the first amendment*. San Francisco: Westview Press.
Montoya, M. (1994). Mascaras, trenzas, y greñas: Un/masking the self while un/braiding Latina stories and legal discourse. *Chicano-Latino Law Review, 15*, 1–26.
Nieto, S. (2002). *Language, culture, and teaching: Critical perspectives for a new century*. Mahwah, NJ: Lawrence Erlbaum Associates.
Skutnabb-Kangas, T. (1988). Multilingualism and the education of minority children.
In T. Skutnabb-Kangas & J. Cummins (Eds.), *Minority education: From shame to struggle* (pp. 9–44). Clevedon, UK: Multilingual Matters.
Smith, W. A. (2004). Black faculty coping with racial battle fatigue: The campus-racial climate in a post–civil rights era. In D. Cleveland (Ed.), *A long way to go: Conversations about race by African American faculty and graduate students at predominantly white institutions* (pp. 171–190). New York: Peter Lang.
Sue, D. W., Capodilupo, C. M., Torino, G. C., Bucceri, J. M., Holder, A. M. B., Nadal, K.L., & Esquilin, M. (2007). Racial microaggressions in everyday life: Implications for clinical practice. *American Psychologist, 62*(4), 271–286.
Yosso, T. J., Smith, W. A., Ceja, M., & Solórzano, D. G. (2009). Critical race theory, racial microaggressions, and campus racial climate for Latina/o undergraduates. *Harvard Educational Review, 79*(4), 659–656.

Part II

Unmasking the Wretchedness of Neoliberalism and Neocolonialism

10 Marxist Scholarship in Neoliberal Times

Social Imagination or Social Revolution?[1]

Antonia Darder

And here is the decisive point: as soon as the productive power of human labour has developed to this height, every excuse disappears for the existence of a ruling class. Was not the final reason with which class differences were defended always: there must be a class which need not plague itself with the production of its daily subsistence, in order that it may have time to look after the intellectual work of society?

—Friedrich Engels, *The Housing Question* (1872)[2]

These words by Friedrich Engels set the stage for one of the most powerful contradictions faced by Marxist intellectuals in the course of our labor. In light of his pointed question, it is interesting to consider for a moment the 2011 theme of the American Educational Research Association annual meeting—*Inciting the Social Imagination: Education Research for the Public Good*, which, despite its well-meaning intent, failed to dispel the notion that the primary purpose of intellectuals in education is, in fact, to produce "social imagination" for the rest of the populace.

What is most striking here is that this should occur at what could well be a most decisive historical junction, when protests and uprisings are occurring in this country and around the world, at a rate only reminiscent of the 1960s. In so doing, one of the most prestigious educational conferences in the world continues to protect its cherished liberal tradition, even in the midst of much radical fervor out on the streets. Hence, true to its roots, the conference proposes to incite "social imagination" through the production of more liberal scholarship, when the kind of social imagination we so desperately need today is that which must be inspired by and rooted in the labor of social revolution.

While many well-meaning colleagues persist, for example, in deploying the idea of "social capital" (an oxymoron if there ever was one) in their analysis of inequalities of schooling, what seems to be missing is a deeper understanding of the changing nature of work in the United States and its ravaging impact on working people. What good does it do for students to gain the "social capital" afforded them by a college degree, if jobs are being eliminated at an unprecedented pace, wages are stagnant, worker protections dwindling, and incarceration or the military inscription are the few likely pipelines for poor and working-class youth?

Hence, social capital is indeed a slippery concept; a metaphor generally used to refer to formal and informal social and knowledge networks, which can enable people to mobilize resources and achieve common goals. Underlying the notion, however, is a tacit acceptance of the market as a legitimate mechanism by which the successful accumulation of so-called social capital by disenfranchised populations can create the conditions for greater civic engagement, political participation, community mobilization, and social cohesion. Pierre Bourdieu, Glen Loury, James Coleman, and more recently Robert Putnam are among the most pivotal and celebrated scholars associated with this idea.[3] By pushing reliance upon markets, community networks and other forms of social cohesion are transformed into "capital" to be accumulated by the poor. It is important to note here that even in the more progressive employment of the term as "symbolic,"[4] arguments related to social conflict are not necessarily grounded in relations of production or the consequence of capitalist exploitation.

Thus, poverty and many other social problems are considered to be caused by a decline or deficit of social capital. Not unlike, the market model of neoclassical orthodoxy, the individual engagement with social networks and social cohesion occurs outside the context of the geo-political economy and are substituted for discourses, policies, and practices that could genuinely attack material poverty and unequal power. Thus, market-driven policies, as witnessed worldwide, are more likely, if anything, to make our problems worse. Hence, it makes much more sense to move in promising (although difficult) counterhegemonic directions than to pursue policies, which are more likely to intensify, rather than to solve, two of the most distinctive features of U.S. life today—increasing poverty and social polarization.

What is lacking in the building of flexible decentralization in working class communities of color, for example, need not commonsensically translate to public-private "partnerships" or other euphemisms for increased marketization. Instead, flexible decentralization can mean empowered participation and democratic renewal in the struggle for emancipatory education for these communities. This would indeed be a kind of "third way" between traditional social democratic emphasis on centralized statist regulation of capitalism and anti-statist free market positions. What is needed is an increase, not decrease, in *social regulation* of the market, but a form of regulation that is executed through empowered forms of popular democratic participation. This is a call for the deepening of *democracy,* rather than reliance on a narrow rationality whose primary intent is to extend and advance the interests of the marketplace.[5]

After more than fifty years of civil rights efforts, recent census data confirm economic inequality levels that rival the 1930s! *Mother Jones* magazine published eleven charts under the title *It's the Inequality, Stupid*,[6] graphically illustrating how domestic economic policy has well protected the private interests of the "super rich;" whose elite well-being is well guarded by congress, where more than 50% of its members are themselves multimillionaires. So, it should be of no surprise that Wall Street was bailed out, while the average worker barely ekes out a living; or that, from 2007 to 2009, Wall Street profits increased by 720%, while unemployment increased by 102%; or that CEO earnings are 185 times greater than that of the average worker; or that the tax rate of the wealthy has steadily and consistently decreased since 1945, including a 200% decrease in the income tax paid by corporations. Not to mention that the federal government spends over a trillion dollars a year on defense, which is not only as much as the rest of the world's defense budgets combined, but also 200% more that what will be spent nationwide on education at all levels this year;[7] and the increasing amount spent on law enforcement and the incarceration of almost 2.5 million people (a population that is actually greater than that of twelve states). And none of these numbers speak to the cost of war, incarceration, or poverty on the lives of working people and their communities; nor do they factor in racialized, gendered, and disabled exclusions, which would constitute even more staggering rates of inequality. So much so that we can't help but recall the words of Engels, as did Rosa Luxembourg in the *Junius Pamphlet*: "At this moment, one glance about us will show us what a reversion to barbarism in capitalist society means." [8]

Given the stark political-economic picture, the central question that we must ask is not whether education scholars and researchers can incite "social imagination" but, rather, whether we can hold clear and steady a collective emancipatory vision for social and material transformation—and with that, a politics of teaching and research that challenges us to retain the dialectic between "what is to be done?" and "what is to be undone?" in the midst of powerful contradictions that serve the interest of the wealthy, as Michael Harrington argued in *The Other America*.[9] In light of all this, we as Marxist scholars must ask ourselves: Do we have the will to struggle against the major contradictions we face in our work and the wherewithal to fight against the degradation of our humanity? And if we answer yes, then what shall be our praxis?

LIMITS OF *SOCIAL IMAGINATION* IN NEOLIBERAL TIMES

> *The bourgeoisie has resolved personal worth into exchange value, and in place of the numberless indefeasible chartered freedoms, has set up that single, unconscionable freedom—Free Trade. In one word, for exploitation . . ."*
>
> —Karl Marx (Manifesto of the Communist Party, 1848)[10]

Among the variety of ways in which C. Wright Mills's notion has been conceptualized, one often cited definition for *sociological imagination* is "the capacity to shift from one perspective to another—from the political to the psychological; from examination of a single family to comparative assessment of the national budgets of the world; from the theological school to the military establishment; from considerations of an oil industry to studies of contemporary poetry. . . . The sociological imagination enables us to grasp history and biography and the relations between the two within society. *That is its task and its promise*"[11] (the italic emphasis here is mine).

And although it is true that in his studies of the American social structure, C. Wright Mills summoned a broader outlook in sociological theory and analysis; attacked positivist intellectuals; sought to lift the academic boycott of Marxism; and breached the uniformity and conformity of official sociology, to embrace his notion of social imagination as our intellectual compass is simply insufficient. In contrast, Karl Marx provided us a powerfully dialectic *and* materialist understanding of history, in which history fundamentally evolves through various forms of class struggle. More importantly, in *Introduction to the Critique of Political Economy*, Marx[12] sketches out for us, in general terms, a process for social revolution, when he writes,

> At a certain stage of their development, the material forces of production in society come in conflict with the existing relations of production, or—what is but a legal expression for the same thing—with the property relations, within which, they have been at work before. From forms of development of the forces of production these relations turn into their fetters. Then begins an epoch of social revolution.[13]

Since the mid-1970s, capitalism has been undergoing vital changes. There was a shift from traditional industrial manufacture to a "postindustrial" culture of consumerism, communications, information technology, and the service industry. Markets were deregulated, and the working-class movement was subjected to brutal legal and political assaults under the Reagan administration. Traditional class allegiances were weakened, as social struggle consolidated around identity politics. In the wake of neoliberal explosion, racism morphed into an unrelenting quest for recognition, whereas the Marxist vision for universal emancipation and equality of workers was systematically eroded, as even scholars on the left lost confidence in the future of socialism and, instead, became apologist for capitalist rule. Terry Eagleton in *Was Marx Right?* argues,

> It was not illusions about the new capitalism, but disillusion about the possibility of changing it, which proved decisive. There were, to be sure, plenty of former socialists who rationalized their gloom by claiming that if the system could not be changed, neither did it need to be. But it was lack of faith in an alternative that proved conclusive. Because the working-class movement had been so battered and bloodied, and the political Left so robustly rolled back, the future seemed to have vanished without trace.[14]

Paul D'Amato notes that "during the neoliberal economic boom, it became very fashionable to declare Marxism dead. But now that we are facing the deepest economic crisis since the 1930s, Karl Marx is suddenly alive again."[15] Yet, for many it is not only a matter of revisiting Marx but, rather, also rethinking our labor as Marxist scholars. As D'Amato and others in the field suggest, if there ever was a moment when we needed to embrace more fully the social revolutionary potential of Marxism, it is precisely in these times; for implicit to Marx's economic analysis is the idea that capitalism creates the conditions for its own abolition; in Marx's words, "It brings into the world the material means of its own destruction."[16] Hence, our capacity to grapple, in theory and practice, with the material and social manifestations of neoliberalism today, within the context of schooling and society, must serve as the political motivation of our scholarship, teaching, and activism, within and across communities.

We are in the midst of a disastrous internationalizing project of neoliberalism. Michael Peters,[17] in *Poststructuralism, Marxism, and Neoliberalism: Between Theory and Politics*, argues that neoliberalism provides "a Universalist foundation for an extreme form of economic rationalism," which can be regarded as the latest political-economic formation of advanced capitalism in the West. Further, Peters insists that "such a philosophy is ultimately destructive of any full-fledged notions of community—national or international, imagined or otherwise."[18] This political reasoning of neoliberalism, unfortunately, has come to dominate policy agendas in education since it's emergence in the early 1980s, with a deeply rationalistic and totalizing effect.

> In simplest terms, we might say that this form of reason is motivated by an extreme economic rationalism that views the market as a superior allocative mechanism for the distribution of scarce public resources, but also a morally superior form of political economy. The central tenet of the theories underlying public-sector restructuring, including changes to both the core and the residual public sector and welfare state, is a

> philosophy of individualism . . . [which] asserts that all human behavior is dominated by self-interest.[19]

Collective social action, accordingly, is seen as a gross obstacle to the freedom of individuals and privatization of what, at another time in our history, would have been the public good. Its rampant individualism functions as a means to end state regulation and control, which neoliberal advocates consider the major culprit in stifling the free market's ability to flourish and its capacity to protect private interests. Thus, it is not surprising that corporations have vied for federal protections as "individual" entities—to pursue more effectively their self-interests.

Hence, what we see is neoliberal policies and practices clearly grounded upon a particular form of rationality that creates a narrow intellectual anchor from which ultraconservatives, conservatives, and neoliberals alike can vie for control of not only the marketplace but all public and private institutions, including those tied to human welfare and education. Neoliberal rhetoric has also become the rallying cry of elite ultraconservative supporters of the Tea Party, such as the Koch brothers, who seek to turn back the clock on democratic gains, in order to line their own silky pockets.

Similarly, given its international nature, the impact of neoliberalism is well at work in the economies of almost every sovereign nation in the world. Through the power and influence of the International Monetary Fund, the World Bank, and a host of NGOs, countries have been coerced, in the name of freedom, democracy, and progress to acquiesce to neoliberal principles, in order to position themselves as recognizable players within the global arena.

The negative impact of these policies and practices, in both particularistic and universal ways, has been directly responsible for a great deal of the poverty and human suffering that has finally led to many of the recent uprisings and protests in Arab and North African nations, as well as right here in the United States—movements that are, by no means, ideologically homogenous and—although too early to tell—may signal the beginning of epochal change.

SOCIAL MOVEMENT AND THE EROS EFFECT

> *New forces and new passions spring up in the bosom of society . . .*
>
> —Karl Marx, *Capital*[20]

Over the last two months there has been a swelling movement worldwide, along with the accompanying violence and impunity so common in circumstances where the powerful are challenged to defer their illegitimate authority over the people. And even now, the self-serving individualism of neoliberal advocates, along with their lack of concern for the distress of workers' lives, attempt to dispel and distract us from the powerful meaning of what is happening at this historical juncture in this country. Yet, when police officers side with protesting masses, as they did in Cairo and in Wisconsin, one can no longer pretend that "an epoch of social revolution" may not be in the air, no matter how many illegitimate governmental actions are attempted or passed by representatives of the state.

In Wisconsin, for example—even with its incredible progressive history—the uprising and occupation of the statehouse would not have been possible without the collective participation of union activists, community workers, teachers, nurses, university students, firefighters, and others, who acted upon their lived empirical knowledge that the quality of their lives and those of other workers in this country were quickly plummeting. In concert with Raya Dunayevskaya, the worker does indeed "grasp the truth of the present";[21] working people know when things are not looking good for them or for their children and they have been willing to act in solidarity upon their knowledge—and through their collective action, a new social imagination can be born. For, as Che Guevara insisted, "Even if the theory is not known, the revolution can succeed if historical reality is interpreted correctly."[22] That is, interpreted within the material contexts of change.

In these passing weeks, as we have witnessed the collective strength of people coming together, sending virtual communiqués, and protestors expressing their hope and love for one another in interviews with journalists—whether in Tunisia, Cairo, or Wisconsin—it has brought to mind what George Katsiaficas, who has studied social movements for almost four decades, terms "the Eros effect"; when "there is a sudden spread of people governed movements and a rapid and massive diffusion of the human need for justice and freedom."[23] In his study of movements in Europe, Asia, and the Americas, Katsiaficas discusses how, in each case, the goal surrounds similar concerns: to reconstitute and reconfigure power in order to abolish hunger and poverty, to give people freedom, and to produce a more genuine praxis of democracy.

The Eros effect, then, functions to not only awaken collective human agency, but also to dispel, for example, long-standing and commonsensical myths that demonize or demean collective action and community participation in the interest of democratic life. Moreover, the Eros effect counters media illusions that portray people as apathetic and uninformed. In civilian-led demonstrations, as in Wisconsin, solidarity has steadily built, inspiring others who have simply had enough!

The transformation of self-interest into species interest is the essential communal dimension of the Eros effect, where an intuitive process of identification occurs in which individual and group self-interest transcends, as the universalized interest of the species emerges. In my own work, I term this collective force "political grace"—a force that unites us collectively, through our labor and relationships of struggle, to those material conditions and social relations that break our alienation and support social revolution.

What the current conditions of struggle can do for us is to inspire us, in our teaching, scholarship, and activism, to revisit the meaning of democracy in the United States and to contend with the manner in which prevailing social values, instilled by capitalism in its current neoliberal formation, obstruct all sense of the public good in ways that debilitate the larger human struggle for social justice in this country and around the world.

SOCIAL IMAGINATION BORN OF SOCIAL REVOLUTION

> *It is not the consciousness of men that determines their being, but, on the contrary, their social being that determines their consciousness.*
>
> —Karl Marx, *A Contribution to the Critique of Political Economy*[24]

If, as Marx argues, social being determines consciousness, then all this begs the question How do we make sense of what is happening around us, if we are not in it? How do we need to think differently about scholarship? How do we need to teach differently *in the world*? How can we establish new forms of relationships within neighborhoods, between parents and teachers, as well as other working people? What new forms of organic pedagogy can produce the social change necessary to incite social imagination? And most importantly, for those of us in the academy, how do we propose to keep higher education open to all, in light of the unrelenting forces of privatization? In these times, more than ever, a focus on abstract theorization, rather than social revolution, can unfortunately result in a tendency to over-ideologize our subject of study, which can deaden the impact of our contribution and can alienate us, despite our best intentions.

For decades, one of the main problems dividing radical intellectuals, and one that continues to plague our scholarly work in education, has been an obsessive compulsion to define ideology first, rather than laboring toward greater unity on the basis of action and a larger political project. This, inadvertently, points to an over-theoretical orientation in naming social relations, of which one often knows little regarding the material conditions or regional and cultural histories that might inform their formation. An exaggerated emphasis on defining ideology then can shroud our understanding of how particularities within social relations can impact questions of struggle and social change.

The predominance of an individualist or careerist agenda in the construction of theory and, thus, the formation of social imagination is an unfortunate consequence of liberal-minded scholarship. Unlike the Marxist imperative for class struggle to emerge from the consciousness of social being and, thus, signaling a collective social project as a means for transforming the material conditions of the working class—in the short run under capitalism and in the long run toward a larger socialist transformation—the task of the project of social imagination has been principally "to enable us to grasp history and biography and the relations between the two within society." As important as this may be to progressive intellectual pursuit, what remains missing from C. Wright Mills's eloquent articulation of "social imagination" is a grounded political project or social objective that is clearly delineated as the purpose of study. Noble though his idea may be, it simply remains insufficient as a foundation for a radical political praxis of transformation.

As Marxist scholars, we are challenged by the dialectical principles of historical materialism to push for the evolution of a grounded, collective, and richly historical understanding of the politics which shape, for example, structural conditions within schools and society and how these impact the lives of teachers, students, and communities—an understanding which must be inextricably linked to our participation in transforming those conditions as part of the praxis of our teaching and research. The consequences of spending too much time theorizing, in the comfort of our classroom, office, or home, has resulted in an unexpected counterrevolution inside the progressive education movement that has led to a waste of activist labor, which has devolved our scholarship into what Marx calls "the prevalence of dead labor, weighing like a nightmare on the brains of the living."[25]

On an even more acerbic note, Frantz Fanon in *The Wretched of the Earth* was concerned with what he considered to be the laziness of intellectuals. He warned that "History teaches us clearly that the battle against colonialism does not run straight away along the lines of nationalism . . . It so happens that the *unpreparedness of the educated classes*, the lack of practical links between them and the mass of the people, their laziness, and let it be said, their cowardice at the decisive moment of the struggle will give rise to tragic mishaps."[26] Dunayevskaya, in *Philosophy and Revolution,* confirms that Fanon is very much in concert with Marx, who "stressed that thought can transcend only other thought; but to reconstruct society itself, only actions of men and women, masses in motion, will do the 'transcending,' and thereby 'realize' philosophy, make freedom and whole men and women a reality."[27]

As such, scholarly labor, alienated from the material conditions that produce the very suffering and oppression we seek to transform, can have little impact on our reimagining of the material conditions of inequalities and injustice. Put another way, social revolution is an organic, living, and communal process. In our teaching, research, and activism we must work to cultivate faith in the people, so that our eyes will remain open to the "relationship of theory to history as a historical relationship *made by masses in motion*."[28] And as such, it must retain the historical material dialectic of theory and practice proposed by Marx, if we are to effectively situate the formation of social imagination squarely within class struggle for societal transformation. But this cannot happen without entering into those public spaces where people can labor and unite, in their universality and diversity, as they make social revolution—a revolution anchored to the power and knowledge of our lived histories, ancestral knowledges, and shared dreams for a just world.

NOTES

1. Keynote presented at the Marxism Analysis of Society, School and Education SIG meeting at the American Educational Research Association meeting in New Orleans on April 8, 2011.
2. Engels, F. (1872). *The Housing Question.* Published as a pamphlet. See: http://www.marxists.org/archive/marx/works/1872/housing-question/index.htm.
3. See: Portes, A. (1998). *Social Capital: Its Origins and Application in Modern Sociology in Annual Review of Sociology.* Vol 24, pp. 1–24. See: http://www.soc.washington.edu/users/matsueda/Portes.pdf
4. Bourdieu, P. 1977. Outline of a Theory of Practice. Cambridge and New York: Cambridge University Press.
5. See: Darder, A. & Torres, R. (forthcoming). Introduction to *Latinos and Education: A Critical Reader.* New York: Routledge.
6. See: http://motherjones.com/politics/2011/02/income-inequality-in-america-chart-graph.
7. See: http://www2.ed.gov/about/overview/fed/role.html.
8. See; Rosa Luxembourg's (1971) *The Mass Strike: The Political Party and the Trade Unions and The Junius Pamphlet.* New York: Harper & Row (111).
9. M. Harrington (1962). *The Other American.* New York: Macmillan.
10. Marx, K. and F. Engles (1848). *The Communist Manifesto.* See: http://www.marxists.org/archive/marx/works/1848/communist-manifesto/.
11. Mills, C. W. (1959). *The Sociological Imagination.* New York: Oxford University Press (pp. 6–7).
12. Marx, K. (1859). *Introduction to the Critique of Political Economy.* Moscow: Progress Publishers. See http://www.marxists.org/archive/marx/works/1859/critique-pol-economy/index.htm.
13. Ibid. See: http://www.marxists.org/archive/marx/works/1859/critique-pol-economy/preface-abs.htm.
14. See: http://www.faqs.org/periodicals/201104/2333848481.html.
15. See: http://socialistworker.org/2009/05/11/the-point-is-to-change-it.
16. Ibid.
17. Peters. M. (2001). *Poststructuralism, Marxism, and Neoliberalism: Between Theory and Politics.* New York: Rowman and Littlefield.
18. Op cit. p.117.
19. Ibid.
20. Marx, K. (1867). *Das Kapital.* Republished later by Progress Publishers in Moscow.
21. Dunayevskya, R. (2000). *Marxism and Freedom.* New York: Humanity Books (p. 106).
22. Guevara, E. C. (1960). *Notes for the Study of the Ideology of the Cuban Revolution.* See http://www.marxists.org/archive/guevara/1960/10/08.htm.
23. Katsiaficas, G. (2009). *The Eros Effect: People Power and People's Uprisings.* See http://video.google.com/videoplay?docid=2409454858610160198&hl=en.
24. Marx, K. (1859). *A Contribution to the Critique of Political Economy.* See http://www.marxists.org/archive/marx/works/1859/critique-pol-economy/index.htm.

25. Marx, K. (1852). *The Eighteenth Brumaire of Louis Bonaparte*. See http://www.marxists.org/archive/marx/works/1852/18th-brumaire/ch01.htm.
26. Fanon, F. (1961). *Wretched of the Earth*. Chapter 3. See http://www.marxists.org/subject/africa/fanon/pitfalls-national.htm.
27. Dunayevskaya, R. (1973). *Philosophy and Revolution*. See http://www.marxists.org/archive/dunayevskaya/works/phil-rev/dunayev9.htm.
28. Ibid.

11 A Critical Pedagogy of Revolutionary Solidarity Against Neoliberal, White-Supremacist, Petrochemical Plunder

A Conversation with Curry Stephenson Malott

Orelus: *Most progressive educators have faced obstacles teaching at institutions that are capitalist market driven and therefore leave insufficient space for them to do critical and social justice–type of work. How have you witnessed and experienced this form of corporatization of schools?*

Malott: Not good. It is a constant battle fighting for real academic rigor beyond standardization. The discourse of business is increasingly employed by educational leaders to frame issues around profitability and consumer satisfaction. Rigor is being equated to increased standardization. Engaging these battles is time consuming and emotionally draining. One must, therefore, weight the effectiveness of fighting each individual battle as it presents itself and decide where your time and energy would be best spent in the service of the larger movement against neoliberal global capitalism and for humanity, to paraphrase the Zapatistas. It is easy to get lost in never-ending battles resulting in the feeling of losing control of your labor power. I have found that in environments where the administration and most of the faculty support market-driven approaches, it is smart to focus on working with like-minded colleagues on constructing critical pedagogies we can use with our own students. This includes maintaining an active schedule of research, conference presentations, and critical networking.

Market approaches to education have just reinforced the idea that capitalism is not some abstract thing, but is the product of a perpetually shifting set of relationships between people. Treating professors as an investment, where the managers of education seek to constantly lower wages to increase profitability, is a human-created policy informed by a specific ideology. For this policy to work, wage earners must either consent to the terms of the relationship, or they must be forced, physically. Because capitalism, within the discourse of domination, is equated with democracy, physical force is not an option for maintaining the hegemony. The larger population, who hold democratic values, would not stand for it. The system therefore relies on consent and the fear of redundancy.

Consent is achieved through a complex system of propaganda and indoctrination mechanisms in schools and the corporate media, as is very well documented in the literature. Market approaches to education not only view educators in economic terms, but they also view students as a source of income and, if managers are successful, a source of profit. I have therefore witnessed academic vice presidents compromise academic rigor in hopes of satisfying customers (students) who just want their degree and straight A's. The idea is that if the program is viewed as an easy path to teacher certification, then market demand will rise, and more consumers will seek this product (a degree from the institution). Working at one of these certification factories, I have overheard students saying to one another, "I just want my twenty thousand dollar A," referring to the cost of tuition. For a time, this worked: student enrollment soared, profits were high, more workers (professors) were hired, and life was good at the factory.

Then in 2008 the stock market crashed; working people took the heat, losing retirements and homes at alarming rates, and, consequently, customers (students) quit coming. We were in a recession. We had more supply (knowledge units represented in full- and part-time faculty members) than demand (students wanting degrees from our programs). The institution was in crisis. Workers (professors) were laid off. The smell of fear was strong. A new dean was hired to straighten things out. A new marketing strategy, a new business model, was employed: Rather than focus on quantity, the new call was for quality, which is what consumers really want, we were told. If the reputation can be altered from a program of low quality to one of high quality, then students will come, we were reassured, because it is not simply just a degree that consumers want, but a degree with merit.

The business model continues. This is an important point. The institution of higher learning is part of how the settler society reproduces itself. It exists to perpetuate the capitalist system. But this purpose is not overt. Capitalism and colonial occupation and economic plunder of indigenous lands have been normalized and naturalized to such an extent that their practices are not even named, but are presumed to represent the natural, objective outcome of human progress linearly marching forward toward a one-world empire of Eurocentric domination. Challenging this destructive process—a process that does not even spare its most loyal followers, White people—is the task of critical pedagogy in the 21st century.

Orelus: *What have you learned from these experiences?*

Malott: I have learned that if one produces a mountain of publications and books, and is able to provide publishing opportunities for their colleagues, the institution will pretty much leave you alone. In most contexts White radicals like myself can survive under the radar. Does this hold true for critical colleagues of color? While I can only speak for myself, I do know that White students, especially, are more likely to complain about critical colleagues of color than White critical colleagues.

Orelus: *Building alliances across the racial and gender lines has proven to be effective in fighting against racial and gender oppression. As a White ally who has been battling against racism in schools and beyond, what are some of the obstacles you have faced challenging people, including your students and family members, who may have held racist and sexist views about people of color and women?*

Malott: The challenge, of course, is the challenge of hegemony. That is, it is the challenge of successfully disrupting taken-for-granted perceptions of the world. This is no easy task. We are talking about our perceptual frameworks here, which people hold on to very tightly because they are what ground us in the world. Psychologically, it is not in our nature to seek feelings of uncertainty and insecurity. We want to be right and just. We want to be on the side of justice. When someone comes along and tells us we are not right, we naturally become very defensive.

Setting out to challenge people to become less racist and sexist therefore requires great sensitivity because it is too easy to offend and end all possibility of transformation. While keeping this contextualization in mind, we also need to be aware of the ways students tend to view the world based on their hegemonic socialization. Consider this myth: Learning occurs when students remember what they read and what was told to them by their teachers. Education, according to this ontological epistemology, is something that is done to you. It is a passive act. Knowledge here is not constructed but is predetermined, transcending time and culture. This point of view comes from the traditions of idealism and realism. Learning, according to students who have internalized the dominant paradigm, is therefore considered to be objective. There exists a right answer. Everything else is wrong. Critical scholar Joe Kincheloe has dubbed this tendency a machine cosmology/ontology, thereby critiquing the Cartesian reductionism of Descartes.

The danger of reducing one's understanding of the world and the relationships within it to a one-right-answer approach is that the Western Eurocentric perspective gets presented not as a philosophy or point of view, but as just how it is. That is, it is presented as existing independent of what people construct in their minds. The Eurocentric perspective of the ruling elite is, therefore, treated as objective reality, thereby subjugating the many African American, Black, Native American, Latina/o, working-class Whites' point of view and other points of view and experience. Because this hegemony is all-encompassing, all students, regardless of their positionality, gender, ethnicity, or race, tend to internalize it. This was the explicit goal of the Indian Boarding School project that the United States and Canada engaged in to assimilate Native Americans into the settler society as low-level wage earners. That is, Indians had to abandon their own ontologies and epistemologies and adopt Western philosophy that positions indigeneity as objectively primitive and inferior to the Western model.

This is significant because it teaches people who do not fit within current conceptions of Whiteness (in this case, students of color) to hate themselves or the backgrounds from which they came. It also highlights the Eurocentrism within the idea that capitalism represents the most advanced stage of human social evolution. That is, because capitalism is attributed to European sources within the discourse of empire, and because capitalism is presented as the end of rational history, and because world powers such as the United States and Great Britain paternalistically see themselves as the spreaders of capitalism, which they call democracy because they want to associate it with purity and supremacy, neoliberal capitalism since World War II has increasingly taken the form of Eurocentric imperialism.

Students, as a result, tend not to view their ideas as racist or Eurocentric, but as unbiased and objective. Herein lies the heart of the challenge: Students become confused and highly agitated when everything they have learned that represents what is good and democratic in the world is critiqued for representing everything that is bad and negative. When challenging students, family members or anyone else, the critical pedagogue must therefore not come across as elitist, paternalistic, or in any way superior.

We must demonstrate a genuine respect for all people so we will not blame the individual for internalizing the racist and sexist values, ideas, and beliefs of the dominant society. Again, the greatest challenge of the critical educator engaging in transformative, counterhegemonic work is not necessarily the racist or sexist student or person, although this factor is undoubtedly significant. The most challenging barrier is the self-righteousness of the critical pedagogue.

It is far too easy to blame the racist student or family member for their racism, leaving the larger racist society and our own teaching practices unexamined. To even begin thinking about student resistance, we must first ensure we are as effective as we can possibly be, and we must constantly be improving our own practice. That is, far too often substandard critical educators blame students for their disengagement, failing to take responsibility for their own shortcomings. As critical educators, we must therefore be lifelong learners staying up on the latest research while simultaneously contributing to it.

Orelus: *As you know, the social/political system of a country directly or indirectly influences the school system of this country. In your experience, to what extent has the U.S.-capitalist system affected the U.S.-school system, teachers' performance, and student learning?*

Malott: The system of mass, compulsory schooling in the U.S. was constructed as part of the ideological system of perpetuating the capitalist system. It is therefore not surprising that schooling continues to be directed by such capitalistic imperatives. After the Great Depression of 1929, the U.S.

working-class was radicalized. Since that time there has been a widespread culture of resistance that has grown and permeated the entire population, to greater and lesser extents.

Many teachers, like most other workers, are therefore concerned about earning a paycheck and not giving too much of themselves to a system they know is not just. We have especially witnessed this happen after the passage of the No Child Left Behind (NCLB) mandate, which has turned schooling, particularly at the secondary level, into a perpetual cycle of test prep. It has been widely argued by critical educators that NCLB is nothing more than a backdoor maneuver designed to set schools up to fail so they can be handed over to private for-profit managing companies.

For example, some critical scholars have suggested that NCLB is not really designed to increase learning and understanding, but to guarantee that schools will be graded as failing through a federally mandated system of high-stakes testing. That is, the testing would document students' failure, which would be ensured by selecting the least relevant, least contextualized approach to literacy development available, phonics. A phonics-based approach is only concerned with decoding words or sounding them out devoid of meaning or context. This vulgar reductionism is so intense that many phonics-based curricula use nonsense words to teach subjects how to decode sounds, such as *thop jop gack*. Part of what was excluded by the architects of NCLB in their review of the studies on how students learn to read was the long and rich tradition of qualitative research teeming with highly effective, engaging, contextualized, rigorous, complex, critical approaches to reading the word and the world.

These methods, many of which are philosophical antimethods, have proven highly engaging and conducive for fostering high-level, lifelong learners actively engaged in knowledge production as political praxis. It is therefore not surprising that the media have played a central role in perpetuating this fraudulent system by serving a propaganda function and setting the parameters of the debate, for example. Consequently, student learning and teachers' practices have been highly influenced by NCLB, and therefore capitalism.

Orelus: *Capitalism is essentially about profit. Therefore, capitalists' goals are to maximize their profits at the expense of workers. Do you then believe that we can still have equity and social equality in a capitalist society such as the U.S.? If so, how do you think this is possible? If not, why not?*

Malott: History has proven that the system can be made more or less oppressive through the regulation of capital (i.e., Bretton Woods and the New Deal) and social institutions (i.e., civil rights legislation). However, as long as the process of value production is in place, as McLaren and other Marxist educators have consistently pointed out, then the complete eradication of inequality and exploitation is, by definition, as you allude to in your question, not possible. It is therefore necessary to advocate for socially just reforms that offer relief for the most oppressed members of our communities while the larger vision of life after capital is simultaneously pursued. What this looks like in practice is a matter of tactics and should vary according to context. It is too easy to get caught up in reform movements and lose sight of larger postcapital/colonial goals.

Orelus: *What is your take on U.S. model of democracy? Also, what is your position on U.S. exportation of its form of democracy to developing countries?*

Malott: The U.S. model of democracy is based on the upstate New York Native American confederation of Six Nations, that is, the Haudenosaunee, who the French called the Iroquois. The idea was to unite all peoples around ideas of peace and coexistence for long-term sustainability. However, the founding fathers, as it were, of the United States were unwilling to deal with contradictions that would prevent the fledgling nation from achieving a viable nation. For example, they were unwilling to eradicate systems of coercive power and privilege from slavery to capitalism. Consequently, U.S. democracy has not been very democratic. It has been a model of imperial expansionism drawing on the paternalistic language of doing the inferior a favor, that is, giving them democracy allowing them to transcend the savagery of their own inferior traditions. This is U.S. democracy. It is a system of conquest that has thoroughly co-opted the language of democracy and social justice.

However, there is the potential of democratizing U.S. democracy, which requires subverting corporate influence over the governmental apparatus. It is the corporate agenda that has led U.S. foreign policy down the invading, antidemocratic path of imposing U.S. democracy around the world since WWII. What can be done to put the government into the hands of working people? We have to oppose corporate power. We have to fight today's global bosses who are at the head of the major corporations. However, rather than focusing exclusively on individual CEOs, we must depose the legal structure of corporate power that affords corporations the power of citizenship without the liability of actual people.

Orelus: *What role would you suggest that concerned citizens play in building a democratic society where people can freely express themselves without jeopardizing the freedom and life of others?*

Malott: According to the neoliberals, such as Friedman, intelligence and drive are naturally hierarchically distributed and thus any attempt to mandate equality is an attack on freedom because it prevents the naturally superior individuals or so-called races from rising to their predetermined place of power and dominance. Because my critical pedagogy and engagement with accepted cognitive science rejects these notions as propaganda designed to perpetuate a system of privilege and oppression, a true democracy will jeopardize what the ruling class views as their inherited and entitled freedoms. This does not bother me. The question I am interested in is how do we best ensure a new oppressive, exploitative ruling class does not rise out of the ashes of the old one, which is now the current one?

For me, the answer lies in critical education and avoiding an approach to movement building that follows the old model of building an army of mindless followers carrying out the orders of the vanguard or revolutionary leaders. I am therefore interested in horizontal movement structures where power and decision making are collective endeavors designed to build global solidarity networks sensitive to the complexity and diversity of the world's peoples. It is a movement that resists romantic conceptions of the working class unaffected by the hegemonic indoctrination the vast majority of the world's schools and corporate media expose all peoples to.

Orelus: *How would you imagine citizens being active participants in political and educational decision-making processes?*

Malott: Anarchist and indigenous traditions have a lot to offer here. There are tried and true structures people can experiment with. That takes the form of collectives and councils based not on majority rules but on consensus where decisions are not made until everyone agrees, not just most. This takes more time but, in the long run, is the only way to ensure some are not left behind. There is a vast body of work that documents this critical pedagogical approach to educational leadership. Consider the following examples:

In "Teacher Councils: Tools for Change," Bob Peterson (2003a) reflects on "a network of teacher-led, district wide councils" that operated within the Milwaukee Public Schools (MPS) during the 1990s having a "significant impact on reform in MPS" (p. 287). Peterson (2003a) describes this initiative and the resulting councils as significant because they "provided a way for progressive teachers to promote student-centered, anti-racist curricular reform" (p. 8). Conducive to our democratic choice for educational leadership, Peterson (2003a) describes the structure of these teacher councils—including, among many others, the Multicultural Curriculum Council, the Whole Language Council, the Humanities Council, and the Bilingual Council—as representing "a strategy that contrasts sharply with the top-down approaches that characterize many school reform initiatives" (p. 287). That is, "instead of imposing an external agenda developed far from classroom life, the teacher councils represented an opportunity for teachers to help shape the reform agenda and to bring credibility and leadership to the effort" (Peterson, 2003a, pp. 287–288) for school improvement.

The power of this movement of councils resided within the fact that it had been "integrated into a district wide curriculum reform effort with explicitly anti-racist goals" (Peterson, 2003a, p. 288). Also contributing to their effectiveness was the promotion of unity and solidarity through encouraging classroom teachers to "share their best practices" (Peterson, 2003a, p. 288), which stands in stark contrast to many school cultures where teachers view themselves as in competition with one another, and therefore never share teaching strategies or curriculum ideas. Peterson (2003a) also points to the model of formalizing "teacher collaboration, mobilization, and training," which transcends the limited reach of "one-time in services" (p. 288) creating the necessary spaces for long-term transformation, which many educational leaders would argue are cultural changes, that is, changes to the culture of the school, the district, the state, the country, and so on.

Because the model of professional development embraced by the councils required such a large time commitment on the part of teachers, the success of the councils was based on the district's decision to allocate funds to pay for substitute teachers. Again, adopting a teacher-led policy proved to be an effective way for the councils to work as peer-review structures ensuring that new practices were informed by sound research. Peterson (2003a) offers a number of factors that contributed to the demise of the councils, "including budget cuts, the push for radical, school-based decentralization, a shift away from the K–12 curriculum effort towards a school-to-work-focus, a national reform effort driven by standardized test scores, and some weaknesses within the councils themselves" (p. 294).

In *Summer Camp' for Teachers: Alternative Staff Development,* S. J. Childs (2003) provides another example of an educational reform effort informed by a democratic approach to leadership and a rigorous engagement with research. In this model of professional development the traditional top-down approach guided by outside experts is rejected for a teacher-led initiative. The rotating leadership method adopted by this Portland, Oregon–based Summer Literacy Institute, and the fact that it is fully funded by the district, has resulted in "the majority of Portland Public Schools' 175 high school language arts teachers" have been through the program and many have "led workshops during the year" (Childs, 2003, p. 297). The institute consists of "one week of intensive collaboration among teachers to develop curriculum units and workshops around multicultural texts" (Childs, 2003, p. 297). Childs reports that it has also been an effective way to train new teachers as they are paired with veteran, expert multicultural, critical pedagogues.

This model grew out of the dissatisfaction of being subjected to traditional in-service lecture formats where the experiences and professional knowledge of teachers tend to be ignored. The vision and goal of the Summer Literacy Institute, according to Childs (2003), is to achieve district-wide reform, which, it is believed, will provide safety to progressive educators who stand out and are therefore often targeted for harassment and demotion in uncritical, Eurocentric contexts.

Providing a more detailed picture of what these institutes look like in practice, Childs (2003) notes that "teachers engage in three main activities.

First, they read research articles on literacy, language, and achievement. Second, mornings are devoted to teachers sharing lessons" (p. 298). The third activity, which is designed to bring it all together, "in the afternoon teams of teachers meet to develop units filled with literacy lessons and strategies around a book or theme that are available for other teachers to use throughout the year" (Childs, 2003, p. 299). As an example of something created out of this democratic approach to curriculum development, Childs (2003) reflects on their desire to encourage teacher-facilitators to adopt books that "puts traditionally marginalized groups at the center" (p. 300). As a result, during the first year of the institute, the organizers adopted a set of guidelines for text selection, including "reflect high literary quality, have cross-cultural themes, actively challenge stereotypes, raise issues of class, race, gender, and justice, move beyond victimization and show resistance and empowerment, provide historical context and deepen cultural knowledge, and have the potential for use across the curriculum" (Childs, 2003, p. 300).

Here, in "Survival and Justice: Twin Goals for Teacher Unions," Peterson (2003b) makes a case for a social justice–oriented approach to teacher unionism, which, again, is conducive to our radically democratic call for educational leadership as critical pedagogy. Peterson describes two models of traditional unionism, industrial and professional, which he argues could better serve their constituencies and the communities in which they are situated by adopting "a new vision of unionism" (p. 309) he calls "social justice unionism." However, Peterson (2003b) notes that "these are somewhat arbitrary distinctions, most useful in helping to frame discussion. In practice, the models often overlap, blending into one another depending on circumstances" (p. 305). In general, though, Peterson (2003b) defines the industrial model as primarily concerned with "defending the working conditions and rights of teachers" (p. 305). The professional model, according to Peterson (2003b), "incorporates, yet moves beyond, the industrial model and suggests that unions also play a leading role in professional issues, such as teacher accountability and quality of school programs" (pp. 305–306). The social-justice model, while incorporating the practices of the industrial and professional models, "is linked to a tradition that views unions as part of a broader movement for social progress. It calls for participatory union membership; education reform focused on serving all children, with special attention to collaboration with parents and community organizations; and a concern for broader issues of equity throughout society" (p. 306).

Orelus: *Now we have the first Black U.S. president, Barack Obama. Throughout the presidential campaign, many people, including some of my progressive colleagues. were very hopeful that under Obama's administration the U.S. foreign policy toward other countries, particularly former colonized countries and currently U.S.-occupied territories, would not be as bad as it was under Georges Bush. Are you also hopeful in this regard?*

Malott: Of course we always hope for the best, but to believe this will happen without widespread movement from working people is naïve. Obama is a corporate guy. He works for the corporate power structure. He does not work for poor people despite his lofty rhetoric. His administration, in its first year of practice, has proven just as war-hawkish as George W. Bush and Dick Cheney. His increased activity in Afghanistan, now the longest running war in U.S. history, is a case in point. There were high hopes that Obama would usher in a new more humane era in U.S. foreign and domestic policy. Unfortunately, such hopes have not materialized, and the Left is now more divided, fractured, and confused than it was during George W. Bush, who represented a symbol of White male privilege and arrogance activists could easily rally support against.

Obama, on the other hand, is much more difficult for the Left to oppose. A large part of this failure, I would argue, stems from White people in general not knowing how to comfortably and counterhegemonically talk about race. That is, many Whites on the Left are scared that challenging Obama will make them look like racists. That is, people in general in the U.S. do not know how to talk about race in complex nonessentializing, nonromantic, or nondemonizing, racist ways. To put the necessary pressure on the Obama administration to embrace less imperialistic foreign policies, the White Left must become more adept at dealing with race and its historical development with the capitalist relations of productions situated in a homophobic and sexist dominant cultural context.

Orelus: *Do you foresee U.S. imperialism taking a different form or direction, hopefully a less ugly one, in the next decade to come?*

Malott: Only if working people are able to overcome our hegemonic indoctrination, work together and depose unjust policies and corporate power structures. It could happen, but it is not looking good. This is not surprising given the tendency for working-class Whites to be more susceptible to overtly racist politics at times when the working class's ability to demand high wages, a clean environment, and decent education, for example, is minimal, such as today. That is, working people throughout the world, and in the United States in particular, are more broke and less secure than they were twenty years ago, even just a couple of years ago before the financial crisis of 2009, the costs of which are always externalized to working people.

Because schools overwhelmingly tend not to provide working and middle-class students the intellectual tools needed to critically read not only the written word but their world and their place in it as well, we tend to be highly vulnerable to external propaganda campaigns. Consequently, White males in the United States are being told by populist-posing, corporate-backed groups like the Tea Party that their relative poverty is the consequence of being persecuted by non-Whites who have seized power and enacted affirmative action–type policies designed to redistribute their hard-earned wealth to undeserving Black welfare mothers and resource draining, tax-evading, non-English-speaking, Brown illegal immigrants from south of the border. As frightening as well it should be, far too many White males, and even people of color, are buying into this rhetoric, paving the way for very scary times ahead if the Left fails to offer a viable counter-hegemony that is far-reaching and readily accessible.

Again, rather than focusing on the rise in corporate power that is oppressing all of humanity, people of color most viciously, Whites are buying the racial scapegoating of Blacks and immigrants. This is very scary and very real as evidence by recent racist immigration laws in Arizona and New York. The only way U.S. policy will become less destructive, less imperialistic, is if we, as critical educators and revolutionary activists, are able to reach White people and assist them in developing more accurate analyses and embrace the long tradition of White criticality embodied by the White abolitionist John Brown, and the recently deceased Howard Zinn and Joe Kincheloe.

Poor Whites and people of color alike need to be reminded that real populism has never been divisive and never been funded and supported by corporate interests such as *Fox News*. Real populism would never receive the amount of airplay the Tea Party receives from all the major networks, especially *Fox News*. Real populism has never had a self-centered focus, but has always been about solidarity and supporting, first and foremost, those most oppressed by corporate greed and enslaving practices and institutions. This is our immediate challenge—reaching poor Whites who remain the vast majority of the U.S. population.

In addition to embracing our tragically lost White brothers and sisters, one of our other centrally important campaigns, based on my own analysis, is slowing down and eventually completely stopping the destructive path of industrialism and the global race for oil, which has not only spawned seemingly never-ending wars and occupations, but is threatening life itself. The challenge against oil is one of those issues that has the potential to unite the world because it is a practice that is destroying and toxifying the planet as one large living entity.

We need a new order, a new paradigm that rejects viewing the world as a series of natural resources whose sole purpose for existence is enriching and serving the needs of people. We need a way of being informed by the vision that acknowledges that all life has an inherent right to exist in its own environment. This vision rejects making decisions based on profitability. Economic decisions, rather, would be based on how they supported human and ecological diversity. Such practices as offshore oil drilling, oil drilling and using fossil fuels in general, for example, would never happen or even come close to happening. What I am describing here is an ontological shift. In other words, a shift in what one sees when one looks at the world. Rather than looking at a river and seeing potential hydroelectrical profits, one sees a fragile life giving force all species are dependent on for their health and perpetuation. From such a point of view, a society would not allow private interests to disrupt its internal ecosystem through any means such as damming or excessive irrigation and the introduction of petrochemical pesticides.

In short, this is revolutionary change, but real revolutionary change, a complete change, happens nonviolently, democratically, and is nonprescripted. Again, we come full circle. That is, nonprescripted change comes from an informed and critically conscious population, and this, of course, requires a critical education or some sort of critical socialization. Education just happens to be a tool already in place that can be subverted by critical educators and transformed from an indoctrinating system of hegemonic perpetuation into a liberating force against the very structures it was designed to reproduce.

REFERENCES

Childs, S.J. (2003). "'Summer Camp' for Teachers: Alternative Staff Development." In Linda Christensen and Stan Karp (Eds.). *Rethinking School Reform: Views from the Classroom*. Milwaukee, WI: Rethinking Schools.

Peterson, B. (2003a). Teacher Councils: Tools for Change." In Linda Christensen and Stan Karp (Eds.). *Rethinking School Reform: Views from the Classroom*. Milwaukee, WI: Rethinking Schools.

Peterson, B. (2003b). "Survival and Justice: Twin Goals for Teacher Unions." In Linda Christensen and Stan Karp (Eds.). *Rethinking School Reform: Views from the Classroom*. Milwaukee, WI: Rethinking Schools.

12 Understanding History From the Standpoint of the Oppressed

Pierre Wilbert Orelus

History and context are crucial for anti-colonial undertakings. Understanding our collective past is significant for pursuing political resistance.

—George J. Sefa Dei, *Anti-Colonialism and Education*

'History is the memory of states,' wrote Henry Kissinger in his first book, A World Restored, *in which he proceeded to tell the history of nineteenth-century Europe from the viewpoint of the leaders of Austria and England, ignoring the Millions who suffered from those statesmen's policies. From his standpoint, the "peace" that Europe had before the French Revolution was "restored" by the diplomacy of a few national leaders. But for factory workers in England, farmers in France, colored people in Asia and Africa, women and children everywhere except in the upper classes, it was a world of conquest, violence, hunger, exploitation—a world not restored but disintegrate.*

—Howard Zinn, *People's History of the United States*

The looking-glass school teaches us to suffer, not change it; to forget the past, not learn from it; to accept the future, not invent it.

—Eduardo Galeano, *Upside Down*

History as a discipline should not be simply about past narratives. Nor should it be a discipline that allows students to merely hear about their past and move on. History should be a vehicle through which students question and "deconstruct" (Derida, 1976) the past and connect it to the present in order to impact future events. History has of course been taught in school. But whose history has it been? Has it been the version of history that reflects the reality of both the Western and the Third World? Or has it been the one that glorified Napoleon Bonaparte and Christopher Columbus while rarely acknowledging, for example, the greatness of Toussaint-Louverture and Simón Bolívar, who, without sophisticated technology at their disposable, defeated the French and Spanish armies to set their people free from colonial subjugation and slavery? Drawing on historical events that shaped both the West and the Rest, in this chapter I analyze World History with a different eye, the oppressed's eyes.

Given the social milieu where I grew up, it took me decades to understand the dialectical relationship between the past, the present, and the future. This dialectical relationship, in my view, constitutes the fundamental triangle of humanity. For adults in my social milieu, however, it seems that one of the components of the triangle, the past, was a painful thing to talk about. They seemed to have an easier time to talk about its other two parts, the present and the future. Were not they right? Is not it a waste of human investment and intellectual energy talking about the past, which is already gone? Is not it sorrowful referring to a past marked by imperialism, bloodshed, human degradation, exploitation, and misery? Is not it a self-torture to speak of one's past that might haunt one's spirit and remind one of the devastating effects of slavery, as Alex Haley brilliantly illustrated in *Roots*. Is not it too dangerous for the mind of young people to allow them to be aware of the cruel brutality of human subjects that colonialism caused, as evidenced in the movie *The Battle of Algiers*? Finally, is not Wane (2006) right when she asserts, "The struggle to retrieve the past and survive the present is an arduous journey"? (p. 34).

Analyzing these questions in a very superficial way, one might agree with the adults in my neighborhood who subconsciously seemed to fear the past while embracing the present and the future. Furthermore, given that one cannot shape or reconstruct the past, it seems logical to simply forget about it and focus on the present and the future. However, I ask: (1) What sense would have the world made to one's mind if it had only entailed the happening of the present and the uncertainty of the future? Alluding to one of the themes, colonialism, which I elaborate on later in this chapter, I ask: (2) Would its legacy and impact on human subjects get registered in one's mind if there were no critical questioning of the past? Finally, how would one be informed of the role that women played in the fight against slavery and colonization if one did not have a clear understanding of the past? In this regard, Dei (2006) notes,

> For colonized peoples decolonization involves reclamation of the past, previously excluded in the history of the colonial and colonized nations. They must identify the colonial historical period from the perspectives of their places and their peoples. Knowledge of the past is also relevant in so far as we as people must use that knowledge 'responsibly.' (p. 1)

Therefore, as one can infer from Dei's argument, trying to discourage the oppressed from critically questioning the "pastness of the past," Eliot (1932) is historically and humanly harmful. However, this has been the ideological tool used by the dominant class to maintain the status quo. Edward Said (1993) noted, "How we formulate or represent the past shapes our understanding and views of the present" (p. 65). Said's idea is clearly understood and appropriated by the dominant class, who has been trying to control the mind of the oppressed through public consent so that the latter will not interrogate the past. This dominant class also understands that allowing the oppressed to interrogate the past might enable them to understand their present situation and how it came into being. For this reason, it is too dangerous to let the oppressed discover the truth about their past. Such a discovery is too threatening to the interest of the oppressing class. This logical reasoning that I am making hopes to help the reader unveil the hidden agenda of the ideological game that the dominant class has played to control the mind of oppressed people. The logic behind this ideological game is that once the mind of the oppressed is domesticated, they most likely will be unable to revolt against their present inhuman economic and social conditions, which usually result from past historical events.

Going back to pertinent issues such as slavery and colonization mentioned earlier, I argue that encouraging silence about these issues is not only humanly harmful but it is also intellectually irresponsible, as Said (1993) reminds us. Said states:

> One cannot postpone discussions of slavery, colonialism, racism in any serious investigations of modern Indian, African, Latin and North American, Arabic, Caribbean, and Commonwealth literature. Nor is it intellectually responsible to discuss them without referring to their embattled circumstances either in post-colonial societies or as marginalized and/or subjugated subjects confined to secondary spots in the curricula in metropolitan centers. (p. 316)

Postponing discussions of important issues, such as slavery, colonialism, and racism, as Said noted above, has been the tireless ideological strategy that the White dominant class has used to stay in powerful positions in society. Institutions such as school, the media, and church have been in some cases the channels through which outright lies and silence about these issues have been circulated. In other words, these institutions have been used as an ideological apparatus tool to freeze people's "presence of mind" (Leistyna, 1999) so that they can become docile recipients of the dominant class's lies aimed to make the oppressed loyal and obedient servants of the imperial world.

It is no accident that history of colonialism and neocolonialism is rarely taught in most universities here in the United States. It is not an accident either that postcolonial studies have not been funded at some universities in the United States. However, disciplines such as engineering, business administration, and computer science, which generally do not question the status quo, have been greatly funded. It will be simply too dangerous to allow neocolonial subjects to have access to true historical facts that might empower them to stand against their longtime oppressors. It will be even more dangerous to allow "this group of people," as often described by the dominant class, to find out that the true version of world history has been mostly confiscated by White Western conservative dominant groups. The artificial version of world history that they have made available to neocolonized subjects has been written in a way that serves their interest. Had the oppressed group been allowed to know the truth about past events that shaped their lives, they would have certainly demanded world history to be rewritten in a way that is not biased, that is, in a way that recognizes and values the heroic action and powerful voices of Toussaint-Louverture, Patrice Lumumba, Simón Bolívar, Amilcar Cabral, Cesar Chavez, Thomas Sankara, and Walter Rodney, among others, who have been silenced and put in a narrow historical box through the Western version of world history written by the White dominant class. Furthermore, the oppressed would have been knowledgeably well prepared to refute "lies that they have been told in school by their teachers," as Loewen (1995) pointed out, about Christopher Columbus, the so-called discoverer of the New World. They would also have wanted to know, as brilliantly captured by Howard Zinn (2003), what "Columbus did to the Arawaks of the Bahamas, Cortes did to the Aztecs of Mexico, Pizarro to the Incas of Peru, and the English settlers of Virginia and Massachusetts to the Powhatans and the Pequots" (p.34). Equally crucial, they would have wanted to have access to the truth about their own history, that is, history of their people who were great scientists, philosophers, inventors, real warriors, and yet have been shadowed throughout the Western version of world history. Finally, had the oppressed been taught the Third World version of world history, they would have certainly known the following historical facts:

1. The Indians invented a nascent form of calculus centuries before Leibniz invented calculus in Europe (Joseph, 1991, p. 67).
2. The Arabs coined the term "algebra" and invented decimal fractions: point twenty-five for one over four (Ibid., p. 29).
3. The Indians developed the use of zero and negative numbers perhaps a thousand years before these concepts were accepted in Europe (Teresi, 2002 p. 28).
4. The Mayans invented zero about the same time as the Indians, and practiced a math and astronomy far beyond that of medieval Europe (Ibid., p. 13).
5. Native Americans built pyramids and other structures in the American Midwest larger than anything then in Europe (Teresi, 2002, p. 67).
6. The Egyptians also developed the concept of the lowest common denominator, as well as a fraction table that modern scholars estimate required eight thousand tedious calculations to compile (Hogben, 1993, p. 89).

7. The Olmecs and Zapotes in Southern Mexico, the Maya in Southern Mexico, Guatemala, and Belize, and finally the Aztecs were founding civilizations before the Spaniards conquered Central America, murdered the native people, and exhausted their resources (Teresi, 2002, p. 69).
8. Aristotle struggled to accept the fact that the Egyptians developed math before his countrymen. He argued: "The mathematical sciences originated in the neighborhood of Egypt because there the priestly class was allowed leisure" (Fowler, 1987, p. 45).
9. "The mathematical foundations of Western science is an intelligent gift from the Indians, Egyptians, Chinese, Arabs, Babylonians, and others" (Teresi, 2002, p. 34).
10. Finally, in spite of the fact that we were told that Democritus was the first particle physicist, his idea was not a new idea (Teresi, 2002, 1999). According to Steven Weinberg (1992), "Indian metaphysicists came upon the idea of atoms centuries before Democritus" (p. 88), who drew upon the ideas of his predecessors to come up with many of ideas endorsed today by physicists.

The historical facts cited above make clear that history needs to be retold in a way that encompasses and captures the significant contributions of Third World scientists and inventors to the scientific advancement of the world. Once the prohibited historical truth is told, Third World scientists and inventors will no longer be denied full credit for their discovery and inventions. No longer will their legacy be shadowed in Western history textbooks. My contention is that oppressed groups need to have access to the truth about Third World scientists, inventors, and heroic historical figures who shaped world history.

As noted earlier, history has been taught al all levels in school from kindergarten to college levels. But from what and whose perspective has it been taught? Has not it been the history that reflects and protects the interest of the Western world? Has the history of the neocolonial subjects and the oppressed been taught to them? If so, has it been taught by teachers emerging from the group of the neocolonized? Or, alternatively, has it been taught by those who are knowledgeable and historically conscious and sensitive to neocolonial subjects' long historical struggle?

History should be a fountain of knowledge from which one can retrieve varying historical features of the past. Such historical features of the past should aim to empower oppressed people so they can make sense of what shapes their historical being, as well as what informs or should inform their present and future beings. In other words, history should be used as a tool to interrogate or, better yet, "deconstruct" (Derrida, 1976) the past in order to have a better understanding of it. In short, as Zinn (2003) notes:

> If history is to be creative, to anticipate a possible future without denying the past, it should, I believe, emphasize new possibilities by disclosing

those hidden episodes of the past when, even if in brief flashes, people showed their ability to resist, to join together, occasionally to win. I am supposing, or perhaps only hoping, that our future may be found in the past's fugitive moments of compassion rather than in its solid centuries of warfare. (p. 11)

REVITALIZING AND HONORING THE PAST

Any society that genuinely cares for the intellectual nourishment and growth of the youth should strongly encourage them to critically analyze historical events that have shaped the past. I argue that analyzing these events would help them become culturally and historically informed critical beings. Past events should not be frozen or buried in the past. Rather, they should be revitalized, cherished, honored, and used to inform us what path to take in order to enlighten our present life with hope, whose power would enable us to shape or at least imagine a world of possibilities for everyone regardless of their racial, ethnic, linguistic, social class backgrounds, and sexual orientation. As Trask (1991) argues, "We do not need, nor do we want to be liberated from our past because it is source of our understanding . . . We stand firmly in the present, with our back to the future, and our eyes fixed upon the past, seeking historical answers for present-day dilemmas" (Trask as cited in Dei & Kempf, 2006, p. 33). Unfortunately, standing in and blocking the path to a clear understanding of the past have been Western colonialists' and neocolonialists' ideological agenda. An agenda that reveals itself in preventing neocolonial subjects and oppressed groups from having access to a collective critical and accurate knowledge of their past. Western neocolonialists' fear is that if neocolonized people and other oppressed groups had a critical and sound understanding of their past, they would then dare imagine and fight for a better world where resources will be justly distributed between Third World people and Westerners. Nonetheless, despite the ideological apparatus that has allowed Western dominant groups to tell outright lies about the history of the world, some scholars emerging from oppressed groups in society have challenged those lies and insisted on finding out other versions of world history. They realize that if they fail to do so they will be just like zombies deprived of recollection of who their ancestors were. Thus, it goes without saying that a critical analysis and understanding of the past is quintessential to one's historical being.

Historians and anthropologists, such as Cheikh Anta Diop (1991) and Walter Rodney (1972), are prime examples of scholars who refused to stay on the margin of world history. They urged their contemporaries and future generations not to live in the shadow of world history. In Cheikh Anta Diop's view, historical factor is of paramount importance. He believed that such a factor contributes to a sense of collectiveness and unity among people. Diop (1991) maintained, "The historical factor is the cultural cement that unifies the disparate elements of a people to make them into a whole, by the particular slant of the feeling of historical community lived by the totality of the collective" (p.45). Like the Antiguan historian Walter Rodney, Cheick Anta Diop tirelessly fought with his pen and brain against the dominant ideology of the European class that has strived to make oppressed groups become spectators of historical events. The scholarly work and intellectual activism of this prominent Senegalese critical thinker have inspired many "postcolonial" subjects, including myself, to be actors/actresses and makers of history, rather than passive historical events recipients. More importantly, Diop has encouraged the oppressed to not miss the historical rendezvous to collectively and actively reflect on their past, act on their present, and envision a bright future for themselves and fellow human beings. This of course has made him and others become what I would call dangerous historical critical thinkers of the imperial world.

"These people," as the Western conservative dominant class usually calls them, are fully aware that the past is such a great treasure to lose or waste. Therefore, they have fought to keep it alive through critical political analysis and social activism. They are cognizant of the fact that whoever has monopoly over the past will be in the best ideological position to invent and manipulate the law to control the disinherited. This is precisely the reason why these dangerous historical critical thinkers deem it imperative to interrogate the past and engage in an ideological battle with those who have been tirelessly trying to control it. They also understood that the propaganda that has been circulated through the mass media, schools, and churches to convince the marginalized to "get over" history of colonialism and slavery is a mechanism used by the Western conservative dominant class to win the battle over the past.

It must be emphasized here that the battle over the hegemonic control of the past has always been between those who have been exploited and those who have been profiting from their exploitation. Therefore, it is not unusual to find privileged groups in society telling oppressed groups to move on with their lives and leave behind the sad historical past of their countries or people. Their convincing sounding slogan usually goes like this: This is the past; this happened years ago; we are in the 21st century; get over it, young men or women; move on. This type of slogan is not neutral; nor is it innocent. In fact, I argue that it aims to serve the interest of the Western conservative dominant group that has worked tirelessly to make the "subaltern" (Spivak, 1988) ignorant of their history, their past. The Western conservative dominant class does not want the dominate group to understand that "The starting-point of critical elaboration is the consciousness of what one really is, and is 'knowing thyself' as a product of the historical process to date, which has deposited in you an infinity of traces, without leaving an inventory. Therefore, it is imperative at the outset to compile such an inventory" (Gramsci, 1971, p. 67).

This dominant group clearly understands that individuals who are able to critically assess and analyze their historical past can become a threat to corporate interests. Therefore, these individuals must be kept ignorant of their history. This has been the political and ideological strategy used by the conservative dominant group in Western capitalist countries. Though sad, this conservative dominant group has been thus far successful with this strategy. How has it been successful? How did this happen? My contention is that one can find answers to these questions by carefully studying the right-wing dominant groups in society. In other words, one must study the right wings in order to know how they think, operate, and act. Otherwise, ideologically one probably would not be in the best position to strategically counter their hegemonic actions against oppressed people.

In ending this chapter, I want to emphasize that economic, social, and political dominations of the "other" by the oppressing group have been made possible by the latter's hegemonic control of the past. By maintaining oppressed groups in an ocean of lies circulated through Western canonical texts and the mass corporate media, the oppressing group has been able to dictate what parts of world history to which the former is allowed to have access. The oppressed group thus far has been simply allowed to know "facts" about world history that would not threaten the status quo. Unless history is rewritten in a way that reflects the voice of the enslaved, the neocolonized, and Third World historical figures, the neocolonized and oppressed groups will merely be allowed to know the romantic version of their own history but not the true and real version of their historical past. As a result, this lack of historical awareness might lead them to narrate their story in a way that is not authentic, that is, in a way that merely reflects the Western dictatorship of truth. Fortunately, as previously noted, there have been historians and anthropologists, such as Walter Rodney and Cheick Anta Diop, among others, who have challenged and resisted the historical dictatorship of Western empires. They have done so by refusing to be simply observers of historical events that have shaped their lives and that of others. They have refused to be absent at the historical rendezvous where the ideological battle over the monopoly of the past has been taking place. They want to be continuously there so that they can design or redesign current and past historical events based on their own understanding of the world history. Neocolonized and occupied people need to join them in the struggle to interrogate and rewrite world history through the lens of historical, socioeconomic, and political realities of both the so-called Third World and the Western world.

REFERENCES

Dei, S. G., & Kempf, A. (2006). (Eds.). *Anti-colonialism and education*. Rotterdam/Taipei: Sense Publishers.

Derida, J. (1976). *Of grammatology*. Baltimore: Johns Hopkins Press.

Diop, A. C. (1991). *Civilization or barbarism: An authentic anthropology*. New York: Lawrence Hill Books.

Eliot, T. S. (1932). *Critical essays*. London: Faber & Faber.
Fowler, H. D. (1987). *The mathematics of Plato's academy*. Oxford: Clarendon Press.
Gramsci, A. (1971). *Selections from the prison notebooks*. New York: International.
Hogben, L. (1993). *Mathematics for the million*: How to master the magic of millions New York: W. W. Norton & Company.
Joseph, G. G. (1991). *The crest of the peacok: Now-European roots of mathematiques*. London: Penguin Books.
Leistyna, P. (1999). *Presence of mind: Education and the politics of deception*. Oxford: Westview Press.
Loewen, J. (1995). *Lies my teacher told me: Everything your American history textbook got wrong*. New York: New Press.
Rodney, W. (1972). *How Europe underdeveloped Africa*. Washington, DC: Howard University Press.
Said, E. (1993). *Culture and imperialism*. New York: Vintage Books.
Spivak, G. (1988). Can the subaltern speak? In C. Nelson & L. Grossberg (Eds.), *Marxism and the interpretation of culture*. Chicago: University of Illinois Press.
Teresi, D. (2002). *Lost discoveries: The ancient roots of modern science—from the Babylonians to the Maya*. New York: Simon & Schuster.
Wane, N. N. (2006). Is decolonization possible? In G. J. Sefa & A. Kempf (Eds.), *Anti-colonialism and education: The politics of resistance* (pp. 87–106). Rotterdam/Taipei: Sense Publishers.
Zinn, H. (2003). *A people's history of the United States*. New York: Harper & Row.

13 Uncovering Racial, Socioeconomic, and Political Domination Through the Western Neocolonial and Neoliberal Agenda

A Conversation With Sangeeta Kamat

Orelus: Professor Sangeeta, would you begin by saying a little bit about yourself? Perhaps you can start by talking about where you're from and grew up and what you have been doing, say, the ten years or so?

Sangeeta: I grew up in Bombay in a middle class family. No one in my family is from the academic field. My mother was a school teacher, and I always promised myself that I would not be a school teacher but here I am. I ended up in this field. So it's kind of ironic. Growing up in Bombay and probably this is true in any Third World city, you cannot escape being politicized in some way just through daily observation and every day encounters. My parents had migrated from a rural area to Bombay. They were the first generation that migrated from the rural area to the big city for jobs, for better opportunities. I grew up in a middle class locality in a modest one bedroom apartment. When you step out of that sort of comfortable life, of the middle class colony (and these are called colonies!) where everyone is like you, the first thing you encounter in a city like Bombay are people living on the sidewalks, in slums, and you start having to question why they are where they are and why are you where you are. It's not an accident that they end up where they are; there has to be a logic to this, a system by which these different conditions of life are produced—Why? How? These were questions I had no answers to but was troubled by the obvious unfairness of it all. I remember asking the question, and my grandmother replying 'they are lazy therefore they are poor'. But that seemed so patently false even to my child's mind, because what you see quite visibly — because their lives are so exposed, they have no privacy — is that they work all the time! Growing up in Bombay, you see poor people differently, for instance, from the way they are constructed in the development literature. You see them trying to make a life for themselves and their children. They have children; they have joyous weddings in the slums. There's humor and playfulness. You also see a sense of resilience among the poor. Regardless of circumstances, they try to make a life for themselves. The way that they preserve their humanity is incredible, and you have to recognize it because it's there; visually it's on display. Going back and forth from school or going to college you get to chat with them. It was during the time when I was in college and through my involvement in a women's organization in Bombay I started becoming a political person. Forum Against Oppression of Women, a new organization had been launched in the 1980s in Bombay. It was a remarkable thing. This group was composed of middle class and lower middle class women. It had started off as a shelter for women who were escaping abusive, violent households. I frequently attended meetings that this group organized, as a silent participant, learning, absorbing. I was in junior college at the time, (11th and 12th grade here) not having any feminist framework or language, but it was a visceral connection to women's issues at the time. My father is a very liberal, modern father; he would encourage discussion and questions. It's my mother who was deeply sexist—in how she treated my brother differently from me and my sister, in her expectations, the traditions we were expected to follow, she laid the line. So that was my first lesson, that women could be sexist and anti-feminist. Feminist theory, its analysis of patriarchy and how men and women are part of reproducing patriarchy, helped me make sense of these paradoxes, but that came much later. Though we sharply disagreed, feminist theory helped me understand and empathize with my mother. From seeing her as my oppressor, I began to understand these things systemically, historically, politically.

I did my Master's in social work. The social work program in India is designed very differently from here. It's not the professional training to be part of the state bureaucracy kind of thing. There's a whole lot of activist and more community based engagement. The training and the people who were our teachers and the kinds of field placements we had helped us understand the lived reality of poverty and social inequality. We learned that there were people doing all kinds of things in the cities and the rural areas outside of Bombay, like creating slum dweller organizations, mobilizing peasant women, conscientizing tribal youth and organizing women's forums where strategies for action were mapped out. The focus wasn't service work or individual case work like social work programs in the U.S. There was plenty of political activity going on in the city and around, and these activists would come to our classrooms; it opened up a whole new world for me that was incredibly inspiring. Our teachers were part of those kinds of involvements and they would come and teach us about them, share their work and their experiences. These were feminists, social activists, political activists in the mid 1980s. The anti-dam movement with a woman, Medha Patkar as its leader, who had graduated from my institute was making national headlines. The movement had a deep impact on my generation of students. There were other teachers who had started organizing slum dwellers on housing rights. It was a dynamic time of independent political organizing, anti-state, separate from Left party politics, and was before NGOs came on the scene and professionalized such work. My first book is about understanding the transformation of this political culture of independent grassroots organizing into a professional depoliticized NGO culture.

With the exposure and the influence of Paulo Freire's work, I came to see education as a key to social transformation. When I learned about a program in Pittsburgh on International Development and Education, that is, education as it applies to developing country contexts, I said, "Oh, that's what I want to do." This kind of a program wasn't available in India. In India, education degrees are very much about teacher training. On a lark I applied to Pittsburgh and got accepted. Otherwise, I would have gone to a university in India, most likely studying anthropology or history in Delhi.

When I came here, I realized that development education programs within Schools of Education are so much part of the cold war history of this country. These programs were founded to ensure that education in Third World countries remained within the U.S. sphere of influence. It wasn't out of a commitment or solidarity with Third World societies and their education needs. Rather, it was cold war interventionist politics where education faculty were enlisted to write textbooks and manage adult literacy programs in Third World countries funded by the U.S. state department that sustained these graduate programs. These programs were founded in the 1960s when the US state department was looking for academics to train entire ministries of education in developing countries, who wanted to ensure American influence on education policy in Africa, Latin America, the Middle East and Asia. If one follows the kind of projects that faculty worked on in these programs, and in which countries, you can see a clear line that connects these to the geopolitical interests of the US at the time. So really it was the imperialist project in action all over again, through the benign path of education. It really brought me face to face with the benevolent face of imperialism, what others have called 'soft imperialism'. I did not realize this until after I joined. As for me, I joined this program with a commitment to social justice, to figure out how I can use education to effect social change. I felt out of synch in that program because I followed a different trajectory from most of my professors and class mates, many who were training to be bureaucrats in their respective countries or become consultants for the World Bank. These were well-meaning people, I respected them as experts in their field but you could not escape the fact that they/we were part of the institutional network that keeps poor countries in debt that manages neocolonial relations for the U.S. I was lucky that there were a few faculty who were critical scholars, one of them was my PhD supervisor.

Orelus: You moved from India to the United States. You've been a Professor for over10 years now? Would you share how your experience in the U.S. Academy has been?

Sangeeta: There's no preparation of what to really expect as a woman faculty of color, there was no mentorship, to anticipate what it is like to be the odd one out, because I think for the most part professors who had taught me, all white American, hadn't gone through it themselves. The unstated norm in these programs is that 'we will train you so you can return to your country to practice what you have been taught.' To be a colleague, to be on equal terms, to question the teaching and propose different course materials, that is not part of the expectation. For me, it's been a learning curve, a very steep learning curve.

There's a whole liberal discourse around multiculturalism, diversity, affirmative action, and the importance of having faculty of color at universities. When you enter these institutions, you realize that there's so little in terms of actual recognition, appreciation, and respect for faculty of color and for diversity. As a new assistant professor I remember American students in the program expected me to teach a course on yoga! You are a token, and they'd like you to stay that way. There are exceptions of course, individual colleagues who don't fall in this category, but for the most part, the entire culture of the institution, departments as a whole would rather you operate as a token, and not bring yourself, your questions, your perspective into the academic space. When I came in I found that there's this constant pressure to prove oneself over and over again. There's constant questioning of one's capabilities, competency, and contribution. And also because I think one's particular kind of political commitments to Third World people and their struggles—- this directs my work very differently. So the work has to emerge from the issues and questions that are coming up in those regions, from the people's struggles in particular places rather than from what funding is available at the moment or what the USAID or World Bank is interested in funding at this point. I find in my field a certain kind of fickleness, in what people research or write about. For the most part, faculty are chasing the funding, overnight they become experts and consultants in a completely new part of the world, in a country they have never stepped into, just because that's where the money is, the grants and projects are, typically from the US government or from large aid agencies. Once the funding stops, they are out of there. The place, the people, the issues are left behind. They move on to a new project. These shifts in funding and therefore their academic engagement mirrors the shifts in the US government's geopolitical interests. It is no surprise therefore that Guatemala and El Salvador were once the flavor of the season, and now it is Afghanistan and Pakistan. So programs such as mine are reduced to becoming the handmaidens of U.S. interests. Students who criticize academia as the ivory tower removed from the real world have got it so wrong. The university is deeply engaged with real world politics, representing the interests of the powerful. That's what needs to change. There is no space for a different kind of investment in scholarly political work, a commitment to a people. And budget cuts, the entrepreneurial university makes it that much harder to balance these commitments.

I was the first woman of color to be hired in 36 years. To my knowledge there had not been--in my program a faculty of color since its inception. It was a lonely time. I survived by reaching out to people that I could count on as allies and people that I could draw strength from in other departments and in other parts of the university. There is no point feeling sorry for oneself. One always finds like-minded people in every institution. Today there are many more of us in the university. But even then my experience is that race and gender are, even though we get hired, sort of off the table. There's almost no space to discuss or raise these issues. I think the rise of neoliberalism has increased that gap in terms of being able to tackle issues of social justice and race and gender. In the context of academic or intellectual scholarship or programming or course work that gap has only gotten wider. There is an instrumentalism that has become all pervasive that neoliberalism thrives on.

Orelus: *Speaking of that many institutions have been following the corporate model of education including University of Massachusetts where you are currently teaching and where I got my doctorate from. So what is your take on that?*

Sangeeta: There is a lot of good scholarship on the corporatization of universities. It's a global phenomenon. Higher education is being modeled along the lines of a market economy. As in a market economy, the more scarce the good, the more it is valued. So reproduction of inequalities of all kinds is part of the logic of the education market. Thus Ivy leagues need to be only of a certain number with limited enrolments to maintain their prestige. If we were to make Ivy leagues the universal standard, the educational norm, they would lose their position in the education market.

At a basic level therefore markets in education are undemocratic, though neoliberals would have us believe otherwise. Stratification is built into the market and everybody is vying to move up in the hierarchy or to improve their position in this market. If you buy into the rules of the game, into education being part of a market economy, then you enter into this competition with other universities to better your position, no matter the costs to minority students, to first generation college goers, no matter the mission of higher education. And this is what public universities like UMass are engaged in. It is a losing battle though because the elite universities will do things to improve their position, and the competition just keeps getting tougher, and in the process we lose track of why we came into academia to begin with or what is the purpose of higher education. And certainly minority students have taken a hit. You see less and less of the working class population in public universities. And at the same time there is a lot of pressure on faculty to raise money. Faculty are expected to generate revenue, and students are seen as a source of revenue. The identity of being an academic, an intellectual, a scholar engaged in making sense of the world along with one's students is fast disappearing and there's pressure to see yourself as somebody who is a revenue generator. I think of Eqbal Ahmed who taught here at Hampshire College for a number of years, a Pakistani scholar in exile, he was part of that generation of an engaged academic. The way he did his work in the academic institution, the way he taught, the way he connected to students, it is faculty like him who are my inspiration and whose example I wish to follow.

Orelus: *Throughout your work you talk about how globalization and capitalism have affected people in the Third World, especially women. How do you think your work has contributed to a sound understanding of these issues?*

Sangeeta: It always feels a bit of schizophrenic for me, living and teaching here in the U.S., and spending a fair amount of my time every year in India. For instance, structural adjustment policies of the World Bank and the IMF had been in full force in so many parts of Africa and Latin America. In the 1990s, it had just started in South Asia. And over here there was the prison industrial complex, the gutting of welfare programs, divestment from the public sector and public schools that were the order of the day. There was not really a common language across First and Third World contexts to talk about this, though the phenomenon was the same. U.S. activists campaigning against World Bank policies in the South were not drawing the connection that the similar policies were being unleashed here on the American public, it was the U.S. government doing it to its own people. But them and us, North and South divide prevented us from seeing these links, which was really the precursor to neoliberalism becoming a full-fledged global regime. The Reagan era, the 1980's and early 90's something akin to structural adjustment policies were already being put into place here. Teachers, scholars of education here, were often not aware of these institutions and their policies and conditionalities in the Third World leading to very similar kinds of exclusions faced here. And not making the connection that it's the very same thing that your government here in the U.S. is doing to its own people. It was not some external institution but the U.S. government was unrolling these same policies out here that impacted education and schools in similar ways as in the Third World.

Drawing these connections and having my graduate students see these connections for example in my seminar on globalization and education, that was important to me. I realized there isn't a course like it in the School of Education where, graduate students from the North and South are talking about globalization and how it impacts their work, and recognize the parallels. Typically U.S. education and education in other countries are not studied together as part of the same universe. Being able to see the connections to how, what's happening in other parts of the world--I think that's been eye opening for students to recognize neo-liberalism as a world wide regime. And that the U.S. is not in any way immune from it, or protected from it. And to understand therefore class in this country, deepening class inequalities because there's very little attention to class among student here.

I think certainly now there's a very different level of consciousness with the financial collapse and with the U.S. economy in a recession. There's much more willingness now to make these connections between North and South than when I started teaching these courses in early 2000. At that time the war on terror set the context for what students were prepared to hear.

And so teaching about international issues, about the South Asian region for instance, or about Orientalism, or about the Middle East, has been a challenge. The only lens available to students was Islamic fundamentalism. It was difficult during those years right after 9/11 to teach about U.S. neocolonialism, about U.S. imperialist adventures in Africa and Asia, about IMF and World Bank credit policies that are very much controlled by the U.S., and to understand the development of these countries in that context and not because of some kind of cultural backwardness, but putting the economic and cultural together. These were difficult things to teach, especially as a woman from the South. There was much resistance from students. In the post 9/11 world, they were the victims, and they didn't want to see it any other way.

I think this was a huge gap in the educational curriculum here that I felt urgently needed to be addressed. It's the same thing with teaching about gender and development because the stereotypes about women in the third world is that they are oppressed. Some students do not seem to have a complex view of third world societies, of women's movements and struggles in these countries and the agency of women. At the same time patriarchy and capitalism and colonialism work together to subordinate women. So oppression is there, but that's not all there is. Making these connections in my teaching was important for me.

Orelus: Some have argued that neo liberalism can be all a new form of colonialism disguised with a different mask; would you support that argument?

Sangeeta: There are definitely parts of the colonial project that carry forward into neo-liberalism. There are continuities in this history of world capitalism, but also very important breaks with the past. The colonial conquest through appropriation of resources and racist logic justified colonization of a people, appropriation of their territory and the accumulation of wealth. So these two things—capitalism and colonialism — have worked hand in hand.

But the terrain has shifted significantly now with neo-liberalism, with globalization and the opening of trade barriers so on and so forth. Now there is a transnational capitalist class that is in place. A class that does not have loyalty to any particular nation state. Neoliberalism projects an equal opportunity kind of capitalism, as recruiting anyone from across the globe who has the requisite skills for the job.

So one finds people of different nationalities and racial backgrounds in a corporation, but they are likely to identify with one another than with people from their own countries. Second, the imperial occupations of today, Iraq and Afghanistan, shares features of colonial conquest from earlier times, but too different to be termed colonialism. A select number of American companies are profiting from the 'war on terror', but it's not as if the U.S. economy as a whole is being enriched because of these wars like Britain or France was from its colonial conquests. Instead neoliberal policies are being put into effect here, in the heart of empire.

Orelus: *Some Marxist would argue that race doesn't matter much when it comes to capitalism because both whites and black are exploited by the system. So how would you change this view?*

Sangeeta: Whites and blacks are exploited but not in the same way and not to the same extent. The nature of exploitation is specific and different just as women from different groups (religion, class etc.) experience patriarchy in different ways. Race plays a huge part and gender too plays a big part. The way race plays out is similar to how caste plays out in India. So you could be a not-so-well-off Brahmin, or an upper caste in India but from a modest or struggling background right? like my parents were. They were 'fish eating Brahmins', not the most elevated kind, but Brahmins nevertheless, in economically difficult circumstances; but it's their caste privilege that allowed them in less than a generation to make the transition from village to city, to secure professional jobs and gain a middle class status. This kind of upward mobility cannot be accessed by those designated as low caste. There is no such thing as a purely economic calculation, of how much to pay someone, how much labor to extract. The economic calculation will have a racist dimension, a sexist dimension so it will have different consequences for different people, though none of these are fixed or fully determined. Yes, all workers are exploited, but if we don't pay serious attention to race and gender inequalities and focus only on class, then these will be reproduced in new forms regardless of changes in the economy, and second, we will be unable to organize effectively toward a radical politics.

Orelus: In a conversation that I had with a professor from India, he argues that neo-liberalism does not only emerge from the West but also from Third World countries. Where do you stand on this issue?

Sangeeta: I wouldn't say that it emerges from Third World countries but certainly they are agents of neoliberal reform. It is a much more limited small capitalist class in the Third World, they wouldn't be able to install neoliberalism as a global project. It is as allies of the capitalist class and political leadership of the West that the Third World elite is able to advance the neoliberal project at home. It is the World Bank and IMF that have driven the neoliberal agenda along with the United States and its investor class at the forefront. The idea that if we marketize everything, including all of the social sectors, then more wealth will be created and the good society will emerge from that. You really don't need the state or you don't need a concept of the public good or public interest that is distinct from individual interest.

Thatcher's notorious statement , "There is no such thing as society. There are only individuals." So in a sense it is like saying there's no such thing as a social good or the commons. Or that we shouldn't construct anything like a public good because there is no such thing as society; all we have is individual self interest. This is the essence of neoliberalism, and being able to translate it into an ideology, a program of action that binds the capitalist classes of India, Russia, South Africa and the U.S., this is a totally new phase of capitalism that sheds it colonial baggage. This doesn't mean that colonial practices are not part and parcel of this new economy, but it is altogether a different scenario we are dealing with, the colonial subject is different, postcolonial nations are differently positioned, in India's case quite dramatically.

The Indian bourgeoisie and I'm sure other sort of capital classes in other Third World countries might be feeling a bit alike in terms of not being able to expand the way they would like to. The state was very much at the helm, controlling mining, the steel industry, telecommunications, the insurance sector, banking, all the major industries. And what neo-liberalism allowed is for the national bourgeoisie in these countries that was feeling constrained, it allowed them to become part of this new global economic regime and become part of the reform process. And to the extent that it is beneficial to them they advance the neoliberal project.

The slogan in India launched in the mid 90's was Shining India. An India with world class airports, highways, shopping malls, gated communities with villas, golf courses where you don't see the poor and --the poor are really invisible while the interests of the entrepreneurial class are protected and promoted. In fact, the poor are also expected to become entrepreneurs. Neoliberalism has given a major boost to the capitalist class in these ertsewhile Third World countries. They have seized the opportunities, but I wouldn't say that they are equal players in driving the neoliberal agenda. There is not a perfect consensus within the Indian state or the Indian elite on certain neoliberal reforms. The development welfare state is also transforming its character to become subservient to this new dynamic capitalist class, the domestic capitalist class that is going global.

For people's movements and struggles the question is: How does one bring the state back in to represent the larger interest, the larger good? Because the state was in a sense the bulwark, maintaining a certain balance of forces in a country like India and not allowing the national bourgeoisie to simply take the reins of the economy. But now with neoliberalism and market is the way to go as common sense, the space for being able to hold the state accountable is really receding. So the struggle becomes equally, if not more urgently, about reclaiming the state, and not just about opposing the World Bank or U.S. policies. What I am saying is we cannot organize simply on the platform of anti-imperialism or decolonization, at least not in India. We need a new discourse of resistance that accounts for this changed scenario.

Orelus: When people talk about neo-liberalism, they tend to focus on the United States? But we have some emerging powers such as China and even India that have adopted and implemented neoliberal policies. For instance, China has invested quite a bit in some African countries, and the agenda is not to necessarily help Africa but rather to maximize its profits. So should we shift a little bit from the United States and focus on those emerging powers to look at how they may have impacted other countries through their neoliberal economic policy, even though they are themselves confronted with internal problems such as poverty and wealth disparity?

Sangeeta: Sociologist Roland Robertson was among the early academics in this country to write about globalization. He draws attention to the universalization of the nation state form. The modern state form itself is an imperialist form that is modeled along the lines of western imperial states. When the former colonized countries became independent, they adopted the same modern state form of the former colonial power.

The modern state form is supposed to represent the greatest good and the public interest, but it is also part of an international system of nation states that compete with one another for power. The global system is set up in a way where nation states are forced to be in competition and create a competitive edge for themselves. As a result of this competition we see the emergence of regional hubs that emulate the core nation-states such as the United States or the U.K. Within that there's going to be a jockeying for power trying to be big brother in your particular region.

So certainly what we see now in the Asian region is this jockeying for power. China and India are the two rising powers that are finding ways to exploit poorer regions of the world, buying land cheaply in these countries, sourcing minerals cheaply, similar to what imperial states earlier have done. These emerging regional economies form strategic alliances with the core imperial states, at the same time seek to displace them politically and economically. We are now in a phase where it is neither colonialism nor neocolonialism, in that these regional powers are not in a subservient relation to the core states.

President Obama's recent visit to India was very much about saying India is going to be part of a global club, and part of being recognized as a global leader entails acting in concert with the United States, not following the dictat of the U.S. necessarily, but being in alliance. So we shouldn't be surprised that India is the largest recipient of military equipment from Israel and is one of its leading business partners. The irony is that India was the one country that did not recognize Israel in solidarity with the people of Palestine. Only in 1992 did India establish formal relations with Israel. So you can see a real shift within the so-called post-colonial state where there is a new configuration of power relations that don't necessarily displace the earlier ones but work in conjunction with them. I think race will play an important role in the way Africa will be positioned in this new power compact.

Orelus: *You have been working in India. Have you witnessed the extent to which the U.S. neoliberal agenda has impacted farmers and factory workers? Could you share that experience?*

Sangeeta: The World Bank and IMF are the visible actors but it is the United States and Western Europe that make the rules and appoint the presidents of these organizations. It is an official agreement that Western Europe appoints the president of the IMF and the U.S. the World Bank president. Their policies are impacting India in dramatic ways. In a largely agrarian economy, farmer suicides have assumed epidemic levels in India. So that tells you something. There was a news item about a village that got together and did a mock sale of their village. The village as a whole had decided to sell their village to the highest bidder. So we are in a situation where it is better to be owned by someone than be a citizen of a free country. Staggering farmer suicides are happening where the farmers are drinking the pesticide that they took loans for to grow their crops.

Multi nationals are marketing genetically modified crops, that comes with its own package of expensive fertilizers and pesticides stripping farmers of their agricultural sovereignty and their knowledge systems. Hundreds of thousand of farmers have committed suicide. Your land is gone, so there's no reason for you to live; there's no material basis on which you can live. You can imagine the impact on the women in these families and their children because they are left behind. The money lenders come knocking, and the government blames the farmers for their plight and refuses to help. However, people's movements have tried to provide some kind of relief to distressed farmers and landless peasants.

Two years ago the right to work bill was passed by the Indian parliament after protracted struggle and lobbying by activist groups (Left parties and academics were also part of the effort). The Act now requires the Indian government to provide at least a hundred days of employment a year at the minimum wage. A livable wage is also a demand of the movement. The Act also specifies that the employment has to be 'meaningful'. Meaningful work means it has to be part of the development of the community. The effort is to connect it back to community development goals. The community has to decide what they need. Roads, schools, irrigation works. Now it's one of the largest public financed programs in the country. It is only 100 days of employment. It doesn't really help people get out of poverty. But we have to understand its value in the larger context. It's part of the struggle to maintain some kind of democratic space and the obligations of the state in the face of the onslaught of neo-liberalism.

Orelus: *Given the damages, the pain, and suffering that neo-liberalism has caused to the poor, are you hopeful that in ten years or so we'll be entering a new era where there will be some level of equity?*

Sangeeta: Yes and no. What we have seen happen from just the last two years in Wall street has led to a new kind of questioning even among mainstream economists who say this economic system is not sustainable. Financial speculation and the deregulation of the economy are not sustainable. The mainstream argument is that we need to find a way to stabilize and make capitalism sustainable. But Marxist analysis of capitalism tells us this is an impossible task. The movements against neoliberalism in South America, particularly in Venezuela, Brazil, Ecuador, and Bolivia, are hopeful. The movements in Egypt, Tunisia, Syria, and Bahrain make me hopeful. Occupy Wall Street makes me hopeful. The democratic opposition is growing. Being involved and invested in struggles is very important.

Orelus: Would you propose to defeat neoliberalism? How should one go about to do that?

Sangeeta: Being part of social movements where you can bring people together who are really facing the impact of neoliberalism, organizing as well as conceptualizing and constructing alternatives is a very important step. Also, being engaged in social movement and organizations, building them up, strengthening them is a very important part of dismantling neoliberalism.

Perry Anderson writes about the history of the Left in England. He documents the cultural work that working class people were engaged in: their own newspapers, theater, and music. This cannot be underestimated. We need this more than ever now in terms of creative media and public forums for people to express themselves and come together, so that they can eventually take the movement forward. We need these within institutional spaces and outside. That's why the university and the academic space is a very important site as well to build a critical politics. We cannot have the idea of the entrepreneurial university take over. We have to keep creating ways for faculty and students to come together, discuss and be involved in issues at the university level and at the same time in other parts of society. If our task is to defeat neo-liberalism, then being part of that struggle inside and outside the institution is the necessary task.

Orelus: Is there anything else you would like to share with regarding neoliberalism? Any final thought or comment?

Sangeeta: I will simply reiterate what I just said earlier. In every period people are faced with a historic task. It's about being able to identify what the historic task is and playing a part in it. I think the historic task for us is really about neo-liberalism that needs to be contested, opposed, defeated. It's operating as a global economic regime that is not quite fully stabilized. As neoliberalism is gaining momentum, it is also creating more ruptures and contradictions. So, I do feel hopeful. I don't think there's any other way to act in this world except from a position of hope.

14 Education, Neoliberalism, Neoconservatism, and Class Struggle in Britain and Europe

Dave Hill

INTRODUCTION

Neoliberalism—marked, *inter alia,* by the marketization, commodification, degradation, managerialization and privatization/preprivatization of public services (Giroux , 2004; Harvey, 2005; Hill, 2013a, b; Hill and Kumar, 2009; Hill and Rosskam, 2009)—does not come unaccompanied. It has a twin—neoconservatism— albeit, a twin with which it has an often fractured relationship. Today we have been experiencing both neoliberalization and neoconservatization in England, in Europe generally, and globally. There are, of course, resistances within neoliberalized states, and isolated states resisting neoliberalism, such as the governments and states of Cuba and Venezuela. Britain, in contrast, with the United States, is and has been one of the centers of this neoliberal/neoconservative transformation of economy, society, and of education. At this stage, it is important to make clear that neoliberalism is simply the latest stage of capitalism. This chapter is written as a critique of neoliberal capitalism but, importantly, this critique is, in essence, a critique of capitalism itself, of capitalist economic relations, of capitalist social relations, the Capital-Labour relation.

NEOLIBERAL/NEOCONSERVATIVE EDUCATION REVOLUTION IN BRITAIN

Education, and other public services in Britain, have been subject to neoliberalization since the Thatcher governments of 1979–90, in particular with the Education Reform Act of 1988. This established classic neoliberal policies of prompting the marketization of schooling (through "parental choice" and through "league tables" of schools by academic results.) It also (together with the 1986 Education Act and subsequent legislation) changed the composition of school-governing bodies, adding "business" governors, and reducing the numbers and influence of governors appointed by locally democratically elected councils. And under the "Local Management of Schools" (LMS) section of the 1988 act, local authority/school district influence was further weakened, when most budgetary control was handed to school head teachers/principals and governing bodies (Ball, 1990; Hill, 1997, 2001).

Since then, successive Conservative (1979–87) New Labour (1997–2010) and Conservative-Liberal Democrat Coalition (2010-) governments have intensified the neoliberalization of schools and of universities dramatically, alongside cuts in funding. One notable recent cut was (from September 2011) that of EMAs, education maintenance allowances, paid to young people aged 16–19 from poor families, of (usually) £30 a week, to encourage them to stay on at school. I benefited from a similar scheme in the 1960s; one of my grandsons received an EMA, 2006–2009. For university students the free university education that, for example, I received has been replaced by the imposition of annual university tuition fees of (usually) £9,000 per annum (see Hill, 2010a). (The New Labour—i.e., neoliberalized Labour government of Tony Blair—abandoned free university education and introduced tuition fees in 1998.)

Ideologically these neoliberal developments can be interpreted as "the businessification" of education, the softening up, the preparation for the wholesale privatization of schools, vocational colleges (called, in Britain, further education colleges) and universities.

Currently (2013) there is only one private university in Britain, but degree-awarding powers have been granted to a number of other organizations, and the current (2010-) Conservative–Liberal Democrat coalition government in Britain is planning more private universities. It is, indeed, likely that in the fairly near future, some, currently public/state universities in Britain will become private, bought and sold on international stock markets by transnational corporations and hedge funds. Ball (2012) is very clear on such developments, regarding schools, colleges, and universities, a development warned about/foreseen by Rikowski (2003) and by Hirtt (2004). Hirtt warned, in 2004, about state education provision and state health provision being "the last great El Dorados" for capitalist privatization and profit from public-sector-provided services.

MARKETIZATION/COMPETITION/CHOICE: "PARENTAL CHOICE," LEAGUE TABLES, AND HIGH-STAKES TESTING

Let me now go into more detail about some of the main aspects of neoliberalism, marketization, and privatization/preprivatization in schools and universities in Britain (or, to be more precise, England Wales, Scotland, and Northern Ireland have a degree of autonomy/self-government regarding education policy and provision).

Neoliberalization affects schools; it affects universities. With schools there is now a system of market competition between schools. Under the 1944 Education Act, which the Thatcher 1988 Education Act replaced, local authorities/

school districts had allocated children/students to schools, sometimes taking into account a degree of parental choice, but sometimes attempting to ensure that within a largely "comprehensive"/all-ability intake of students, there was a mix of students of all "bands" of ability/attainment (Hill, 1997, 2001).

The conservative governments in Britain, those of Thatcher (1979–1990) and of John Major (1990–1997), introduced and extended what they termed "school choice," or, more specifically, "parental choice." But, of course, it is not the parents who choose; it is the schools which choose the children/students, the "preferred" children/students being those with high test scores and "acceptable" (high status, "middle class" cultural capital. This leads to much increased hierarchy and elitism within the state education system, elitism which is "raced" social-class based. That is one aspect of the neoliberalization in schooling, a class-based increased hierarchicalization of schools. And this choice is facilitated by the creation of the league tables of schools and of universities, league tables of schools (and universities) sorted by exam results, by "high-stakes testing."

Neoliberalism requires that in a market, it is necessary to be able to test what you think is the efficiency and value of the products. So in England there is now a very rigid system of testing children at different ages, even, when they first enter the schools. That could be either at age four or five. As result of the exam results of the children, of the assessment results of the children, there becomes a league table in every municipality; in every part of the country, in every area, there are league tables of schools. And, of course, it is middle-class parents who have the means, the cars, the ability to pay transport costs, to take the children to the schools, which have higher results, which may be some distance away.

As a result of "parental choice" and published/public league tables, there has been a big increase in differentiation between the high-achieving schools and low-achieving schools. In Britain 13% of children have "free school meals" (FSM); the poorest 13% have free dinners at school. I did when I was a boy. If we look at two maps in England, the map showing who receives free school dinners, and the map of exam results, the maps are virtually identical. We know that the map showing assessments at tests and exams, the map of high and low attainment in school tests, mirrors the map of the existing income inequality.

PRIVATIZATION/ PREPRIVATIZATION OF SCHOOLING: THE ACADEMY (SCHOOLS)

In Britain, the government is engaging with schools on a program of preprivatization, setting up a so-called "academy system" where numerous state schools remain state funded, and within the state system, but are redesignated as "academies."

Thus, in the school sector, state-funded schools are being handed over to private companies, to chains of schools, to a variety of religious organizations, lock, stock, and barrel, to become "academies" (formerly City Academy Schools) (Beckett, 2007; see also Benn, 2011; and Anti-Academies Alliance, n.d.). These schools (currently more than half of all state secondary high schools, and increasing numbers of primary/elementary schools) are taken away from democratically elected local authority/school district control and residual funding, to become quasi-independent schools, actually receiving their funding directly from central government. At the stroke of a ministerial pen they could easily, at some stage, become fully independent, fully private schools, offered for sale on the market.

What is an academy? An academy is where government gives to any religious group, Muslim, Jewish, Christian, or to any rich businessmen or any rich businesswomen, for example, and can say, "Look, have this school; you can call it and name it with your name and you can name it after your wife or your business/company," or, I guess, even name it after your pet dog. "You can name it, and then you can have control over the school! You can appoint a majority of the governors, the people who run the schools, the people who oversee the head teacher." You can change the contracts of the teachers ultimately. You can change the skill mix of staff, that is, the numbers of fully qualified teachers, and the numbers of less-well-qualified (and much-lower-paid) "teaching assistants." You can have less teachers and more teaching assistants. You can change the length of the school day and you can change the curriculum. You have to follow the national curriculum, but if you want much more religion, for example, fundamentalist religion, more fundamentalist Christian religion, then the government says that is fine.

This, academy schools, is an aspect of preprivatization. At the moment all these academies are "not-for-profit" organizations. At the minute, in England, you cannot make a profit from running schools. But we can look at the United States, where there are charter schools, and we can see that some of them are "for profit," with multinational and national capital companies making profits from running state schools!

NEOCONSERVATISM

Neoliberalism is always accompanied with neoconservatism. Because the capitalist class, and the governments they control, have to make sure that this freedom in the market is controlled, in Britain the Thatcher government in the 1988 Education Reform Act instituted a national curriculum. Prior to 1988, schools and local education authorities (LEAs)/school districts had considerable autonomy over curriculum design and also teaching methods/pedagogies. However, the national curriculum for state is quite rigid, and it is a conservative curriculum. Margaret Thatcher herself looked at some of the curriculum proposals and said "No, that is too liberal." She herself, and I have written on this (Hill, 1997), changed the curriculum. That is an element of state control, control of the free market: an example of where neoliberalism, "free choice," is accompanied by state supervision/

control, and a rigid control of the curriculum for state schools. Not, interestingly, for private schools. They decide their own curriculum. (In Britain, approximately 7% of children go to private schools.)

For teachers and schools, the (privatized) school-inspection system, the Office for Standards in Schools, Ofsted, has changed from its (pre-1988) role of "light touch"/supportive school inspection to its current feared draconian role with regularly used powers to close what it regards as "failing" schools and/or force them to become Academies—often against the wishes of parents, teachers, and governors (Anti- Academies Alliance, n.d.; Benn, 2011; Local Schools Network, n.d.).

And for radical and critical educators in general, those of us trying to engage in "deep critique" (Rikowski, 2008) of capitalism, of capitalist economic, social, and political relations, and how these operate within schools and universities, there is often marginalization, nonpromotion, dismissal, pressure to conform to procapitalist norms in ideology, performativity, compliance.

SCHOOLS AND UNIVERSITIES AS IDEOLOGICAL STATE APPARATUSES: STIMULATING INDIVIDUALISTIC COMPETITIVE ENTREPRENEURSHIP IN SCHOOLS AND UNIVERSITIES.

In many countries there is now in schools and in universities an emphasis on designing, applying, and updating education and school teaching programs that seek to develop and stimulate students to become entrepreneurial, competitive. For example, some British universities now have institutional targets such as "at least 7% of students will go on to set up their own business."

This is very good demonstration of what Louis Althusser (1971) said about education being one of the major ideological state apparatuses. The major ideological state apparatuses are the capitalist-controlled mass media and the (again, capitalist-controlled, through governments of political parties–bankrolled capital) state education systems. In every capitalist country, and in England, capitalists have an ideological agenda. Children are told to be competitive, individualistic; children are told to set up businesses, to value moneymaking, and "the spirit of enterprise." This is against leftist notions of collectivity, solidarity, public service, and public good.

CRITICAL EDUCATION AND CRITICAL EDUCATORS

In schools, colleges, universities, many radical and Marxist critical educators try to affect four aspects of learning and teaching, asking questions about (at least) four aspects (see Hill, 2012b, c,).

Some critical educators question the teacher-centred pedagogy, the pattern of teaching and learning relationships and interaction, and try to use democratic participative pedagogy which breaks down patterns of domination and submission and listens to children's, students' and local communities' voices- but not uncritically. Critical Marxist educators engage in critique that frames educational experiences within the conditions of Capitalism and its current neoliberal form. Critical Marxist educators also attempt to utilise different types of pedagogy in teaching, to engage in non-hierarchical, democratic, participative, teaching and research, while by virtue of their role in actually teaching, may maintain an authoritative stance where appropriate. Such approaches are rooted in social constructivist Vygotskyan understandings of learning, and are also aimed both at producing co-learning, by teachers as well as taught, and at overtly welcoming and valuing more cultures than are commonly valued in a transmission mode of teaching. Of course critiques of such teacher-centred pedagogy are not restricted to Marxist educators. They are also made by liberal-progressive, child/ student-centred educators and by some conservative educators, concerned about teaching effectiveness and preparation for the workplace.

But critical education is about far more than pedagogy (Hill, 2014). Indeed, it takes place outside schools and universities as well as inside (Hill, 2012a, 2013a,), as the rise of alternatives to the English university indicates. (Canaan et al, 2013; Hill, 2013b). There is educational resistance outside the state-controlled education structures, in connection with the teach-ins at Tent Cities, a Free University movement, and through oppositional media and cultural workers, as well as within trade union and student groups.

A second question is about the curriculum- who selected the content and how rigid is it? Even where the curriculum is very tightly controlled, even where it is very rigidly prescribed, there are, as Gramsci, taught us, always spaces, little spaces for us to infiltrate, to use, to colonise. For example this can be seen in the teaching of the three of us writing this chapter, in primary/ elementary schools, secondary / high schools, prison, youth clubs, universities and vocational colleges and in 'tent cities', teach-ins and teach-outs and in emergent alternatives.

Marxist educators, indeed critical educators in general, can, with students, look at the curriculum and ask, 'Who do you think wrote this? 'Who do you think decided on including this in the curriculum'?,'What do you/ we think should be in the curriculum that is currently absent?' 'Why do you think it is absent? 'Who do you think benefits and who loses from this curriculum?', 'What is the ideology behind this book/ task/ lesson/ curriculum piece?' We believe that this can be done with ten year olds, 16 year olds, 40 or 70 year olds.

However limited the spaces are, within a school, university or educational site, within a curriculum, we can always find some possibility to question and to encourage the children/ students to do this as well so that they are, in effect, developing an awareness of what can be called 'ideology critique' (Kelsh and Hill, 2006). And then we can suggest, and seek from students, an alternative, perhaps even if only for five minutes in a lesson/

session. We can question existing versions of history. We can ask, 'Is there a different version or view of the past, the present, or the future?'. So, looking at the work of Marxist and Communist teachers and Critical Educators, we can affect the content of curriculum, or, if that is, at any particular time/space, almost impossible, we can seek to develop ideology critique, an understanding of the Capital-Labour relation, of capitalism and its relationship to education systems, of ideological and repressive state apparatuses, and of how schools and universities are shaped and controlled into producing politically and ideologically quiescent and hierarchically organised and rewarded labour power. Where Marxist educators, and Revolutionary Critical Educators (McLaren, 2005; McLaren and Jaramillo, 2010) differ from more social democratic and liberal critical educators is in the emphasis placed on resistance and socialist transformation (Kelsh and Hill, 2006; Skordoulis and Hill, 2012; Hill, 2014).

A third question in education that critical/ Marxist educators can and should ask is 'how should children of different social class, gender, and ethnic backgrounds and different sexual orientations be organised within classrooms, within institutions such as schools and universities, and within national education systems? Are some groups in fact labelled, segregated, divided, demeaned? In some countries virtually all children go to the same *type* of school. But children tend to go to schools where their own class predominates. There is also a question of how the education system inculcates a differentiated sense of class awareness in working, middle and ruling class students. And it tries to keep the working class as a working class that is obedient, subservient, individualistic, interested in only themselves not in collectivity, not in community. Marxist educators clearly prefer and work for what in Britain is called 'comprehensive' schools, and in India, for example, is called 'the common school'. But then, even where this happens (as in Finland, where there are only a single handful of private schools, where students up to the age of sixteen are taught in common/ comprehensive schools in 'mixed ability' classes) there are internal informal mechanisms, the hidden curriculum of differential ('raced', gendered' and 'sexually oriented' expectations and responses to different cultural capitals (Reay, 2006; Hill, 2009).

A fourth question Marxist educators ask is 'who should own, control and govern schools, further education (vocational) colleges and universities? Of course we cannot change the law at a stroke, but we can lead a movement that at some stage- in two years time, ten years time, twenty years time- the ownership and governance of schools can be changed, made democratic, and secular and can attempt to be egalitarian. Instead of, as in some countries, schools, colleges and universities being run by a religious state, by transnational corporations (Ball, 2012), or by religious organisations themselves, by 'for-profit' private companies, by companies that are in theory and public discourse 'not-for-profit (but which reward handsomely their executives and their friends), or schools that are run and governed by rich businessmen or women. Marxist educators (and others, of course) believe that schools, colleges and universities should be run democratically, with education workers and students, as well as elected representatives of local communities, having powers in and over those education institutions, within a secular, democratic national framework. Explicit in this is the assertion that education is a public good and a public right that should not be distorted and corrupted by private ownership- there should be no private schools, colleges or universities. (For an attempt to address these various aspects of education, in developing a socialist policy for education, see Hill, 2010c).

Of course the number of critical, radical, Marxist, counter-hegemonic school teachers and university teachers is limited, and it takes courage to be one, in the face of the repressive aspects (non-promotion, dismissals, harassment by management) of and within the education state apparatuses.

EFFECTS OF NEOLIBERALISM AND CONSERVATISM ON TEACHERS IN SCHOOLS: MANAGERIALISM, SURVEILLANCE, AND CONTROL

Stevenson (2007) is one of many analysts (see also Lewis, Hill, and Fawcett, 2009) who note that

> A key feature of current school-sector reform in England is the restructuring of teachers' work and the increased use of support staff to undertake a range of activities previously undertaken by teachers. Supporters speak of a new teacher professionalism focused on the "core task" of teaching. Critics fear deprofessionalization through a process of deskilling, work intensification, and labor substitution.

Stevenson continues, describing a

> relentless drive to raise productivity, teachers have often found themselves the victims of unwelcome change in which they have had their professional judgment curtailed, witnessed the increasing managerialization of the educational process, and been subjected to ever more forensic scrutiny of their work by external agencies (Ball, 2003). . . . These developments have inevitably affected the work pressures on teachers and resulted in an intensification of the labor process of teaching. . . . (*Smyth, Dow, Hattam, Reid, & Shacklock, 2000*).

In the section below I use some primary research about "teachers' work" carried out between September 2012 and January 2013 by James Lloyd Hill, who has worked in four different secondary (high) schools in England (Hill, J., 2013).

James quotes a colleague who

> summarised her view of being a teacher as 'you're not a teacher anymore, you're someone who works in a school'—she's been teaching 6 months, and was backed up by another colleague in the room with 12 years teaching experience behind her. The same teacher also said 'I didn't get into teaching to deliver lessons which are already pre-planned for me which I have to follow, or teach subjects which I never trained for and to only deliver other peoples' resources, I wanted to inspire them to learn History' (her subject).

James's view is that

> It seems to me the ability (time/insight) to inspire is taken up with filling in tracking data, data in-putting, filling in spreadsheets when homework has been set, making sure your room is not untidy for fear of senior management noticing and 'having a word'. The extra work that teachers now have to do has very little to do with the delivery of lessons, but ticking the boxes which senior management feel they should have ticked, in case Ofsted come calling. There is a lot of talk among heads of department about 'how can we show this?' and 'where's our evidence for that?', and as a result, we don't hear as much of 'I think I'm going to try this with that group of students'.

This view exemplifies research carried out by McBeath in 1995 (p. 12), not long after the National Curriculum and its testing and surveillance regime came into operation. McBeath quotes a student teacher as saying "I used to feel that this school cared about how well I was doing. Now I just think it cares about how well it's doing."

James continues,

> I'm not suggesting that as teachers we are not accountable for students' attainment in our lessons, but there is a limit on our ability to be accountable, and certainly a limit on how that accountability is tracked; lesson plans, intervention documentation by teachers—what have you done about student x, y and z? Why are they still failing?! Documentation on each student, and each aspect of a student accounted for on your lesson plan (such as average reading age; SEN status; Gifted and Talented status; preferred learning style (VAK), learning goal; current grade.

James talks not just of the intensification of accountability, but of a managerial culture of control and fear:

> The voices of the Unions are quieter than they once were in schools, there are still those brave enough to speak out on behalf of those who must not be named to senior management, even though they do ask 'and who thinks that?' but more recently it has had to be a case of

safety in large numbers. We had a Joint Union meeting of the NUT (National Union of Teachers) and 'NASUWT' (National Association of Schoolmasters/Union of Women Teachers) 'where we agreed on 'work to rule' principles the unions had set out, but the added pressures being placed on staff meant that we signed a petition. One member of staff set it up, and had to guarantee at least 60 signatures before he would show it to the head. Staff feel they can be got rid of so easily now. Having spoken to a Union leader in the school, she said staff are just too afraid to speak out now, because they know that if senior management want rid of you, they can do it now.

Senior management can observe you with their performance management duties (in some schools this may be once a year, in this, once every term). There are the 'learning walks' where they can 'pop into' your lesson (for how ever long they choose—this may have a different label, but it has the same effect on their view of your teaching, and your anxiety levels). There are also 'book looks', which have always been done, but now they must be standardised (making sure there are comments on how students can improve, and asking a 'Learning Development Question', which the students must answer. This is to tick another box in case Ofsted arrive). And the over-riding view of the reasons for many of these quality initiatives, is that if Management want you out, they will force you out with the amount of pressure they will place on you from the observations, or you will slip up in an observation, which can then be used against you.

I was observed on a learning walk by a member of senior management, she came in as the class were doing an activity, there was music on in the background, I was sat at my desk looking over a student's book. The member of staff left after a few minutes. At the end of the day I received an email from my head of department, who had received an email from the senior management observer. It was a complaint that I hadn't got up and gone over to greet her at the door. She didn't see the reason why I was playing that music and so therefore thought it questionable. The fact I was sat at my desk also gave her cause for concern, especially as another member of staff had also seen me sat at my desk once when they had walked past my classroom and looked inside through the window in the door.

This type of micro management is something you may expect from working in a cubicle in an office. How teachers relate to students, how they engage them, is being written out in a memo, so Ofsted can tick it off.

McBeath (1995) is among many who note that

inspections carry high stakes for schools and teachers and where the press for accountability overshadows the improvement motive. It also

> assumes that inspectors are able not only to 'see' schools as they are but are able to tell the story in ways that depict the complexity, vitality and dynamic of a school's character. Snapshots are by nature limited by both frame and focus.

James continues,

> You hear they're (Ofsted) in the area, you panic. They call, you plan like you've never planned before (because it's impossible to do that amount of planning for 9 different teaching groups who you see at least 2/3 times a week, with the amount of detail the school thinks Ofsted require). They observe your lesson, the students are amazing, because there's a new person in the room who looks important. Your nerves are hanging by a thread because you don't know if you've demonstrated 3 levels of progress in the 15 minutes the inspector has been in your room (possibly not, because they came in right in the middle of the activity). By the end of the lesson, the students may have learnt something, but if it hasn't been measured by the inspector, you're not a 'good' teacher. So you'll be observed again, and again, and again.

NEOLIBERALISM, NEOCONSERVATISM, AND RESISTANCE: WHAT IS HAPPENING IN THE OTHER EUROPEAN COUNTRIES: THE SIMILARITIES

The paths of neoliberalization and neoconservatism are similar in many countries. But each country has its own history, has its own particular context; each country has its own balance of class forces, its own level of organization of the working class. So in some countries where resistance to neoliberalism is very strong, as in Greece, then the government has found it actually so far very difficult to have large-scale privatization. Because just about every time the Greek government tries to privatize, just about every public-sector activity, the ports, the buses, the trains, the museums, and so on, almost every time there is a general strike. Working-class consciousness and class organization, in a situation of naked class war from above, are highly developed.

But in some countries, where trade-union resistance and working-class organizations' resistance are historically very weak, for example, Ireland, the United States, in those countries neoliberalism has, and the capitalist class has, an easier path. There has been little resistance even to extreme measures taken by, for example, recently in Wisconsin in the United States, the state government's passing a law which made it illegal to negotiate with trade unions. In other words, it has said there would be no more collective bargaining with trade unions. There were big protests, big demonstrations, big union protests—but the law passed, even if it did electrify the left and the trade union movement in the US.

To us in Britain, that was incredible, because although we have neoliberal and neoconservative governments in Britain, both Conservative and New Labour, the trade unions still have great strength. The Trade Unions Congress (TUC) in Britain has around six million members. On October 20, 2012, one hundred fifty thousand of us went on the march in London against austerity. That followed the student and worker marches against education cuts referred to earlier.

When the organized working class wakes up, then we can take very strong action. But some trade-union leaders sometimes live comfortable lives; sometimes they have good relations with the government. Not all the trade-union leaders are radical. However, some union leaderships are Marxist. In Britain the Communist Party of Britain has some power in unions at the top level; so does the Trotskyist group called the Socialist Party, the Committee for a Workers International, and so does the Socialist Workers Party. And of course, socialists and Marxists are very active within the membership of trade unions, pushing the leaderships into more radical action. The power of the organized working class, if it is spurred into action, can have veryconsiderable impact. We hope in Britain to have a general strike against 'Austerity Capitalism'. We (Marxists, activists) are working towards that. This would be only the second general strike in British history, the first since 1926.

Levels of resistance vary very march in different countries. In Portugal, for example, recently there were one million on strike, one million in demonstrations. That is in a small country of eight million people. In Ireland, there are very small demonstrations. The most noteworthy action in Ireland against austerity and neoliberalism was one worker driving his big digger truck into the gates of parliament.

EDUCATE, AGITATE, ORGANIZE

We Marxists, and critical educators in general, seek to serve and advance the interests of the working class. We, as teachers, as educators, are working class, too, we sell our labor power to capitalists and to the apparatuses of the capitalist state, such as schools and universities. All the time we have to challenge the dominant ideology, the hegemony of the ruling class, the bourgeoisie, the capitalist class. We are in a battle for dominance of our ideas; there are "culture wars" between different ways of looking at/interpreting the world. We have to contest the currently hegemonic control of ideas by the capitalist state, schools, media, and their allies in the religions. If we sit and do nothing, if their ideas are not contested, then capitalism will continue to rule, to demean, to divide, to impoverish us, and the planet.

At certain times in history, and in certain locations, the disjunction—the gap, the difference—between the material conditions of workers' existence on the one hand, our daily lived experience, and, on the other hand, what the newspapers and the media and the imam and the priest and the rabbi say/preach, that gap becomes so stark, so obvious, that workers' subjective consciousness changes. At this moment—now—in some countries in the world, the gap between the "official" ideology that "we are all in together" and that "there is no alternative" (to austerity), or, in schools and universities faced by commodification and managerialism and (pre-)privatization—that gap becomes so large that the ruling party, and the ruling capitalist class, and capitalism itself, loses legitimacy. And so, as in Greece now, and in Portugal, in Spain, in Turkey and Brazil, and in other countries such as Britain, we Marxists are necessary. Necessary in leading and developing changes in consciousness, a change in class consciousness, and in playing a leading role in organizing for the replacement of capitalism.

1938, in "The Transitional Programme", Trotsky addresses the types of programmes moving the discussion beyond minimum programme (minimum acceptable reforms, such as those to protect and improve existing rights and entitlements, such as rights at work, social and political rights)) and maximum programme (socialist revolution, with the type of society ultimately envisaged by Marx, a socialist non-capitalist/ post-capitalist society) that were advanced by late nineteenth and earlt twentieth century social democrats and by communists of the 3rd international and articulates a new type of programme: the transitional programme.

Trotsky, with a distinct resonance to today's struggles, wrote:

> The strategic task of the next period—prerevolutionary period of agitation, propaganda and organization—consists in overcoming the contradiction between the maturity of the objective revolutionary conditions and the immaturity of the proletariat and its vanguard (the confusion and disappointment of the older generation, the inexperience of the younger generation. It is necessary to help the masses in the process of the daily struggle to find the bridge between present demand and the socialist program of the revolution. This bridge should include a system of transitional demands, stemming from today's conditions and from today's consciousness of wide layers of the working class and unalterably leading to one final conclusion: the conquest of power by the proletariat.
>
> Classical Social Democracy, functioning in an epoch of progressive capitalism, divided its program into two parts independent of each other: the minimum program which limited itself to reforms within the framework of bourgeois society, and the maximum program which promised substitution of socialism for capitalism in the indefinite future. Between the minimum and the maximum program no bridge existed. And indeed Social Democracy has no need of such a bridge,

> since the word socialism is used only for holiday speechifying. The Comintern has set out to follow the path of Social Democracy in an epoch of decaying capitalism: when, in general, there can be no discussion of systematic social reforms and the raising of the masses' living standards; when every serious demand of the proletariat and even every serious demand of the petty bourgeoisie inevitably reaches beyond the limits of capitalist property relations and of the bourgeois state.

Trotsky continued,

> Under the menace of its own disintegration, the proletariat cannot permit the transformation of an increasing section of the workers into chronically unemployed paupers, living off the slops of a crumbling society. The right to employment is the only serious right left to the worker in a society based upon exploitation. This right today is left to the worker in a society based upon exploitation. This right today is being shorn from him at every step. Against unemployment, "structural" as well as "conjunctural," the time is ripe to advance along with the slogan of public works, the slogan of a sliding scale of working hours. Trade unions and other mass organizations should bind the workers and the unemployed together in the solidarity of mutual responsibility. On this basis all the work on hand would then be divided among all existing workers in accordance with how the extent of the working week is defined. The average wage of every worker remains the same as it was under the old working week. Wages, under a strictly guaranteed minimum, would follow the movement of prices. It is impossible to accept any other program for the present catastrophic period.
>
> [. . .] The question is not one of a "normal" collision between opposing material interests. The question is one of guarding the proletariat from decay, demoralization and ruin. The question is one of life or death of the only creative and progressive class, and by that token of the future of mankind. If capitalism is incapable of satisfying the demands inevitably arising from the calamities generated by itself, then let it perish. "Realizability" or "unrealizability" is in the given instance a question of the relationship of forces, which can be decided only by the struggle. By means of this struggle, no matter what immediate practical successes may be, the workers will best come to understand the necessity of liquidating capitalist slavery. (Trotsky, 1938)

The 'decay, demoralisation and ruin' Trotsky speaks of, are, for many many millions of workers' families- including what in the USA and elsewehere are called 'middle class' workers, an everyday reality in this current era of capitalism, neoliberal capitalism, or 'immiseration capitalism'. The precise organisation and characteristics of the resistance to the depradations described in this chapter is a matter for strategic and tactical considerations, relating to the current balance (strength, organisations, (dis-)unity) of class forces in specific local and national contexts. What is clear, though, is that the problematic regarding capitalism, for Marxist activists and educators, is not just to reform it, welcome though such reforms, such as 'minimum programme' are, and active in campaigning for and to protect such reforms we must be. But, regarding capitalism, our task is to replace it with democratic Marxism

ACKNOWLEDGMENTS

This to thank James Lloyd Hill for carrying out a series of semistructured interviews and personal ethnography in relation to the intensification and managerialization of teachers' work.

REFERENCES

Anti-Academies Alliance website. Online at http://antiacademies.org.uk/.

Ball, S. (1990). *Politics and policy-making in education: Explorations in policy sociology*. London and New York: Routledge.

Ball, S. (2003) The teacher's soul and the terrors of performativity, *Journal of Education Policy 18*(2):215–228

Ball, S. (2012). *Global Education Inc.: New policy networks and the neoliberal imaginary*. London and New York: Routledge.

Beckett, F. (2007). *The great city academy fraud*. London: Continuum.

Benn, M. (2011). *School wars: The battle for Britain's education*. London: Verso.

Canaan, J., Hill, D. and Maisuria, A. (2013) Resistance in England. In *Immiseration Capitalism and Education: Austerity, Resistance and Revolt* Brighton, UK: Institute for Education Policy Studies.

Giroux, H. (2004) *The Terror of Neoliberalism: Authoritarianism and the Eclipse of Democracy Boulder*, CO: Paradigm

Harvey, D. (2005(A Brief History of neoliberalism. Oxford, England; Oxford University Press

Hill, D. (1997). Equality in primary schooling: The policy context of the reforms. In M. Cole, D. Hill, and S. Shan (Eds.), *Promoting equality in primary schools* (pp. 15–47). London: Cassell. Online at http://www.ieps.org.uk/papersdh.php.

Hill, D. (2001). Equality, ideology and education policy. In D. Hill and M. Cole (Eds.), *Schooling and equality: Fact, concept and policy* (pp. 7–34). London: Kogan Page. Online at http://www.ieps.org.uk/papersdh.php.

Hill, D. (2009) Theorising Politics and the Curriculum: Understanding and Addressing Inequalities through Critical Pedagogy and Critical Policy Analysis. In D. Hill and L. Helavaara Robertson (eds.) *Equality in the Primary School: Promoting good practice across the curriculum*. London: Continuum. Online at http://www.ieps.org.uk/PDFs/Ch20HillandRobertson2009.pdf

Hill, D. (2010a). Students are revolting—and quite right too. *Radical notes*. Online at http://radicalnotes.com/journal/2010/12/03/students-are-revolting-education-cuts-and-resistance/.

Hill, D. (2010b). A socialist manifesto for education. *Socialist resistance online*. Online at http://socialistresistance.org/?p=905.

Hill, D. (2010c) A Socialist Manifesto for Education. *Socialist Resistance Online*. Online at http://socialistresistance.org/?p=905

Hill, D. (2012a). Immiseration capitalism, activism and education. Resistance, revolt and revenge. *Journal for Critical Education Policy Studies*, *10*(2). Online at http://www.jceps.com/index.php?pageID=article&articleID=259.

Hill, D. (2012b) Fighting Neo-Liberalism with Education and Activism. *Philosophers for Change*. 1 March. Online at http://philosophers.posterous.com/fighting-neo-liberalism-with-education-and-ac

Hill, D. (2012c) The Role of Marxist Educators Against and Within Neoliberal Capitalism. *Socialist Resistance. 26 Feb.* Online at *http://socialistresistance.org/3184/the-role-of-marxist-educators*-against-and-within-neoliberal-capitalism

Hill, D. (2013a) *Marxist Essays on Education: Class and 'Race', Neoliberalism and Capitalism*. Brighton: The Institute for Education Policy Studies

Hill, D., et al. (2013b). *Immiseration Capitalism and Education: Austerity, Resistance and Revolt* Brighton, UK: Institute for Education Policy Studies.

Hill, D. (ed.) (2014 forthcoming) *Critical Education, Critical Pedagogies, Marxist Education*

Hill, D., and Kumar, R. (Eds.) (2009). *Global neoliberalism and education and its consequences*. New York: Routledge.

Hill, D., and Rosskam, E. (Eds.) (2009). *The developing world and state education: Neoliberal depredation and egalitarian alternatives*. New York: Routledge.

Hill, J. L. (2013). Interview and personal ethnography research data gathered on secondary school teachers' perspectives on and reactions to the intensification and managerialisation of teachers' work. Unpublished.

Hirtt, N. (2004). Three axes of merchandisation. *European Educational Research Journal*, *3*(2), 442–453. Online at http://www.wwwords.co.uk/eerj/.

Kelsh, D. and Hill, D. (2006) The Culturalization of Class and the Occluding of Class Consciousness: The Knowledge Industry in/of Education. *Journal for Critical Education Policy Studies*, 4 (1). Online at .http://www.jceps.com/index.php?pageID=article&articleID=59

Lewis, C., Hill, D., & Fawcett, B. (2009). England and Wales: Neoliberalised education and its impacts. In D. Hill (Ed.), *The rich world and the impoverishment of education: Diminishing democracy, equity and workers' rights* (pp. 106–135). New York: Routledge.

Local Schools Network (n.d.). Online at http://www.localschoolsnetwork.org.uk/campaigns/transparency-academies-freeschools/page/3/.

McBeath, J. (1995). Self-evaluation and inspection @ a consultation response, for the National Union of Teachers. London: National Union of Teachers. Online at www.teachers.org.uk/ . . . /Future_of Inspection-MacBeath_response.d.

McLaren, P. (2005) *Capitalists and Conquerors: A Critical Pedagogy Against Empire*. New York: Rowman and Littlefield.

McLaren, P. and Jaramillo, N. (2010) Not Neo-Marxist, Not Post-Marxist, Not Marxian, Not AutonomistMarxism: Reflections on a Revolutionary (Marxist) *Critical Pedagogy. Cultural Studies- Critical Methodologies* XX (X) pp.1–12.

Reay, D. (2006) The Zombie stalking English schools: social class and educational inequality. *British Journal of Education Studies*, 54 (3) pp. 288–307.

Rikowski, G. (2003). The profit virus: The business takeover of schools. *The flow of ideas*. Online at http://www.flowideas.co.uk/?page=articles&sub=The%20Profit%20Virus%20-%20The%20Business%20Takeover%20of%20Schools.

Rikowski, G. (2008). The compression of critical space in education today. *The flow of ideas*. Online at http://www.flowideas.co.uk/?page=articles&sub=Critical%20Space%20in%20Education.

Skordoulis, C. and Hill, D. (eds.) (2012) Introduction. In *Proceedings of the First International Conference on Critical Education*, 2011. Athens: University of Athens.

Smyth. J,, Dow, A., Hattam, R., Reid, A., & Shacklock, G. (2000). *Teachers' work in a globalizing economy*. London: Falmer Press.
Stevenson, H. A. (2007). Restructuring teachers' work and trade union responses in England: Bargaining for change? *American Education Research Journal, 44*(2), 224–251. Online at http://aer.sagepub.com/content/44/2/224.full.
Trotsky, L. (1938) *The Death Agony of Capitalism and the Tasks of the Fourth International: The Transitional Program*. Online at http://www.marxists.org/archive/trotsky/1938/tp/tp-text.htm#m

Conclusion

Offering a departing analysis and reflection for *Colonized Schooling Exposed,* we can turn our attention to the long, violent legacy of paternalism and its educational role in manufacturing consent to the historical process of the expansion and development of capitalism, considering its colonial, neocolonial, and neoliberal manifestations, or periods of development. Offering an historical perspective here will leave us able to begin to envision a world without capitalism and its many consequences from paternalism, alienation, to immiseration (Hill, 2012).

In his critically acclaimed book *Class Dismissed: Why We Cannot Teach or Learn Our Way Out of Poverty*, John Marsh (2011) offers an insightful analysis regarding the paternalism of the dominant colonizing/capitalist class, especially in the context of education. Marsh points to the 19th-century Scottish immigrant who came to be a titan of industrial monopoly capitalism, Andrew Carnegie, because he signifies the deeply paternalistic, philanthropic capitalist. That is, Carnegie believed that capitalists should not hoard their fortunes, but rather redistribute them throughout working-class communities with directed philanthropy, such as the construction of libraries where the poor could improve themselves. Carnegie was adamantly opposed to redistributing wealth to workers in the form of wages for fear that workers would squander the wealth and deteriorate into depravity. Carnegie believed the only proof that was needed for the wisdom and competence of capitalists to direct the affairs of the toiling masses was the fact that they were in fact capitalists. In other words, having successfully appropriated the vast majority of value, as in capitalist production, or land and resources as in the colonialist or ongoing primitive stage of the expansion and development of capitalism, demonstrates a high level of competence. Summarizing Carnegie's position here, Marsh (2011) notes that

> Carnegies' argument led to a bizarre if inescapable conclusion: the poor and working poor must remain poor so that the rich could help them. The rich had to impoverish the poor in order to save them. (p. 96)

It is therefore not surprising that Carnegie was a violent strikebreaker and overall militant opponent of unionism and any form of worker democracy or economic independence. This is the same colonialist paternalism of the White man's burden that viewed the act of colonization as a necessary, if burdensome, favor to all colonized peoples, from Native Americans and Africans to the Irish. As Carnegie dominates workers for their own good, so too do the colonizers colonize in benevolence. Marsh argues that the United States has become a nation of Carnegies with education rather than libraries serving as the primary vehicle through which workers can be saved from their inherently lazy and indolent selves, if they can overcome their natural inferiority and work hard and follow the wisdom of the colonizer and colonialist society.

Historically, the ruling ideology has been designed to convince, first, the former peasants of the colonizers' homeland, the colonized, and the enslaved (all of whom would come to be dominated by capital) of the wisdom and righteousness of the bosses and private property. It is this paternalism that we can trace back to the earliest forms of religious education in the colonies, which portrayed workers as sinful and in need of the wisdom and superiority of the elite. It is the same paternalism of Captain Richard Pratt informing his conceptualization and practice of Indian boarding schools of the 19th century. Pratt, like Thomas Jefferson before him, rejected the determinism of biological racism, and adopted, rather, an equally violent form of cultural racism.

This European conquest of the Americas, which unfolded and spread from the Caribbean to northern North America (lands that would eventually become Canada and the United States), resulted in a deep moral paradox of self-proclaimed loving Christians who were engaged in violent wars of conquest and enslavement. Martha Menchaca (1997), for example, argues that between 1620 and 1870, Whites in North America engaged in large-scale land theft, intentional genocide (i.e., wars of extermination) and unintentional genocide (i.e., the unknowing spread of deadly diseases), and enslaved and subjugated "racial minorities," all because it benefited them economically, which they justified by "promoting various discourses alleging the inferiority of non-whites" (p. 13). For some scholars, this represents the root cause of contemporary capitalistic paternalism and the creation of subservience through internalized oppression.

In her account of events, Menchaca (1997) reminds us that the racism of the Pilgrims merely reflected the dominant discourse of elites and the scientific community in Europe. The stereotypes of the savage, cannibalistic, cognitively inferior, so-called *dark races* were constructed not only through academic discourse but through 17th- and 18th-century popular culture as well as in many of the works by Shakespeare, Cervantes, and others. Pilgrims were therefore conditioned before coming to America to ensure that they would not deviate from their prescribed roles. Summarizing this insight, revolutionary psychologist Franz Fanon (1963), in his widely influential *The Wretched of the Earth*, comments that

> Colonialism is not satisfied merely with holding a people in its grip and emptying the native's brain of all form and content. By a kind of perverted logic, it turns to the past of the oppressed people, and distorts, disfigures, and destroys it. (p. 210)

We might observe that this form of ideological indoctrination is an early example of behaviorism for domination and cultural genocide. This destructive psychological process, for Native Americans, was carried out through a system of boarding schools. In practice, children as young as four years old were physically removed from the love and cultural nurturance of their communities by *coercing* (violently if needed) families into allowing their children to be taken away to schools far from their communities and for years on end. Between the late 1800s and the mid-1900s more than half of all Native American children had been removed from their homes to be forced to act and think like White children and therefore become something *other* than what they formerly *were* through this *boarding school project*. This compulsory form of assimilation was put into practice in *the classroom* by indoctrinating native children with a paradigm or worldview based on the idea that Western civilization, the United States and Canadian governments in particular, and White society in general, represented everything good and civilized and that *Indian* ways were shameful and savage. The *unhappy history* (colonization and genocide) of indigenous peoples was rarely discussed, and if it was, it was to be contrasted with the superior future that is now within their grasp thanks to the generous gifts embedded within *Western, Christian, capitalist civilization* (Churchill, 2004).

In addition to manipulating the curriculum, Native American children were *conditioned* or *modified* by severely controlling their actions and very closely monitoring their *behavior*. The so-called *teachers* accomplished their objectives through a number of means: changing the children's dress and hairstyles from their individualized traditional tribal attire to institutionalized military-style uniforms; destroying all of the cultural materials they brought with them from their home communities, which was everything they brought with them from their home communities; banning all cultural practices and severely punishing *students* for engaging in their indigenous cultures, such as speaking their native tongues, even outside of *class*; and by only allowing English to be spoken while spending the majority of ones time toiling in boarding-school factories (Churchill 2004).

However, regardless of how harmful or destructive our behaviorist conditioning has been, the species, from a scientific point of view (Chomsky, 1988), always retains the ability, due to a biological endowment, to be self-reflective, and thus become conscious of our own conditioned consciousness (Freire, 1998). Consequently, any critical or scientific analysis of behaviorist, dehumanizing colonization must highlight the ways the targeted victims have always fought back, demonstrating the persistent, fixed, or biologically determined nature of the abstract notion of *free will*. For example, summarizing the frequency and ways Native American children fought back, Churchill (2004) notes:

> Native children were not merely the passive victims of all that was being done to them. Virtually without exception, survivor narratives include accounts of subversion, both individual and collective, most commonly involving such activities as 'stealing' and/or foraging food, possessing other 'contraband,' persistence in the speaking of native languages and running away. In many—perhaps most—residential schools, such activities were so common and sustained as to comprise outright 'cultures of resistance.' (p. 51)

Whereas this human propensity for counterhegemony when faced with the persistent oppression of external coercion and degradation cannot be lost sight of because it is the essence of *revolutionary hope*, the larger purpose of a domesticating, dehumanizing behaviorist psychology is worth revisiting, for *transformation* comes from the ashes and rubble of *deconstruction*.

The primary goal of replacing indigenous cultures with the foreign settler *common* culture of domination/subjugation was therefore to transform the peoples' relationship to the land, making them willing accomplices in their own oppression, rendering the process of colonization (i.e., westward expansionism) that much easier for land speculators, investors, and European settlers willing, due to their own behaviorist, Eurocentric, Christian conditioning, to lift themselves out of poverty on wealth extracted from stolen native lands, much of which (especially lands east of the Mississippi) had already been transformed for large-scale corn production by a multitude of indigenous groups distinguished from one another by distinct languages, cultures, and so on.

To destroy the cultural connections between indigenous communities and the productive lands on which they lived, native children were to internalize the same White supremacy and support for the system that other people slated to be workers in the settler communities were to incorporate into their consciousnesses. The psychological implication for White people is to hate the other, whereas the implication for people of color, such as Native Americans, is to hate the self and those who taught them this self-destructive hatred. Consumed by their own guilt, however, many White people wind up hating themselves too. Whereas white supremacy is obviously more harmful to people of color, White people would also be better served by a system based on a more positive, affirming psychology rather than the very negative tendency that exists.

To better understand this psychological process of domination, we can observe the connection between the many mental illnesses of so many people to the boarding-school project and to the model of schooling designed to produce passive workers. This is a challenge because people are not naturally passive. Education must therefore suppress certain drives and desires, such as the free and creative use of language and labor power, to achieve some level of functioning consent. Consequently, workers are mentally sick and forever searching for ways to either rebel or escape the living hell of suppression—the product of a behaviorist social order.

The educational goal for native children and the majority of Europeans and Africans brought to North America to be put to work for the investors was therefore to instill a fear of God, that is, the ruling authority, and a commitment to sacrifice and hard work because it would appease the fearful God and lead to salvation. Whereas the schoolhouse was often used for Europeans and Native Americans, the classroom for Africans was more often the plantation. While White laborers, often flogged or whipped for falling victim to Satan, that is, showing any signs of free thinking, they were nevertheless born into the Western world and therefore tended not to possess worldviews that challenged the occupier's use and control of the land. This, in part, helps to explain the harsher measures the U.S. and Canadian governments have taken against native children, reaching genocidal proportions. In other words, those raised in the settler communities were born and bred to be wage earners, to be externally controlled, which essentially is to be a slave. Native American communities with an independent existence from the settler states socialize themselves to be free and not externally commanded. The true goal of boarding schools was therefore to colonize the mind and enslave the body.

The goal of education for those deemed most suitable for manual labor (Native and African Americans and the vast majority of Whites) was designed to replace any previous conception of self with "worker." That is, to define oneself as a slave, a worker. If the only thing your identity is based on is being a worker, then you will feel incomplete if not working, or taking orders. This sense of dependency was and continues to be reinforced in the schools through a banking model of education where the teacher and/or the creators of curricula are deemed to be the sole possessors of valuable knowledge and the students therefore are void of useful information and understandings. In this model, education is something that is done to you—you go to school to *be* educated. In this context the student's success is measured by how well he or she can follow directions and regurgitate prepackaged knowledge (Freire 1998).

REFERENCES

Chomsky, N. (1988). *Language and problems of knowledge: The Managua Lectures*. Cambridge, MA: The MIT Press.
Churchill, W. (2004). *Kill the Indian, save the man: The genocidal impact of American Indian residential schools*. San Francisco: City Lights.
Fanon, F. (1963). *The wretched of the earth*. New York: Grove Press.
Freire, P. (1998). *Pedagogy of the oppressed*. New York: Continuum.

Hill, D. (2012). Immiseration Capitalism, Activism and Education: Resistance, Revolt and Revenge. *Journal for Critical Education Policy Studies*, *10*(2).
Marsh, J. (2011). *Class Dismissed: Why we cannot teach of learn our way out of inequality*. New York: Monthly Review.
Menchaca, M. (1997). Early racist discourse: The roots of deficit thinking. In Richard Valencia (Ed.), *The evolution of deficit thinking: Educational thought and practice*. New York: Falmer.

Contributors

Antonia Darder is an internationally recognized Freirian scholar. She holds the Leavey Presidential Chair of Ethics and Moral Leadership at Loyola Marymount University, Los Angeles, and is Professor Emerita at the University of Illinois at Urbana–Champaign. Her scholarship critically focuses on social inequalities within schools and society. She is the author of *Culture and Power in the Classroom, Reinventing Paulo Freire: A Pedagogy of Love* and A Dissident Voice: Essays on Culture, Pedagogy, and Power; coauthor of *After Race: Racism After Multiculturalism*; and coeditor of *Latinos and Education: The Latino Studies Reader*, and *The Critical Pedagogy Reader.*

Vijay Prashad is an Indian historian, journalist, and commentator. He is the George and Martha Kellner Chair in South Asian History and Professor of International Studies at Trinity College in Hartford, Connecticut, United States. In 2013–2014, he will be the Edward Said Chair at the American University of Beirut. Prashad is the author of fifteen books. In 2012, he published five books, including *Arab Spring, Libyan Winter* (AK Press) and *Uncle Swami: South Asians in America Today* (The New Press). Two of his most well-known books, *Karma of Brown Folk* (2000) and *Everybody Was Kung Fu Fighting* (2002), were chosen by the *Village Voice* as books of the year.

Manal Hamzeh is an associate professor in the Women's Studies Program at New Mexico State University. Her research focuses on gendering discourses shaping Muslim girls' bodily experiences. She is interested in antiracist/decolonizing educational theories, the Egyptian's January 25th Revolution, and the politics of gender and sexuality. She teaches courses on Arab-Muslim feminisms, feminist research methodologies, and transnational feminisms. Her latest book is *Pedagogies of Deveiling: Muslim Girls* and the hijab discourse (Charlotte: NC, Information Age Press). Her articles are published in several journals, including *Race, Ethnicity & Education* and *International Journal of Qualitative Studies in Education.*

David Hill is Research Professor of Education at Anglia Ruskin University, England; Visiting Professor in Athens, Greece, and Limerick, Ireland. He chief edits the *Journal for Critical Education Policy Studies* (www.jceps.com) and has published twenty books and over a hundred chapters and academic articles. Dave is a Marxist academic and political activist. His academic work focuses on issues of neoliberalism, capitalism, class, "race," resistance, and socialist education/education for equality. As a socialist political activist, has fought thirteen elections at local, national, and European levels and been a regional trade-union leader. He lectures worldwide to academic and activist/trade-union groups and co-organizes the annual ICCE conference (International Conference on Critical Education) (http://www.icce-2013.org/).

Sangeeta Kamat is Associate Professor in the School of Education at the University of Massachusetts at Amherst. Her research is on education policy and politics in South Asia, neoliberalism and the cultural politics of globalization, critical development studies, and NGOs and social movements in India. She is author of Development Hegemony: NGOs and the State in India (OUP, 2002) and is working on a new book on neoliberal urbanisms and the education economy in India as well as a collaborative project on Dalit issues and caste dynamics in higher education.

Marivel Oropeza was born and raised in El Paso, Texas, where she attended public primary and secondary schools in El Paso's Lower Valley. She graduated from Vassar College, where she obtained her bachelor of arts degree in political science. Oropeza earned a master of arts degree in postsecondary education and a doctor of philosophy in educational leadership from New Mexico State University. Oropeza has a special interest in how she and others can make institutions of learning more sensitive to students' and families' needs—culturally, financially, linguistically, and so on. She is passionate about helping students to not only matriculate in and graduate from, but more importantly, thrive in college.

Loren Ola Delaney is an Afro-Canadian Diasporic woman with Caribbean ancestry. She recently graduated with a Master's degree in the Leadership Higher and Adult Education Program at the Ontario Institute for Studies in Education at the University of Toronto. Her academic interests span over a diverse array of disciplines. Loren's research, however, has focused on consent literacy in education and empire, and into the complex ways hegemony is produced through constructions of consent in the reality of peoples' lives. At present, Loren is largely invested and engaged in community organizing from a feminist and anti-racist lens, applying her interest in consent literacy to the lived experiences of women who experience commercial sexual exploitation and the implications of consent within the wider structures underpinning Canadian society and nation building. In addition, Loren Delaney has recently partnered with local women from the greater Toronto area to create a clothing line that embodies Diasporic, Indigenous and Urban culture and expression, as a means to creatively resist these complex oppressions and to reclaim one's voice that too often have been silenced. She plans to continue her academic career in the near future.

Dr. Marisol Ruiz is assistant professor at Humboldt State University. Her research interests include bilingual education, youth of color, TESOL/ESL, women's studies, equity in education, and feminist theory.

Dr. Manal Hamzeh is associate professor of women's studies at New Mexico State University. Her research interests include antiracist/decolonizing educational studies, Arabic contemporary literature written by women/queer Arabs. She is the author of *Deveiling Pedagogies: Muslim Girls and the Hijab Discourse*.

Dr. Sandy Grande is chair of the Education Department at Connecticut College. Dr. Grande has served in a number of administrative capacities at the college, including special adviser to the president for institutional equity and diversity (2004–2005) and faculty representative on the Strategic Planning Committee (2003–2004). Among her many honors and awards, Professor Grande was named as a "founding scholar" to The Paulo and Nita Freire International Project for Critical Pedagogy at McGill University, Montreal, Quebec, Canada. As part of this project she was invited to attend an international meeting of Freire-ian scholars in Baeza, Spain (2009). Professor Grande has written several articles, including "Beyond the Ecologically Noble Savage: Deconstructing the White Man's Indian," *Journal of Environmental Ethics*; "Critical Theory and American Indian Identity and Intellectualism," *The International Journal of Qualitative Studies in Education*, and "American Indian Geographies of Identity and Power: At the Crossroads of Indigena and Mestizaje," *Harvard Educational Review*. She has also peer-reviewed and edited articles including the special issue of "Tensôes Mundias/Tensiones Mundales/World Tensions: The Political Economy of Natural Disasters" (forthcoming in 2013) and the "Confessions of a Fulltime Indian" in the *Journal of Curriculum and Pedagogy* (2011). Her current manuscript in progress is titled *Pedagogy of the Dispossessed: Decolonization and the Struggle for Critical Democracy*.

John Katunich is a lecturer in the English Department at the University Kitakyushu, Japan, and a doctoral student at the Center for the Study of Higher and Postsecondary Education at the University of Michigan, United States. His research interests include language and identity, language practices in higher education, and the use of practice theory in EAP/ESP.

George J. Sefa Dei was born in Asokore-Koforidua, in the eastern region of Ghana. He completed his undergraduate education at the University of Ghana, and postgraduate studies at McMaster University and the University of Toronto, Canada. Currently, George is professor and chair, Department of Sociology and Equity Studies, Ontario Institute for Studies in Education of the University of Toronto. Between 1996 and 2000 he served as the first director of the Centre for Integrative Anti-Racism Studies at OISE/UT. Professor Dei's teaching and research interests are in the areas of antiracism, minority schooling, international development, and anticolonial thought. His professional and academic work has led to many conference and workshop invitations in Canada, the United States, Europe, and Africa. He has also appeared on many radio and television shows speaking about academic and research work. Professor Dei has received several awards for his work, including the African-Canadian Outstanding Achievement in Education; the Community Builder Award, Continuing Education Department of the Toronto Catholic District School Board; and the Race, Gender, and Class Project Academic Award (at the Annual Race, Gender, and Class Conference, New Orleans). He is the author, coauthor, and editor of several books on antiracism and education, including *Anti-Racism Education: Theory and Practice; Hardships and Survival in Rural West Africa; Reconstructing 'Drop-Out': A Critical Ethnography of the Dynamics of Black Students' Disengagement from School,* and *Indigenous Knowledge in Global Contexts.*

Myriam N. Torres is an associate professor of curriculum and instruction, College of Education, New Mexico State University. Her areas of specialization are thought, language, and culture; discourse analysis; critical literacy; and participatory action research. Other areas of expertise include language, literacy and culture: living language pedagogy; adult and family literacy; critical media literacy; teacher action research; participatory action research; research in curriculum and pedagogy; democratic education. She is the coauthor of *Research as Praxis* (Lang, 2011).

Index